PARENTS' COMPLETE
SPECIAL-EDUCATION GUIDE

TIPS, TECHNIQUES, AND MATERIALS FOR HELPING YOUR CHILD SUCCEED IN SCHOOL AND LIFE

PARENTS' COMPLETE
SPECIAL-EDUCATION GUIDE

TIPS, TECHNIQUES, AND MATERIALS FOR
HELPING YOUR CHILD SUCCEED IN SCHOOL AND LIFE

ROGER PIERANGELO, PH.D. & ROBERT JACOBY

**THE CENTER FOR APPLIED
RESEARCH IN EDUCATION**
West Nyack, New York 10994

Library of Congress Cataloging in Publication Data

Pierangelo, Roger.
   Parents' complete special education guide : tips, techniques, and materials for
helping your child succeed in school and life / Roger Pierangelo & Robert Jacoby.
     p.   cm.
   Includes bibliographical refernces and index.
   ISBN 0-87628-614-7
   1. Special education—Parent participation—United States. 2. Handicapped
children—Education—United States. I. Jacoby. Robert (Robert C.) II. Title.
LC4031.P487   1996
371.91—dc20   96-2496
                                                         CIP

© 1996 *by* The Center for Applied Research in Education West Nyack, NY

Printed in the United States of America

10 9 8 7 6 5 4 3 2 1

ISBN 0-87628-614-7

ATTENTION: CORPORATIONS AND SCHOOLS

The Center for Applied Research in Education books are available at quantity discounts with bulk purchase for educational, business, or sales promotional use. For information, please write to: Prentice Hall Career & Personal Development Special Sales, 113 Sylvan Avenue, Englewood Cliffs, NJ 07632. Please supply: title of book, ISBN number, quantity, how the book will be used, date needed.

**THE CENTER FOR APPLIED RESEARCH
IN EDUCATION**
West Nyack, NY 10994
A Simon & Schuster Company

On the World Wide Web at http://www.phdirect.com

Prentice Hall International (UK) Limited, *London*
Prentice Hall of Australia Pty. Limited, *Sydney*
Prentice Hall Canada, Inc., *Toronto*
Prentice Hall Hispanoamericana, S.A., *Mexico*
Prentice Hall of India Private Limited, *New Delhi*
Prentice Hall of Japan, Inc., *Tokyo*
Simon & Schuster Asia Pte. Ltd., *Singapore*
Editora Prentice Hall do Brasil, Ltda., *Rio de Janeiro*

About the Authors

Dr. Roger Pierangelo has over 25 years of experience as a classroom teacher, school psychologist in the Herricks Public School system in New Hyde Park, N.Y., administrator of special education programs, full professor in the graduate special education department at Long Island University, private practitioner in psychology, member of Committees on Special Education, evaluator for the New York State Education Department, director of a private clinic, and consultant to numerous private and public schools, PTA and SEPTA groups.

Dr. Pierangelo earned his B.S. degree from St. John's University, M.S. from Queens College, Professional Diploma from Queens College, and Ph.D. from Yeshiva University. Currently he is working as a psychologist both at the college level and in private practice.

Dr. Pierangelo is a member of the American Psychological Association, N.Y., State Psychological Association, Nassau County Psychological Association, New York State Union of Teachers, and Phi Delta Kappa.

Dr. Pierangelo is the author of the *Survival Kit for the Special Education Teacher* and *The Special Education Teacher's Book of Lists* published by Simon & Schuster, and *301 Ways to Be a Loving Parent*, published by Shapolsky Publishers of New York.

Mr. Robert Jacoby has 25 years of experience in the field of Special Education as a regular classroom teacher, classroom teacher in alternative high school programs and hospital settings, resource room teacher and special education teacher on both the elementary and secondary levels, and has been instrumental in the development of two special education facilities in Rockland County and Westchester County, N.Y., principal for a school of developmentally disabled children in Pomona, N.Y., principal for an alternative high school in Lakeland School District, Shrub Oak, N.Y., and pupil personnel director in the Herricks Public Schools, New Hyde Park, N.Y. and East Rockaway School District in East Rockaway N.Y. Mr. Jacoby is currently the principal of the Unity Drive Special Education School in Middle Country School, Centereach district, N.Y.

Mr. Jacoby received his B.A. from Long Island University, M.A. from Manhattan College, and his Certificate of Advanced Study from The State University of New York.

Mr. Jacoby is a member of American Association of Curriculum Development, Long Island Association of Special Education Administrators, Long Island Association of Pupil Personnel Administrators, American Association of Supervisors, New York State United Teachers, and the American Association of Teachers.

About This Book

The *Parents' Complete-Special Education Guide* has been developed to help all parents of disabled children survive the myriad rules and regulations surrounding the educational, social, vocational, and environmental needs of their children. Many texts are filled with theories, but very little practical advice. From our combined experience of 50 years in special education services, we have come to realize the need that all parents have for a wide variety of important and pertinent information that can be obtained at a moment's notice. This book is organized to give parents that wealth of practical advice.

Many parents of disabled children do not have the perspective of the entire special education process as well as the specific knowledge and tools required at each stage. Awareness of this global concept of special education allows parents to fulfill the requirements for any experience that they may encounter.

Filled with practical tools and suggestions, the book takes parents through the various stages required in understanding the processes of early childhood intervention, procedures for school-aged disabled youngsters, how to work with the special education process, placement, Committees on Preschool Special Education and Committees on Special Education, individual educational plans, and practical educational law. It also contains many useful tables and charts.

It is the responsibility of parents of a disabled child to keep themselves abreast of the latest educational processes which involve their children. Having one book that provides all the necessary survival skills can only facilitate the process of assuring that your child receives the best and most appropriate education available in the least-restrictive environment.

How to Use This Book

Parents who are interested in becoming proactive in their child's educational process from preschool through college will find this guide invaluable because of the practical assistance offered through every phase of their child's educational development. The *Parents' Complete Special-Education Guide* can be referred to by parents seeking assistance or guidance for their child from birth to adulthood. Each section of the book enables parents to feel more secure and informed about the sometimes overwhelming process of special education. For example, if a parent is concerned about what to do at a CSE meeting, the chapter on *How to Prepare for an Initial CSE Meeting* will give step-by-step instructions concerning questions to ask, materials to bring, what to expect, and so forth.

From our experience we know that the "aging-out" process and what to do with special education children after 21 is a major concern and fear for all parents. This real issue is covered in the section entitled *Post-High-School Services for the Disabled*, and offers readers alternatives, organizations, forms, materials, and informational resources so that the process can begin before the age of 21 and have positive results.

The section on *How to Examine School Records* provides parents who wish to examine school records with step-by-step directions on what to ask for, who to contact, legal rights, and how to interpret what they have in front of them.

Practical parenting tools so important to parents of special-education children, are provided in useful, easy-to-understand terms and suggestions in the section *Practical Parenting Tools for Parents of Disabled Children.*

In closing, here is an information-packed handbook that you can bring to meetings or refer to on an as-needed basis that offers you expertise in dealing with every facet of the special-education process.

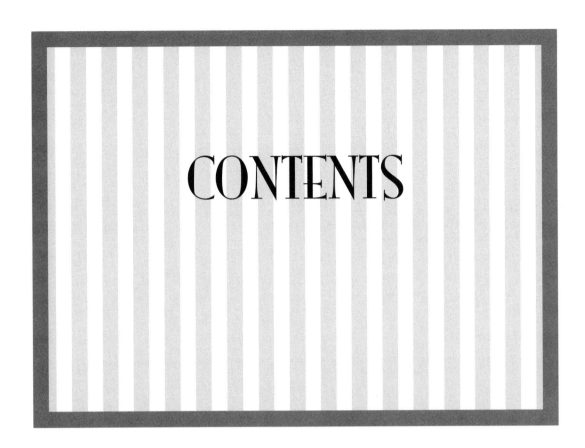

CONTENTS

About This Book   vii

c h a p t e r   o n e
An Introduction to Special Education
1

Modern History of Special Education Services   1

Introduction   1
Background   1
Primary Rights of Parents   2
Relevant Court Cases to Special Education   3
Legislation   3
Right to a Free Appropriate Public Education   4
Education in the Least-Restrictive Environment   4
Right to Due Process and Equal Access   5

chapter two
Child Development Information
7

Normal Development   7

Principles of Normal Development   7
Milestones in Child Development   8

chapter three
Screening Procedures for Suspected Disabilities
21

General Screening Procedures for All Students   21

What is Screening?   21
The Screening Program for New Entrants   22
Representative School District Screening Model   24
Confidentiality   31
Reviewing the Results of the Screening   31
Referring Children Who May Have a Suspected Disability   31

chapter four
How You Can Observe Your Child for Suspected Disabilities
33

School Symptoms Exhibited by High-Risk Students   33

How Emotional Problems Affect a Child's Ability to Function in the Classroom   34

Symptomatic Behavior   34

How to Determine the Severity of a Problem   35

Avoidance Behavior Patterns   36

How Problems May Affect Your Child's Behavior and Ability to Learn   38

Normal Development—Division of Energy   *38*
High Tension Level—Division of Energy   *39*

c h a p t e r   f i v e

Preschool Special Education
43

Early Intervention—Preschool   43

When Should You Be Concerned?   *43*
Why Parents are Important   *44*
Referral of your child   44
Talking with your service coordinator   44
Evaluation   44
Individualized family service plan   44
Review of the individualized family service plan   44
Transition   44
What Is the Early Intervention Program?   *45*
What Determines Your Child's Eligibility for Services?   *46*
What Is the Criteria Used in Determining Eligibility?   *46*

c h a p t e r   s i x

The Special-Education Process
49

The Referral Process—Step 1   49

Contents of a Referral   *49*
Parental Guarantees in the Referral Process   *50*
Suggestions for Parent Participation in the Referral Process   *51*

Record-Keeping Ideas During the Referral Process   *52*

Initial Referral to the CSE from the School Staff   *52*

Example of a Parent Referral Letter to the CSE   *53*

Referral to the CSE From School Staff   *54*

Referral Forms Used by Local Schools   *55*

Rating Scales   *57*

The Evaluation Process—Step 2   57

What Is an Evaluation?   *57*

Components of a Thorough Evaluation   *60*

Parental Consent for Evaluation   *60*

How Parents Should Deal with School Intakes and Interviews   *61*

Parent Consent Form for Evaluation   *62*

How to Examine Your Child's School Records   *63*

Social and Developmental Intakes   *65*

Example of an Intake Form Used by Schools   *65*

Observation Scales   *67*

Classroom Observation Report Form   *69*

Due-Process Guarantees During the Evaluation Phase   *71*

Selected Tests for Special Education   *72*

Types of Tests   *72*

Recommendation—Step 3   73

What Is a Recommendation?   *73*

The CSE: What Is It?   *73*

How Recommendations Are Made by the CSE   *74*

Conditions of Public Law 504   *75*

CSE Procedures   *76*

Specific Responsibilities of the Committee on Special Education (CSE)   *77*

Individual Educational Program Development   *79*

Continuum of Services   *79*

Facts About Inclusion   *81*

Recommended Placements   *83*

Recommendations Made by the CSE   *84*

Parental Guarantees During the Recommendation Phase   *84*

Suggestions for Your Participation   *85*

Record-Keeping Ideas During the Recommendation Phase   *85*

Procedures for Changing a Student's Classification or Placement   *85*

Implementation—Step 4   87

What Is Implementation?   *87*
What You Should Consider During the Implementation Phase   *87*
Educational Considerations   *88*
Diploma Options and Requirements   *89*
Additional Parental Considerations   *90*
Arranging for Implementation: Your Suggestions for Participation   *90*
Record-Keeping Ideas During the Implementation Phase   *91*

Annual Review—Step 5   91

What Is the Annual Review?   *91*
Suggestions for Your Participation in the Annual Review   *92*
Record-keeping Ideas During the Annual Review   *92*
Parent's Preparation Checklist for Annual Review   *93*

The Triennial Evaluation—Step 6   94

What Is the Triennial Evaluation?   *94*
Parental Guarantees During the Triennial Evaluation   *94*
Suggestions for Your Participation in the Triennial Evaluation   *95*
Record-Keeping Ideas During the Triennial Evaluation Phase   *95*

Due Process—Step 7   95

Overall Summary of Due-Process Assurances   *95*
What Is an Impartial Hearing?   *96*
When Are Impartial Hearings Requested?   *98*
Record-Keeping Ideas During Due Process   *98*

chapter seven

Individual Educational Plans
99

IEP Guidelines   99

Student Eligibility and Criteria for Testing Modifications   *105*
Impact of Testing Modifications on Specific Tests   *106*
Roles and Responsibilities for Implementation   *107*

chapter eight

Related Services
111

Overview of Related Services   111

In-School Individual Counseling   *111*

In-School Group Counseling   *111*

Speech/Language Therapy   *112*

Physical and Occupational Therapy   *112*

Art Therapy   *112*

Adaptive Physical Education   *112*

Music Therapy   *112*

Itinerant Services for Hearing Impaired   *113*

Itinerant Services for Visually Impaired   *113*

Sign Language Interpreter   *113*

What You Need to Know About Physical and Occupational Therapy   113

Guidelines for Occupational and Physical Therapy Evaluations   *113*

What You Need to Know About In-School Counseling   *119*

chapter nine

Specific Disabilities
123

The Learning-Disabled Child   123

Diagnosing the Learning-Disabled Child   *123*

Who Is a Student With a Learning Disability?   *126*

Severe Learning Discrepancy   *126*

Characteristics of Children With Dyslexia   *127*

Instructional Considerations for Children With Learning Disabilities   *128*

Characteristics of Writing, Mathematical, and Reading Disorders   *130*

The Emotionally Disabled Child   132

Characteristics of Children With Emotional Disabilities   *132*

Instructional Considerations   *133*
Warning Signs of a Potential Suicide Risk in Adolescents   *135*

The Mentally Disabled Child   137

Residential Alternatives   *137*
Instructional Considerations   *138*
Characteristics of Down's Syndrome   *139*

The Physically Disabled Child   140

Causes of Physical Disabilities   *140*
Infectious Diseases: Modes of Transmission   *142*

The Visually Disabled Child   143

Characteristics of Individuals With Visual Impairments   *143*
What Is Meant by Visual Impairments?   *144*
Causes of Visual Impairments   *144*
The Braille Alphabet   *145*

The Hearing-Impaired Child   146

Causes of Hearing Impairments   *146*
Audiometric Evaluation Measures   *147*
Modes of Communication for the Deaf   *148*
The Manual Alphabet   *149*

Degrees of Hearing Impairment   150

Examples of Typical Sound Intensities   151

The Child With Attention-Deficit/Hyperactivity Disorder   152

Defining Attention-Deficit/Hyperactivity Disorders (ADAD)   *152*
Diagnostic Criteria for ADD/ADHD   *152*
Treatment Plans for Children With ADD/ADHD   *153*
Classroom Management Techniques   *154*

Children With Communication Disorders   157

What You Need to Know If Your Child Has a Communication Disorder   *158*
Characteristics of Communication Disorders   *159*
Summary of Normal Language Development   *160*
Treatment and Remediation of Communication Disorders   *161*
Determining the Presence of a Speech and Language Disability   *162*

The Autistic Child — 163

Criteria Used to Diagnose Autistic Disorder — *163*
Interdisciplinary Diagnosis of Autism — *165*

Tourette's Syndrome — 166

Diagnostic Criteria for Tic Disorders — *167*
Pharmacotherapy and Tourette's Syndrome — *168*
Classroom Strategies for Children With Tourette's Syndrome — *169*

The Bilingual and Culturally Disadvantaged Child — 170

Variables That May Influence an Exceptional Bilingual Child's Placement — *170*
Basic Elements of an Individualized Education Program (IEP) for Exceptional Bilingual Children — *170*
Specific Requirements for Referral of Bilingual Students to the CSE — *171*

The Gifted Child — 172

Evaluation Procedures — *172*
Examples of Classroom Activities — *174*
Approaches to Educational Programming — *175*
Common Characteristics of Program Management — *177*
Terminology for the Gifted — *178*
Characteristics of the Gifted and Talented — *179*

Common Disorders Usually First Diagnosed in Infancy, Childhood, or Adolescence — 180

Developmental Disorders — *180*
Pervasive Developmental Disorders — *181*
Specific Learning Disorders — *182*
Common Disruptive Behavior Disorders — *184*
Common Anxiety Disorders of Childhood — *185*
Common Eating and Tic Disorders — *187*
Other Disorders of Childhood and Adolescence — *188*
Anxiety Disorders — *190*
Mood Disorders — *190*
Specific Personality Disorders — *190*

chapter ten

Common Medication Information
193

Medications Used for Specific Disorders   **193**

    Attention-Deficit/Hyperactivity Disorder   *193*

    Psychosis   *194*

    Tourette's Syndrome   *196*

    Depression   *197*

    Anxiety or Panic Disorders   *198*

Medications by Category   **200**

    Psychostimulants   *200*

    Sedatives/Hypnotics   *200*

    Antipsychotic medications   *201*

    Antidepressant medications   *202*

    Antianxiety medications   *203*

    Anticonvulsive medications   *205*

chapter eleven

Practical Parenting Suggestions
207

How You Can Help Your Children With Homework   207

How You Can Use Effective Discipline   211

How to Communicate Better With Your Children   214

How to Improve Your Child's Self-Esteem   217

How You Can Recognize Possible Learning Disabilities in Your Children   221

Frequently Asked Questions Concerning Learning Disabilities   223

What You Need to Know About Retention   224 chapter twelve

The Transition of Special-Education Students to Adult Life
227

Transitional Services   227

Vocational Assessments   228

Individualized Transitional Education Program (ITEP)   231

Student and Family Participation   232

    Transition Planning Timeline   *233*

Sample Transitional IEP   235

Transition From School to Work   239

Transition to Posthigh-School Programs   240

Postsecondary Schooling   240

Things to Consider When Looking Into Postsecondary Education   241

Practical Adive for Students Considering Postsecondary Education   243

chapter thirteen

Appendices
247

Appendix A—Terminology   248

    Educational Terminology Associated With Special Education   *248*

    Medical Terminology   *252*

    Psychological Terminology   *257*

    Occupational and Physical Therapy Terminology   *259*

    Commonly Used Terms in the Employment of Disabled Individuals   *262*

    Abbreviations Associated With Special Education   *264*

Appendix B—Special-Education Forms   267

    Suggested Materials for CSE Presentations   *267*

Data Processing Sheet — *267*

CSE Packet Checklist — *270*

Initial Referral to CSE From Parent/Guardian — *271*

Parent Consent for Evaluation — *271*

Explanation of Evaluations — *272*

Required Academic Data — *273*

Social and Developmental History Form — *274*

Medical Report for CSE — *276*

Other Required Information and Procedures — *277*

Agreement to Withdraw CSE Referral — *277*

Learning Profile — *278*

Early Childhood Screening Program Checklist — *280*

Elementary Screening Program — *280*

Appendix C—Organizations and Publications — **282**

Selected Organizations for Exceptional Children — *282*

Selected Journal Publications on Exceptional Children — *285*

Publishers of Materials for the Gifted — *288*

Organizations and Publications for the Gifted — *289*

Publications for the Gifted — *290*

Selected Readings on Instruction and Management for the Disabled — *290*

Selected Readings on Assessment and Testing for the Disabled — *292*

Selected Readings for Parents on Specific Disabilities — *293*

Selected Sources of Commercially Produced Instructional Software — *299*

Names and Addresses of Test Publishers — *300*

Appendix D—Reference Lists — **303**

Gross motor skills — *303*

Receptive language skills — *303*

Expressive language skills — *304*

Dressing skills — *304*

Eating skills — *305*

Toileting and grooming skills — *306*

Child Immunization Checklist — *307*

Appendix E—Special-Education Tests — **308**

Intelligence Tests — *308*

Language Tests — *309*

Tests for the Hearing Impaired — *310*

Psychological Tests   *310*

Perceptual Tests   *311*

Rating Scales and Adaptive Behavior Scales   *312*

Reading Tests   *313*

Arithmetic Tests   *314*

Spelling Tests   *314*

Writing Tests   *315*

Comprehensive Academic Skills Tests   *315*

Bilingual Assessment Measures   *316*

Early Childhood and Assessment Scales   *316*

Standardized Tests Used in an Occupational Therapy Evaluation   *317*

Index

321

chapter one

AN INTRODUCTION TO SPECIAL EDUCATION

Modern History of Special-Education Services

Introduction

The passage of Public Law 94–142—Education for All Handicapped Children Act by Congress in November of 1975, was the end result of many years of litigation and state legislation to protect and promote the civil rights of all disabled children. Increasingly the local school districts are becoming aware of the ramifications resulting from the handicapped act, as are the parents of disabled children. You should review the constantly changing legislation under P.L. 94–142 by requesting updated materials from either your local school district or state education agency. You should also be aware of the your rights under these new regulations as they will undoubtedly affect the placement of your disabled child and the curriculum in his/her schools, such as required class size, school district responsibilities, and classroom modifications. This chapter will focus on the legislation as it relates to your rights.

Background

In order to explore what rights you may have concerning the education of your disabled child, a definition of children with disabilities is necessary as a frame of reference. For this chapter the following definition will be used:

1

A disabled child means a person under the age of twenty-one who is entitled to attend public school and who, because of mental, physical, or emotional reasons can receive appropriate educational opportunities from special services and programs to include, but not limited to, transportation, special classes, part-time programs, resource programs, alternate learning centers, home instruction and special teachers; State operated or State supported special school or other special facilities; pupil personnel services and/or those services, facilities, or programs which can be obtained through contracts with boards of cooperative educational services, public school districts, approved nonpublic schools, or other agencies.

The purpose of this chapter is to explain those legislative court actions and Commissioner's regulations which directly affect you as the parent of a child with special needs.

Traditionally, the belief among educators was that the law reflected a social bias that disabled children's best interests were synonymous with those of their parents. Present reforms in the law emphasize a change in children's legal status in two distinct ways: by extending more rights similar to those granted to adults, and by recognizing certain specific interests and needs of children as legally enforceable.

One cause of this law reform was parents exercising their freedom to challenge educational decisions made by the schools. The parents of disabled children used the courts to reshape the educational system. Also, the parents of disabled children have held schools accountable for the kinds of programs which they offer to their children. These actions have resulted in legislation and court decisions regarding "children's rights." It is through these laws and decisions that specific parents' rights have been defined.

Primary Rights of Parents

Landmark decisions have been made regarding the rights of disabled children to a free and appropriate education. These decisions form much of the basis for specific rights of parents. The decisions themselves show that the primary right of parents is to have their children educated. Many states have published pamphlets which describe the rights of children and parents.

Legislation came about because of specific court decisions in many states. These were influenced by several landmark cases, one of which was the *Pennsylvania Association for Retarded Children vs. Commonwealth of Pennsylvania* in 1971. In this case a suit was filed to obtain and guarantee publicly supported education for all mentally retarded children in the state of Pennsylvania. It was felt that the failure to provide any educational opportunities to these children was a denial of equal protection, and that the assignment of children to programs without a hearing was a denial of due process. The decision of the court not only guaranteed the educational rights of the children, but also provided specific requirements to ensure equal protection and due process.

Relevant Court Cases to Special Education

In the case of *Mills vs. Board of Education of the District of Columbia*, the parents and guardians of seven disabled children brought suit for failure to provide all children with a publicly supported education. The court's decision was in favor of education for the disabled.

In one example, the New York State precedent for the right to education for children with disabilities involved the Reid decision, in which a complaint was submitted to the Commissioner of Education concerning the failure of the New York City Board of Education to provide disabled children with suitable education programs. In essence, the Commissioner's ruling ordered that all students diagnosed as disabled be placed in a public or private school setting (depending on availability), and that plans be submitted by February, 1974 to eliminate waiting lists, regionalize evaluation, meet the needs of secondary students, and notify parents of available services.

These are short descriptions of but a few of the many cases throughout the country which have dealt with the right to an education. As more states implemented mandatory legislation, the need for court action has lessened. The previously mentioned legislation and court actions have indeed emphasized the primary right of parents to have their children educated in an appropriate least-restrictive environment. This right is based mostly on the rights guaranteed in the 14th Amendment of the Constitution. It includes the child's right to have equal protection, as well as the benefit of due process under the law.

The modern history of education for students with disabilities stems from court cases filed by parents some thirty years ago. It was not until the 1960s that persons with disabilities received any type of educational services. What they did receive at that time was inadequate, and advocates and parents turned to the courts to address the problems their children faced. As the litigation became more and more successful in the court, Congress began to recognize the need to do something to protect the disabled individual's rights and to ensure that they had an access to education. The parallel of the civil rights movement and that of the handicapped in this country opened many doors for people who previously had no protection under the law.

Legislation

Several laws were passed during this period but the most significant was *Public Law 94–142* which was signed in 1975. This law greatly affected the provision of education for children with disabilities in the United States. The law itself was unique in that it defined its purpose in specificity.

Public Law 94–142 concerned itself with unidentified or unserved children with disabilities. It also focused on the limited resources for such children including preventive and remedial services, proper identification and placement, and related services.

It offered assurances so that children with disabilities would be entitled to a free, appropriate public education, and that the rights of children with disabilities would be protected. It excluded evaluation of program effectiveness and required state and local commitment of resources.

Each state was mandated to put into law and regulation guidelines the fulfillment of the Public Law 94–142 mandates. Remember, if the states didn't provide for the disabled, they would lose federal funding designated to service them.

Since 1975 other laws at the Federal level have been passed extending Public Law 94–142, placing greater emphasis on the role of the parent in the special education process. *Public Laws 98–199, 99–372, 99–457* and *101–476* ensure that each child with a disability will benefit from an equal opportunity, free public education. The right to a free public education in most states begins at the age of five; the specific cut-off date differs from state to state. Simply stated, children with disabilities are eligible to attend the public school in the district where they live, free of tuition. This eligibility continues until a high-school diploma is received or until the year of the student's twenty-first birthday, whichever is earlier. Students who receive an IEP diploma or a local certificate are eligible to continue in school until their twenty-first birthday.

Right to a Free Appropriate Public Education

Students with disabilities are also entitled to receive a free *appropriate* public education. The assurance that disabled students receive an "appropriate" education is a very important concept. It is the basis for all other rights that stem from an equal opportunity to free appropriate education. Once you as a parent understand this concept—that your child is entitled to receive an educational program that enables them to benefit educationally from appropriate instruction—you can start your quest to develop your role as an appropriate advocate for your child.

The educational programs designed for your child should specifically meet the needs of the individual student. They should be reviewed periodically to determine their appropriateness. Hopefully, as your child grows and progresses the need for extra services or programs will decrease. This should be your goal.

Education in the Least-Restrictive Environment

Your child should be educated as closely as possible with his or her peers. That means, all things considered, that your child should be in his or her home school with his or her friends. Many times this concept may be the final goal in a process. You may need to consider alternate programs as well. You should only consider alternate programs when the needs of your child cannot be met within the regular school setting with supplementary aid and services. Students with disabilities should have access to alternate programs that are appropriate to their individual needs. The least-restrictive-environment definition includes three components as it applies to children with disabilities:

1. Appropriateness of programs for meeting student needs.
2. Disabled student involvement with nondisabled peers.
3. Distance of educational facility and/or program to home.

Right to Due Process and Equal Access

If your child has a disability he or she has certain rights protected by law. You and your child have the right to challenge any recommendation made by the school. This right is most important to you as your child's advocate. It encourages schools to seek out and work with parents, ensuring that the child receive a free appropriate education in the least-restrictive environment. You and your school district working as partners in a process have a large responsibility; that responsibility is to work as a team, consider the child's needs, and provide the appropriate program and services accordingly. Should a disagreement arise regarding the process or the outcome, there are formal and informal procedures available to you for recourse including but not limited to an impartial hearing provided by the school district. We will talk more about this later. Hopefully, after reading this book, you will not have a need for any due-process procedures.

Your involvement as you can readily see is a key component for your child. Laws for the education of children with disabilities continue to recognize the pivotal role of parents in the special-education process. These laws only go so far. The continued success of a student depends on the active participation of all persons responsible for the student. Your level of participation will depend on many factors and will vary throughout your child's education. The success of your participation will depend on the following:

1. Maintaining current information about your child.
2. Communicating with your school about your child.
3. Voicing concerns and questioning the school staff when you are unsure.
4. Becoming involved and interested.
5. Providing support to the educational program.
6. Being fully informed about your child's program.
7. Seeing yourself as part of the process and part of the partnership when designing a school program.
8. Knowing your child's rights.

chapter two
CHILD DEVELOPMENT INFORMATION

Normal Development

All children develop differently. No child really develops according to a specific "clock." As a result, while developmental timing may vary from child to child, there are certain general guidelines or principles that can be followed. These guidelines are just that—guidelines. You need to be very cautious in becoming overly anxious because your child did not "reach" a specific task at a given time. If you have any concerns about your child's developmental pattern contact your pediatrician or a child psychologist who will be more than happy to evaluate your particular situation.

The following principles are general developmental patterns included to provide a framework on child development.

Principles of Normal Development

- A child's developmental progression follows orderly step-by-step sequences where each achievement paves the way for the next one.
- Individual differences among children also tend to remain apparent over time.
- As a child's development progresses, small elements of behavior (for instance, finger movements) are combined and linked to larger, practical behaviors (such as grasping objects).
- A child's developmental progress is often intermittent and the rate of change in one area of proficiency may vary while other skills are being learned.

- Growth and development may vary in terms of rate among individual children and between different developmental areas within the same children.
- Individual differences are evident in young children at a very early age.
- Each child develops at his or her own pace and capability.
- Motor development and voluntary movements progress from the head downward and from the trunk outward.
- The continuity of development is basically the same for all children.
- All areas of development (such as motor development and conceptual development) are interrelated.
- Critical periods of learning are part of every child's developmental sequence. There are times when children indicate that they are ready for new learning.
- Preceding and following critical periods of learning, the child may exhibit periods where learning may prove to be more difficult.
- Most children exhibit subtle behavioral mannerisms to their caregivers about their needs and readiness for new learning. A child's learning potential is best served when the stimulation provided matches the child's facility to learn the new task.
- As children develop increasing capacities for learning and doing, they tend to use these capacities.
- The outcome of development is governed by the nature/nurture principle which is influenced by many factors including a child's genetic make-up, social environment, and family structure.

This section deals with general milestones that you may observe in your child at different developmental levels. Again, as you review these guidelines you need to be cautious in your assessment of your child's development. Children attain developmental milestones at different times. In some cases a child who is growing very well may leave out one milestone or may not follow our chart exactly. For example, a child may begin to walk without ever crawling for any significant length of time. One only has to look at adolescents to further see this point. Just observe children in this stage and you will see a variety of children at different points. Some will take years to develop certain characteristics: deep voice, hair growth, growth spurt, and so on—while others will develop in a few months. And the important factor is that they are all within normal levels. As previously mentioned, use these guidelines as a general frame of reference and if you have any concerns consider what we suggested earlier.

Milestones in Child Development

The Newborn (Birth to Four Weeks)

- Your newborn will spend much of the first month sleeping, eating, and needing to be comforted. She will know that she is being comforted by the way you handle her. Be gentle with your child whenever you pick her up or put her down. Remember, a baby's neck muscles are very weak at first, so be sure to support her head.

- Feeding time is a great time for talking to your baby. Occasionally, switch your infant from one arm to the other.
- Your child should be sucking and swallowing well. For safety's sake, don't leave her with a bottle. After each feeding gently burp her, and if you lay her down, place her on her side or belly to prevent possible choking.
- The most important need of a newborn is to know she is cared for and loved. You will not spoil her by meeting her needs. Go to her when she cries. That cry is her language. Does she need to be fed, changed, or held? She needs your love and attention in order to grow strong and healthy.

REFLEXES OF THE NEWBORN Just as you laugh when tickled or blink when you sneeze, your baby has certain "reflex" movements, too. Also, please be aware that premature and handicapped infants may reach certain stages later than they are listed. An infant will squeeze your finger if you put it in her palm, and will turn her head toward your finger if her cheek is touched.

One to Three Months

CHILD GROWTH

- Lifts head up briefly when on belly.
- Reacts to sudden movement or noises.
- Makes "cooing" sounds.
- Follows moving objects with eyes.
- Appears to stare at times.
- Smiles when played with.
- Grasps small object if placed in hand.

YOUR ROLE

- Place your infant on his belly at times (not at night).
- Watch and see if your child reacts to sounds.
- Speak to him in a pleasant voice.
- Hang a mobile two feet in front of your child.
- Move him from room to room.
- Let him watch people and activities.
- Smile and talk softly while holding and touching your infant. Your infant needs as much contact with you as possible.
- Place a small rattle in his hand.

During these first months you and your baby are getting to know each other. Does he seem to be calm, active, or just in-between?

Watching him as he starts to grow and learning how he does things are the first steps toward good parenting. Remember, you are the key observer of your child. Enjoy his growth. However, if you have any questions about his development, please do not hesitate to check with your doctor.

Three to Six Months

CHILD GROWTH

- Lifts head and chest when on belly.
- Tries to roll over.
- Sits with some support.
- Kicks legs and moves arms actively when on back.
- Looks at hands and fingers and sometimes folds hand on chest.
- Tries to reach and hold objects.
- Seems to know familiar objects and is happy to see them; for example, parents' faces, bottle, toys, and mirror.
- Makes babbling sounds such as "ee, ih, uh."
- Sometimes laughs or chuckles.
- Turns head toward sound such as bell, voice, music.

YOUR ROLE

- Place your infant in different positions in crib.
- Hold her in a sitting position on occasion.
- Turn your infant on her back. Do not keep her tightly covered. Allow movement for exercise.
- Give your child a few small, safe objects to play with, such as rattles and plastic rings.
- Hold her in front of a mirror.
- Praise your infant, show pleasure at her first sounds and repeat them back.
- Sing and speak to your child. Play music for your infant. Look at your child when speaking to her.

It is very likely that by the end of six months your child will be very active. This is a very happy time for your child. You can share in his/her happiness by gently holding, talking, and touching your child. You should be concerned if your child suddenly stops "babbling" or has never made sounds at all. Further, you may want to question your doctor if only the top part of the eyeball appears above the lower lid or is unable to focus on objects (roving eye movements). In either case, you should call your doctor.

Six to Nine Months

CHILD GROWTH

- Sits by self when placed.
- Rolls from stomach to back, and back to stomach.
- Begins to creep on belly; may rock back and forth on knees.
- Reaches, holds and puts objects in mouth.
- Feeds self cracker; may pass objects from one hand to another.
- Naps about 1 to 4 hours a day.
- Makes sounds such as, "baba, gugu, didi."
- Uses crying to show different needs, for example, hunger, anger, discomfort.
- Knows strangers from family; cries when parent goes away.
- Begins to play simple games.
- Looks at person speaking; may respond to own name.

YOUR ROLE

- Help your child to a sitting position.
- Place your baby in a playpen or on a blanket on the floor.
- Give him safe play areas. Prevent accidents by "child proofing" your home. Your baby is very active now.
- Introduce finger foods such as crackers, toast, and small pieces of bananas. Watch what your child puts in his mouth.
- Provide a quiet place for him to sleep. In nice weather, place your child outside for a nap.
- Talk to your baby about what you are doing and name objects and foods.
- Try to understand what your child is crying about.
- It is very important to spend as much time as you can touching, playing, and talking with your child. Let him stay by you and get accustomed to new people a little at a time.
- Play peek-a-boo, clap hands, and help your child play with his toys.
- Expose your child to many different sounds.
- Give him noise-making and musical toys.

You will notice that your child may get upset if a new person comes into the home. This is a stage that he needs to go through. Comfort your child and allow him to get used to different people in his own way. During this time, or in other stressful situations, you can help your baby if you remain calm and patient.

Nine to Twelve Months

CHILD GROWTH

- Pulls self to sitting and/or standing positions for short periods of time.
- Creeps or crawls, perhaps backwards at first.
- Develops hand skills; picks things up with thumb and forefinger, looks closely at objects, places objects in and out of containers.
- Can stack two blocks.
- Understands some simple words such as "Mommy," "Daddy," "Dog," "Bye-bye."
- Knows own name.
- Pays attention to simple commands such as "No" and "Give it to me."
- Copies sounds such as clicking and coughing, and words such as "Mama" and "Dada."
- Plays with family members.
- Gives affection and love.

YOUR ROLE

- Provide a safe area where your child can practice these new skills, and help her to do so.
- Give her a safe area in which to move around and exercise.
- Give your child small, safe objects such as cups, cubes, and lids. Provide your infant with containers and pots and pans. Be patient; she needs to practice picking up and dropping things. Let your child use the hand she prefers.
- Tell your child the names of many things such as people, animals, colors, and parts of the body.
- Ask your child to hand you objects and praise her for doing it.
- Provide sounds and simple words that she can mimic.
- Look at simple picture books with your child and point to objects.
- Avoid baby talk. Use simple words and short sentences.
- Continue parent-child games. Roll a big ball with your child.
- Provide your child with a lot of love and attention; always respond to her gift of love.

This is the beginning of your child's active, exploring, and discovering stage. Prepare yourself and your home. Keep cleaning products, glass, and small objects that your child can swallow out of reach. You can make it safe, but make it fun, too! Curiosity is a necessary tool for all learning! Make sure you provide your child with many opportunities to learn and grow.

Twelve to Fifteen Months

CHILD GROWTH

- Begins to walk by himself; may walk by holding onto furniture at first.
- May begin to climb.
- Learns skills such as self-feeding (lifts cup with two hands and drinks, starts using a spoon); turning pages two or three at a time; trying to build and stack objects.
- Experiments with language; talks nonsense words, voice goes up and down as if speaking (jargoning), can usually say two words besides "Mama" and "Dada."
- Understands more of what is being said to him.
- Comes when called by name; starts to be aware of "do's and don'ts" around the house.
- Plays by himself, but also likes to be with other children and adults.

YOUR ROLE

- Provide safe places for your child to practice walking. Praise him for his efforts. Walk hand-in-hand with your child. Watch him in case he falls. Let your child practice climbing at playgrounds, in the backyard and on furniture, but watch your child and try to prevent falls from happening.
- Provide baby-sized cups and spoons for your child. Be patient; your child will be messy.
- Give your child some cloth or cardboard books.
- Give your child objects to stack such as blocks and plastic cups.
- Talk about the day's activities, household objects, toys and people.
- Give only one simple direction at a time.
- Teach your child the "shoulds" and "should nots" for his safety and pleasure.
- Spend some special time with your child.

Is your child making lots of new sounds now? Has he tried to walk yet? Can he feed himself and is he chewing and swallowing well?

Fifteen to Eighteen Months

CHILD GROWTH

- Walks by herself; can often walk upstairs with help and creep backwards downstairs; can throw ball without falling.
- Employs hand skills such as block building (can pile 3–4 blocks).
- Scribbles with crayons; can push and pull toys.
- Experiments with language; imitates simple words (may use 5–10 words).

- Can point to simple pictures such as dog, baby, and car.
- Naps 1 to 3 hours in the afternoon.
- May tell you she has wet her pants.
- Imitates simple actions such as cooking and reading.
- Begins to ask parent for help when needed; enjoys being with other children and adults.

YOUR ROLE

- Take your child on walks. Allow your child to walk barefoot sometimes. Play ball with your child.
- Give your child toys and blocks to play with. Color with your child. Fat crayons are easier for little hands.
- Read out loud to your child. Let her point to known objects. Listen and pay attention to your child.
- Provide a quiet, comfortable area to rest.
- Praise your child if she tells you she is wet.
- Let your child help you with everyday chores.

Get ready, get set, go! You and your child can now become good partners. He/she wants to play and work right alongside with you. Your little one is learning by imitating what you do. He/she will watch you carefully and try hard to copy your actions. Be patient; he/she needs to practice these new activities.

Eighteen to Twenty-Four Months

CHILD GROWTH

- Walks well; may begin to run; can climb stairs and onto adult chairs; throws ball overhand.
- Employs hand skills; can put squares and circles into puzzles, likes to explore and examine all sorts of objects.
- Experiments with language; uses many words to tell you about specific objects, persons, or actions, combines two different words such as "Play ball," or "Want cookie."
- Knows self in mirror or picture. Uses words such as "I," "Me," and "Your."
- Often says "No" to bedtime, certain foods, and simple requests.
- May show some interest in using the toilet.
- Likes to move to music; play periods are longer.
- Will play next to, but not usually with other children.

- Take your child on walks. Go to playgrounds and play catch with him.
- Give him simple puzzles and other objects and show him how to use them.
- Talk about the activities that he is involved with.
- Name foods, toys, and household objects for your child to say.
- Ask your child to name objects for you.
- Make sure your child has some things of his own and places to put them.
- Allow your child to make choices whenever possible; for example, say, "Do you want an apple or an orange?"
- Don't punish your child for any toilet accidents, and praise dryness and the use of a bathroom.
- Provide music for your child and help with simple dance-like movements. Let your child be around other children. Play with your child using different toys.

Your child will be very active now. You may not be used to all his energy and movement. These few months will take much patience and understanding on your part. He will come to you with lots of questions; he wants to learn so much. You are your child's first teacher. Please remember, your child will be growing in his own special way. Your child will usually enjoy moving to music. However, if he rocks back and forth, spins, walks on his toes, and/or bangs his head for long periods of time, we suggest that you mention this to your doctor or clinic.

Twenty-Four to Thirty Months

CHILD GROWTH

- Jumps; runs; kicks a ball; walks up and down stairs.
- Employs hand skills; turns pages one at a time, can help to dress and undress herself, turns door knob and unscrews lids, can feed herself well with a spoon.
- Experiments with language skills; can speak in short sentences.
- Begins to name objects in books; uses many new words.
- Shows understanding; can pay attention to activities for longer periods of time, knows some colors, points to parts of the body, can say first name.
- Begins to ask to use the toilet during the day.
- Plays with other children, usually for short periods of time, with little sharing of toys.

YOUR ROLE

- Encourage your child to play in a safe area.
- Let your child look at books and magazines.
- Hang a full-length mirror at your child's height.

- Teach your child to dress herself; do not rush her.
- Praise her for good feeding skills.
- Listen and talk with your child. Point to pictures in magazines and ask your child to tell you about them. Don't rush your child when she is speaking.
- Answer your child's questions simply and honestly.
- Read simple stories to your child. Let your child use paints, clay, and crayons. Have your child color simple pictures such as fruits and houses. Tell her to choose the crayon that is the same color as the object. Have your child touch her nose, mouth, ears, and other parts of the body.
- Praise her for using the toilet. During the day, try to use training pants instead of diapers.
- Remind your child to use the toilet, especially after mealtime.
- Provide time for your child to play with other children.

Because children during this stage have very definite opinions about things, it is often called the "The Terrible Twos." She may often disagree with you. This is very common. She is not really being bad; she needs to learn that her feelings count and that she is an important member of the family, too.

Thirty to Thirty-Six Months

CHILD GROWTH

- Walks upstairs (one foot on a step); begins to balance on one foot; likes to ride a tricycle.
- Employs hand skills; puts shoes on (no lacing), begins to copy simple shapes, cuts with scissors, brushes teeth with some help.
- Experiments with language skills; says first and last name, knows whether he/she is a boy/girl, repeats some nursery rhymes.
- Shows understanding; knows difference between "big" and "little," follows two or three directions given at one time, begins to count.
- Naps start to disappear (may not nap every day).
- Plays more often with other children (shares, tells stories, likes to play dress-up).

YOUR ROLE

- Take your child to parks and playgrounds.
- Point out things in nature such as flowers, birds, trees.
- Praise your child for his efforts. Encourage him to use materials such as finger paints, blocks, and simple puzzles. Children love to play with water.
- Let your child tell stories and explain pictures.
- It is "normal" for your child to want to look at and touch the parts of the body. Teach your child to say his name and to sing nursery rhymes.

- When you play with your child, help him to understand numbers and ideas such as large/small, under/over, on/off, and open/close.
- Encourage napping when he seems tired.
- Make sure your child has the chance to play with other children. Encourage his imagination. Provide old clothes for dress-up games.

Children grow and mature at different rates. They develop in their own ways. Some children are better at climbing and jumping, others are better at drawing and singing. Your child may not be athletically inclined. However, if your think he is very clumsy and awkward, and does not seem to enjoy any playground equipment, you may want to have him checked by your doctor or a team of professionals.

Three to Four Years

CHILD GROWTH

- Walks and runs well; has good balance.
- Employs hand skills; catches a large ball, begins to copy some capital letters, draws circles, crosses, and squares.
- Exhibits self-help skills; washes and dries herself, brushes teeth, dresses and undresses herself (including buttons).
- Tells you when she needs to use toilet.
- Experiments with language skills; talks about her experiences, makes up stories, asks many questions (why, what, where).
- Names colors.
- Shows understanding; knows difference between part and whole, same and different, begins to understand ideas of past, present, and future. May count from 1–10.
- Plays well with other children (takes turns, shares).
- Interested in new experience; more independent.

YOUR ROLE

- Plays games such as Giant Steps, Red Light/Green Light; and Hide-and-Seek.
- Play ball with your child. Use follow-the-dot outlines for letters and shapes. Let her cut pictures from old magazines and newspapers.
- Help your child when necessary, but allow your child to do as much as she can.
- Encourage your child's questions and talk about her day.
- Be patient, she is learning and is curious.
- Play guessing games; for example, ask her "What is round, red, and good to eat?"
- Take your child to different places such as a firehouse, a bakery, and a library. Talk about feelings with your child. Allow your child freedom, but keep a watchful eye.

- Let her chatter; monsters, trains, Sesame Street, dreams, and camels are a few of the thoughts that your child will want to share with you. Write her stories in a notebook, she will enjoy hearing them over the years.

- In her rush to tell you about everything, she may stumble over words. This is very common. However, if you notice that she often stutters (cannot get her words out), you may want to arrange for a check-up with your doctor or clinic.

This is a very crucial developmental period. However, there will be more diversity of development at this level than at many others. Your child's neurological system is developing and will mature around age 8. Keep in mind that a skill that may not be there during one month, may appear the next month. The child at this stage is going through many changes, some of which can occur within a relatively short period of time. So be patient and don't get anxious if you observe your child playing with a peer and notice differences. It usually all evens-out in the end.

Four to Five Years

CHILD GROWTH

- Skips, hops, swings, climbs, somersaults.
- Employs self-help skills; dresses himself completely (laces shoes, combs hair), serves himself at the table, uses fork, spoon, and sometimes knife, almost always cares for his own toilet needs.
- Experiments with language; uses full sentences, tells longer stories.
- Says name and address.
- Shows understanding; has knowledge of events in time such as "yesterday," "next summer," and "when you grow up."
- Knows about things used everyday in the home such as money, foods, appliances, and furniture.
- Social skills; plays games with other children and can agree to rules. Likes to sing, dance, and act. Shows more independence (may visit a neighbor by himself).
- Interested in physical differences between boys and girls.

YOUR ROLE

- Take your child to the park where he can swing and climb safely.
- Encourage your child to care for himself and his home by giving him simple chores.
- Let your child help pick out his clothing.
- Pay attention when your child speaks to you. Show interest in what he has to say.

- Provide materials for drawing. Help your child to practice printing letters and numbers. It is quite normal for your child to print numbers and letters backwards at first.
- Tell your child as much about the world as you can.
- Help him to learn how to get along with others and to give-and-take.
- Boys and girls should be allowed to choose whatever play activity they want.

If you notice that your "little shadow" is no longer with you all the time, it is because he is now more interested in playing with other children. You may often be called upon to play the part of referee because children of this age are just beginning to learn how to get along with each other. Try to listen to both sides and help them to understand your decision.

You may also be wondering about milestones for specific areas such as toileting, grooming, dressing, eating, and so on. We have included many reference charts and lists in the Appendices on these and other areas.

chapter three

SCREENING PROCEDURES FOR SUSPECTED DISABILITIES

General Screening Procedures for All Students

This chapter is designed to help you become more familiar with the initial stages of the special-education process. The intent of the information and materials presented is to give you an overview of screening requirements for public schools. Although screening has many different meanings, for the purposes of this chapter, screening is defined as a preliminary method of distinguishing from the general population those pupils who may possibly have a disability.

Many local school districts currently conduct screening programs in an attempt to offer students individual assistance as soon as a need is identified. Screening is the first step in the identification process. It will be helpful for you as a parent to understand the general basis for screening.

What Is Screening?

Screening is defined as a method of distinguishing from the general population those pupils who possibly have a disability or those who may possess some other type of exceptionality. *Exceptional children* are defined as those whose school performance shows significant discrepancy between ability and achievement, and as a result require special instruction, assistance, and/or equipment. However, not all exceptional children fall under the Individuals with Disabilities Education Act (IDEA) concept of a disability. Exceptional children who may need special services but may not be considered disabled include gifted, bilingual, slow learners, those who have experienced environmental deprivation, and so forth.

Screening identifies those students in need of further evaluation and should not be viewed as an in-depth method of assessing development. Screening is a quick method of assessing a student's overall performance and should indicate whether or not an in-depth evaluation is necessary. Based upon the results of the screening, students who are in need of further evaluation should be referred to appropriate school and medical personnel.

Your school district is responsible for:

- Screening new entrants.

- Ensuring that students scoring below grade level two on a third-grade reading or mathematics test are screened. Students who obtain a certain percentile score on specific school-administered tests are screened. These are not teacher-made tests but more formal tests.

- Developing a written plan which describes screening procedures.

Transfer students that are from nonpublic schools within a state, from other states, and from other countries are considered to be new entrants and must be screened to determine if they may possibly have a disability or some other type of exceptionality. Student records and information from previous schools need to be reviewed in order to determine if screening has already been conducted.

Screening Program for New Entrants

Screening programs must be designed to obtain preliminary information regarding a child's development in the following areas:

Cognitive Development. Evaluative tools should be selected to provide a method of distinguishing the child's ability to function in an age-appropriate manner. A series of verbal and nonverbal tasks should be utilized to assess concept understanding, word associations, memory, general information, knowledge, and problem-solving ability.

Expressive and Receptive Language Development. The child's ability to understand and process spoken language is assessed through tasks requiring picture identification, following verbal directions, conversation, and direct questioning.

Articulation Skills. The child's ability to reproduce sounds and words are assessed through tasks which require repetition of words, phrases, and sentences. Articulation skills should be assessed, understanding that these skills will not be developed fully until the age of seven or eight.

Motor Development. A child's ability to move in the environment, to manipulate objects and use crayons, scissors, pencils, and so on can be tested by utilizing an obstacle course, drawing, tracing, and other fine and gross motor activities.

Physical Development. Development should include tests of vision and hearing, a review of the child's immunization records, tests for scoliosis, and a physical examination. Health examinations should be conducted by a duly licensed doctor, or evidence should be presented in the form of a health certificate that such an examination has been conducted.

School districts must assure that children are screened in a fair and unbiased manner. Districts must make every effort to screen children in their primary language. Persons conducting screening should ascertain the primary language spoken in the home by giving an oral efficiency test that will answer the following questions:

- Does the student function only in his or her native language?
- Does the student also converse in English?
- Does the student function fully in his or her native language and English?

Procedures for evaluating students with limited English proficiency (LEP) should be detailed in the school district's plan in order to assure that screening procedures are nondiscriminatory.

The tests that may be selected should be administered by appropriately trained paraprofessionals or professionals. Tests which have been designed to give an I.Q. score and are generally part of an in-depth evaluation are not suitable for a preliminary screening.

Where certain tests are not available in the child's primary language, school districts are responsible for providing an interpreter. Either the parent or the school district may request that an interpreter be provided. Your State Education Department can provide information on screening instruments available in languages other than English.

The results of the screening will automatically become part of the student's school records. School districts should ensure that policies regarding confidentiality are established, and that parents and children are informed of their rights to privacy.

The following questions and answers have been developed regarding the purpose and intent of screening requirements. Again, answers will vary state to state. You should take the time to question the following:

1. **How do screening and evaluation differ?**

   Screening is a measure of a pupil's abilities, while evaluation involves a comprehensive assessment of the pupil's abilities.

2. **Who should be screened?**

   New entrants, pupils scoring on the third-grade reading or mathematics tests, and all pupils who obtain a comparable percentile score on the state test.

3. **Should your child be referred for further evaluation?**

   As a result of the screening, only those children who may be referred for possibly having a disability or who may possibly be experiencing some other exceptionality may be referred.

4. Which areas of development should be screened?

Physical, receptive and expressive language, articulation, and motor and cognitive areas—any that will affect the child's ability to function in school.

5. Should school districts conduct screening of new entrants prior to the beginning of the school year?

Screening your child as a new entrant should be conducted prior to the school year, if possible, but no later than December 1 of that school year.

6. Who are the qualified medical personnel required to conduct the educational screening?

Physicians employed by the district, who may be assisted by trained nurses, dentists, dental hygienists, nutritionists, or optometrists.

7. Who is the qualified school person required to conduct physical screening?

Persons selected by the school district who have been trained appropriately. Professionals and/or paraprofessionals.

8. When should your child be referred to the Committee on Special Education (CSE)?

If it is determined that your child has an identified disability.

9. Is there a list of approved screening tests?

No.

10. Who refers a child who may be handicapped or gifted to the CSE or the District Superintendent?

Local procedures will dictate who should make the written referral. Procedures must, however, ensure that referrals to the CSE or District Superintendent should be made within 15 days of the screening.

11. Should your child be screened if identified as disabled prior to school entry?

No. A referral should be made directly to the CSE. (Refer to Chapter 5 for a more in-depth explanation.)

12. Should a child who does not speak English be screened?

Yes. The school district's screening program should include provisions to communicate with the student in his or her native language.

Representative School District Screening Model

School districts should develop a written plan at the beginning of each school year which describes their screening program. A school district should take into account local screening procedures and available resources in the development of the plan. The plan should include, but not be limited to:

- Procedures for developing a list of all students who should be screened.

- Outlines for conducting screening for new entrants, and those scoring below the indicated levels on the state tests.

- Descriptions of the specific screening tests to be used at each level.

- Provisions for a notice of screening to be sent to parents of each child to be screened in advance of the screening date.

- Process for screening non-English-speaking students.

- Process for assuring confidentiality.

- Process for assuring nonbiased testing.

- Process for reporting the results to parents.

- Process for referral to the CSE for a child who may possibly have a handicapping condition, and referral to the Superintendent for a child who may possibly be gifted.

- Descriptions of personnel responsible for supervising and conducting screening.

- Descriptions of procedures used to provide in-service training to all professionals and paraprofessionals involved in screening.

While formal screening procedures are a normal part of every school district, informal screening usually takes place on a regular basis in each school within a district. These local school teams called Child Study Teams, Pupil Personnel Teams, School-Based Support Teams, and so on meet on a regular basis to discuss any potentially high-risk students. The members of these teams work as a single unit in determining the possible cause (etiology), contributing factors, educational status, outcome (prognosis), and recommendations for a student. The concept of bringing many disciplines together to help work on a case is the major objective of such teams. In this way you have many experts covering many fields and disciplines rather than a single individual trying to determine all of the factors.

You as a parent should become familiar with the school procedures that are utilized in screening children for potential problems or a suspected disability. While parents are not members of such school-based teams, your knowledge of how they work can only enhance your understanding of your options.

Membership of the Pupil Personnel Team

This team (for the purpose of clarity we will use the term Pupil Personnel Team or PPT to indicate all such teams) is usually made up of the following individuals:

Administrator. This is usually the principal or assistant principal. This individual leads the team and designates responsibility when required. The administrator can also contribute any information regarding prior family meetings, involvement with other siblings, and so on.

Psychologist. The psychologist is the member of the team who determines the presence of psychological symptoms in the child's profile. He/she is also able to interpret behavior, analyze prior testing, and offer the team insight into the child's intellectual and emotional state.

Nurse Teacher. This professional is valuable in interpreting prior medical history or providing screening in visual and hearing areas.

Classroom Teacher. The teacher provides an experiential profile of your child on a day-to-day basis. He/she can also help the team by providing patterns of behavior and examples of your child's work for interpretation and analysis. The teacher can also provide first-hand knowledge of your child's social interaction and any involvement with you and your concerns.

Social Worker. Many teams may not have a social worker. This individual can provide valuable information on family dynamics and provide information if a home visit is involved.

Special-Education Teacher. This individual is responsible for analyzing academic and perceptual symptoms that your child may be experiencing. The special-education teacher may also be called upon to interpret past evaluations, and Individual Educational Plans or other materials, especially if your child has already been classified.

Guidance Counselor. The guidance counselor, usually a member of a secondary team, can also provide past academic history, prior formal group test results, scheduling factors, teacher comments, and vocational skills.

Reading Teacher. Some teams include the reading teacher if he/she is available. The reading teacher can provide an in-depth analysis of a child's reading skills or alert the team to symptoms that might reflect severe reading problems.

Speech and Language Teacher. This professional provides the team with the ability to diagnose and analyze symptoms that might reflect a receptive or expressive language disorder. Further, this individual can interpret outside speech and language evaluations for the team.

The members of this team usually meet on a regular basis, once or twice a week depending upon the case load. This is a local school-based support team and should not be confused with the Committee on Special Education which is a district-based team with a parent member. The Pupil Personnel Team does not have a parent member and is not required to do so, as is the CSE.

Questions Considered by the Pupil Personnel Team

When a PPT first receives a referral from a teacher it must consider many issues. These may include the following:

1. **Has this child ever been referred to the PPT?**

   Prior referral may indicate a *historical disturbance* (long-term problem) and therefore a more serious situation, especially if the same pattern exists. *Situational disturbances*, (with no prior history of problems indicated) usually have a better outcome.

2. **Do we have any prior psychological, educational, or language evaluations?**

This information is very important so that your child is not put through unnecessary testing. These reports also offer the team another perspective on the problem. If such reports are available you should have copies of all of them. You may want to request copies of all testing, evaluations, and so on from the school. While it is normal procedure to receive a report after an evaluation is completed, some schools may not follow this practice. Regardless, you may request that a copy of your child's report be sent to you. This is your absolute right.

3. Is anyone familiar with other family members?

Family patterns of behavior may help define contributing factors to the child's problem. If you or any family members are experiencing certain issues which might affect your child's performance in school, then it would be helpful for one of the team members to know. It may also offer the team some experience on the best and most delicate approach to take with your family. If you are concerned about telling the school about some personal family issue, then seek advice from an outside professional who may be able to work with the school about your concerns.

4. Are there any medical issues we need to be aware of at this time that might impact this case?

These issues are crucial and the existence of medical problems should always be determined first. Difficulties with hearing, eyesight, taking medication, severe allergies, and so on may be significant contributors to poor performance and may be masked as "unmotivated," "lazy," or "stubborn" behavior. It would be very important for you to allow the school such information. With this in hand, specific symptoms that your child may be exhibiting can be understood and dealt with in a more realistic manner.

5. What do his/her report cards look like? What patterns are exhibited?

Some children have trouble starting off in a new situation and play catch-up the entire year. Others do well the first marking period and slowly decline to a pattern of poor grades. Others exhibit the roller coaster effect with children consistently receiving grades from failing to passing. Knowing your child's report-card "style" may help with the type of support, remediation, and program offered by the school.

6. What are his group achievement test score patterns?

Achievement test scores can offer a great deal of useful information about your child's patterns. If the team suspects a learning disability, then the areas affected should be consistently low from year to year. Many fluctuations of scores and wide ranges of results may indicate more emotional involvement than a learning disability. If your child is not functioning in the classroom but consistently receives achievement scores within the 90th percentile, he/she may not be functioning because of reasons other than suspected learning disabilities.

7. If no prior testing is available, is there any group IQ test information to give us some general idea of ability?

While group IQ tests should never be used to determine your child's true intellectual potential, they may offer a general idea of his/her ability. The problem with group tests for children with learning and emotional problems is that they may lack the energy or motivation to adequately take such tests. Since it is being given to the group, your child's behavior towards the test can be hidden easily or not observed.

8. Has anyone observed this child?

This piece of information is required if the team plans to refer your child to the CSE. In any case, observation should always be a piece of the contributing information presented to the PPT. One member, usually the psychologist, social worker, guidance counselor, or special education teacher, observes your child in a variety of situations prior to the first PPT meeting. It is very important for the team to know how your child functions in structured and unstructured settings.

9. Do we have samples of his classwork?

Samples of your child's classwork over a period of time offer a clearer overview of his or her abilities and attitude towards class work. This also gives several team members an opportunity to observe possible academic symptoms that may first appear in written work.

10. Has the parent been notified of the teacher's concerns?

The team should not be the one to notify you that a problem may exist. It is the responsibility of the classroom teacher to alert you that he or she is concerned and would like the PPT to take a closer look at your child. Unlike the CSE, you do not have a legal right to refuse such a request since it is considered a normal school procedure. You should also be notified by the teacher that someone from the team will be in touch with you to gather more information and to review any findings.

At this point the school may ask you to come in for a *parent intake* in order to gather more information that may assist in the diagnosis of the problem or problems. Do not be afraid of this procedure. However, if you are concerned, first ask to see a copy of the parent intake form or the questions to be asked and consult with an outside professional about the best way to handle your concerns.

Options of the Pupil Personnel Team

In the meantime, the PPT may be discussing the next logical step at a series of meetings that may take up to several weeks depending on delays, conflicts, procedures, organizational ability of the team, and so on. Once the PPT has all the necessary information gathered on your child including:

- evaluations
- observations
- rating scales
- parent intake
- work samples

- academic records
- group achievement scores
- medical records
- past teacher reports

it can determine a direction. There are several directions and recommendations that can be instituted during this process by the PPT, which follow.

PSYCHOEDUCATIONAL EVALUATION: The team may utilize this recommendation when your child's academic skill levels (reading, math, writing, and spelling) are unknown or inconsistent, his/her learning process shows gaps (i.e. memory, expression) or when making a referral to the Committee on Special Education for a suspected disability. This is done in order to rule out or rule in a discrepancy between ability and academic achievement required for the classification of Learning Disabled (LD), or to determine strengths and weaknesses in academic and perceptual (how a child processes information) areas. It is very important for the team to identify any student who is not working up to his/her potential as a result of some factor such as emotional interference or learning disabilities. When a child does not work up to his/her potential as a result of some factor we consider it a discrepancy. Any discrepancy in achievement must be explored for the possibility of a suspected disability. Some symptoms that might suggest this recommendation are:

- Consistently low test scores on group achievement tests.
- Indications of problems in processing information when faced with academic requirements.
- Labored handwriting after grade 3.
- Poor word recall.
- Poor decoding (word attack) skills.
- Discrepancy between achievement and ability. Achievement is usually measured by academic tests, while ability is measured by an intellectual evaluation.
- Consistently low achievement despite remediation.

LANGUAGE EVALUATION: This recommendation usually occurs when the child is experiencing significant delays in speech or language development, problems in articulation, or problems in receptive or expressive language. Some symptoms that might warrant such an evaluation would be:

- Difficulty pronouncing words through grade 3.
- Immature or delayed speech patterns.
- Difficulty labeling thoughts or objects.
- Difficulty putting thoughts into words.

PSYCHOLOGICAL EVALUATION: This recommendation may be suggested by the school when the child's intellectual ability is unknown or there is a questionable factor in his/her ability to learn. Also, this recommendation is used when referring to the CSE for potential learning, emotional, or intellectual problems. The psychological evaluation can rule out or rule in emotionality as a primary cause of a child's problem. Ruling this factor out is required before the diagnosis of LD can be determined. Some symptoms that might signal the need for such an evaluation are:

- High levels of tension and anxiety exhibited in behavior.
- Aggressive behavior.
- Lack of motivation or indications of low energy levels.
- Patterns of denial.
- Oppositional behavior.
- Despondency.
- Inconsistent academic performance ranging from very low to very high.
- History of inappropriate judgment.
- Lack of impulse control.
- Extreme and consistent attention-seeking behavior.
- Pattern of provocative behavior.

REFERRAL TO CSE FOR A MEETING TO DISCUSS THE RECOMMENDATION FOR EVALUATION DENIED BY PARENT(S):   If you refuse to sign a release for testing and the school feels strongly that such a procedure is in the best interests of the child, then a review by the CSE is possible to resolve this dispute. If available, the school may urge you to attend a meeting prior to this referral so that some agreement or compromise can be worked out. While it may be difficult for you to attend due to work schedules, family responsibilities, or other reasons, you should make every attempt to have at least one parent present.

Parents will often ask about their rights concerning an evaluation. You do have the right to refuse an evaluation requested by the school. However, you should make sure that you have valid reasons since the school can take certain actions if it strongly feels the need to evaluate, including making a referral to Child Protective Services for educational neglect. While this is a last resort, many schools feel that in serious cases, such a referral is valid. You are also entitled to go outside of school for an independent evaluation. The school must provide you with a list of low-cost options for such an evaluation. Whenever possible, keep in mind that you can let the school do the evaluation and then take the results to an outside professional for another opinion. Having the testing done does not lock you into anything since your due-process rights are still in effect.

Whatever the recommendation instituted by the Pupil Personnel Team, it should be done with all the most recent available information on a child. Such recommendations may have tremendous implications and should never be taken lightly.

Confidentiality

Information about your child collected through the screening program automatically becomes a part of your child's school records. The school district should have established policies regarding confidentiality of information contained in the school record such as informing you and your children of your right to privacy, of who has access to the information, and to challenge those records should they be inaccurate, misleading, or otherwise inappropriate. To communicate this information to you, handouts describing the district's policy on confidentiality of school records are usually given to you prior to or on the day of the screening.

Since individuals conducting the screening are involved in collecting confidential information about your child's health status and educational development, it is very important that verbal as well as written accounts of the child's performance be held in the strictest confidence. Screening personnel should treat their own impressions and concerns about the children they see in a confidential manner and should refrain from talking about children and their performance with people not directly involved with conducting the screening. If you ask how your child is doing during the screening, do not be upset if the evaluator explains that the screening results are meaningful only after all the testing has been completed and your child's performance in all areas is recorded. The person in charge of screening may choose to designate certain persons responsible for answering specific questions about the screening instruments, children's responses, and screening reports. You might also want to inform the evaluator at this time that you would like to receive a complete typed report from the screening personnel.

Reviewing the Results of the Screening

Screening personnel should be available to you during your review of the results. A summary profile of the results may be helpful when reviewing the information and making decisions regarding the referral of a child identified as having a disability. Criteria should be established for reviewing the results of non-English-speaking students, which takes into consideration the child's native language.

Should further evaluation be indicated, screening records and information along with the reports from screening personnel should accompany all referrals.

Referring Children Who May Have a Suspected Disability

In the review of screening results, personnel should develop criteria for determining which students should be referred as possibly disabled. The results of this review should indicate specific information regarding the reason for the referral. Individuals who are responsible for making such referrals should be identified. The school principal, screening personnel, or you may make the referral.

Referral to the CSE should be in writing and its format similar to the referral forms currently being used by the district. The referral must be made to the CSE as soon as possible. Once the Committee receives the written referral, it collects and reviews all existing information in your child's record including the screening results and the reason for the referral. After review of existing information, the CSE determines the need for additional testing and notifies the parents of the proposed evaluation, its intended uses, and requests written consent for evaluation.

If your child is identified as disabled, at the time a referral is made to the CSE the Individualized Education Program (IEP) process begins for him/her. This process includes evaluation, classification, placement, and the development and implementation of an Individualized Education Program with an annual review.

chapter four
HOW YOU CAN OBSERVE YOUR CHILD FOR SUSPECTED DISABILITIES

School Symptoms Exhibited by High-Risk Students

There are times when you will observe behaviors that confuse your child. Such behaviors may be symptoms of more serious concerns or may be indications of stress within your child. To ignore them will only make them become worse. Many parents may not want to "see" what is happening because they feel helpless and have no idea what to do. But acknowledging that a problem may be present will not only alleviate the child's tension, but ensure a greater chance for successful resolution. The longer the problems fester, the greater the scars.

A high-risk student is usually a student that is experiencing severe emotional, social, environmental, or academic stress. As a result of this intense turmoil, many symptoms are generated in a dynamic attempt to alleviate the anxiety. They can show up in many different behavior patterns. Some of the more common ones that can be exhibited by either elementary or secondary students while in school are:

- A history of adequate or high first-quarter grades followed by a downward trend leading to failures in the final quarter.
- A history of excessive absences.
- A history of excessive lateness.
- Frequently cannot separate from parent at the start of the school day. While this can be normal behavior in very young children, it becomes a more serious symptom after age 6 or 7.

- High achievement scores and high school-abilities index with a history of low academic performance.
- Consistent failure in two or more quarters of at least two subjects.
- Students wandering the halls after school with no direction or purpose.
- A history of constant blame onto others as a reason for a lack of performance, handing in work, failures, or cutting.
- A history of feeling powerless in the student's approach to problems.
- Recent stress-related experiences such as divorce, separation, death of a parent, or parent's loss of employment.
- A history of constant visits to the nurse.
- Social withdrawal from peers with an emphasis on developing relationships with adults.

There may be other patterns as well. However, keep in mind that the *frequency, duration,* and *intensity of symptoms* is crucial in determining a pattern of high-risk. Children with serious problems are not "stubborn" or "lazy." The real reasons for a lack of academic production or inappropriate behavior may lie in their dynamic state of tension and how it affects their abilities to learn in the classroom.

How Emotional Problems Affect a Child's Ability to Function in the Classroom

When children are experiencing serious emotional turmoil, the tension that is generated usually results in *symptoms*. These symptoms become the first signal noticed by parents and teachers. Therefore, it is very important for you to understand the difference between symptoms and problems. If this is not fully understood, a great deal of frustration will occur in trying to extinguish the symptom on both the part of the child and the parent. The identification of symptoms as an indication of something more serious is another first step in helping children work out their problems.

Symptomatic Behavior

Examples of typical symptomatic behavior that may be indicative of more serious concerns may include the following:

Impulsivity	Lies constantly
Frequently hands in incomplete work	Awkward
Gives many excuses for inappropriate behavior	Fearful of adults
Constantly blames others for problems	Fearful of new situations
Panics easily	Verbally hesitant

Distractible

Short attention span

Overreactive

Physical with others

Intrusive

Unable to focus on task

Procrastinates

Squints

Turns head while listening

Disorganization

Inflexibility

Irresponsibility

Poor judgment

Denial

Daydreaming

Unwillingness to venture a guess

Unwillingness to reason

Social withdrawal

Constant use of self-criticism

Bullies other children

Needs constant reassurance

Poor reader

Hypoactive

Hyperactive

Fears criticism

Rarely takes chances

Moody

Defies authority

Anxious

Not able to generalize

Insecure

Trouble starting work

Tires easily

Controlling

Overly critical

Forgetfulness

Painfully shy

Overly social

Slow starter

Argumentative

Destroys property

Lazy

Inconsistency

Poor spelling

How to Determine the Severity of a Problem

While many of these symptoms may indicate a problem, several guidelines should be used to determine the severity of the situation:

Frequency of Symptoms. Consider how often the symptoms occur. The greater the frequency, the greater the chance of a serious problem.

Duration of Symptoms. Consider how long the symptoms last. The longer the duration, the more serious the problem.

Intensity of Symptoms. Consider how serious the reactions are at the time of occurrence. The more intense the symptom, the more serious the problem.

If you suspect serious problems they cannot be ignored. The more immediate the response to such symptoms, the greater the chance of success with the child.

Avoidance Behavior Patterns

Perhaps the first thing you will notice when children are experiencing problems with learning are several Avoidance Symptoms. These are techniques used by children to avoid what they perceive as a failure or an ego-deflating situation. Children will often exhibit these symptoms at home and at school to avoid loss of parental approval, peer humiliation, or fear of failure. In this way, children do not have to:

- Show their parents they are not capable.
- Deal with possible parental anger and frustration.
- Come face-to-face with their own inadequacy.
- Deal with peer pressure and possible ridicule.

Avoidance behaviors are common "tools" utilized by children who are experiencing problems in learning. Some of the more common ones follow.

1. **Selective Forgetting**. This is a symptom in which your child knows the batting averages of all baseball players, the words from most songs on the radio, the times of most TV shows, but "forgets" to bring home his/her math book. The selectivity of the forgetfulness usually centers around areas of learning that may be creating frustration.

2. **Forgets to write down assignments day after day**. This symptom may continue even after repeated requests. The avoidance of a perceived failure experience is accomplished through the use of this behavior.

3. **Takes hours to complete homework**. In this particular case, your child seems to labor or procrastinate over the work. Frequent trips to the kitchen for food, or to the bathroom, or to get a drink, or sharpen a pencil, will delay the possibility of perceived failure. This symptom also occurs if your child is under tension and cannot concentrate for long periods of time. He/she will tend to "burn out" quickly and daydream the night away.

4. **Finishes homework very quickly**. In this type of symptom your child's major objective is to get the ego-threatening situation (homework) over as quickly as possible. Every attempt is made to "rush" through the assignments with little if any care or patience. Getting it over as quickly as possible almost makes it seem as if it never existed.

5. **Can't seem to get started with homework**. When your child's anxiety level is very high it makes it very difficult to "start the engine." Like a cold engine on a winter day, you can turn the key and it revs but never turns over. Your child may act in the same way. He/she may spend a great deal of time getting "ready" for the homework by arranging books, sharpening pencils, getting the paper out, opening the textbooks, getting a glass of water, going to the bathroom and so on, but never really starting the assignments.

6. **Frequently brings home unfinished classwork**. This symptom is frequently exhibited by your child for several reasons. One reason is a low energy level and therefore problems dealing with tasks involving sustained concentration. The second reason may involve the concept of learned helplessness and may arise when, without knowing the implications, you constantly sit next to your child when he/she is doing homework. When this happens, your child becomes conditioned to your assistance and is helpless without it. Since someone sitting next to your child is not recreated in the classroom, your child procrastinates over classwork so that he/she can bring it home and do it with you.

   The third reason may involve your child's need for attention. Bringing home unfinished classwork may necessitate that you sit with him/her and complete the work. This "captive audience" of your attention is reinforced when you try to leave. Your child stops working or complains that he/she can't do it. Consequently, you may remain seated next to your child. Bringing home unfinished classwork extends the period of attention your child may receive from you. However, these types of situations usually become more tense and negative as the hours progress and your patience waivers.

7. **Consistently leaves long-term assignments until the last minute**. Avoidance of school-related tasks, especially long-term ones, is a frequent symptom of children with low energy levels. It would be like avoiding paying a big bill when you have very little money. You may "hide" the bill or forget it exists. Magical thinking is a frequent dynamic/mechanism of children who are highly anxious.

8. **Complains of feeling ill before or after school**. Very high tension levels over an extended period of time may result in somatic (bodily) complaints. These complaints, while real to your child, may indicate an avoidance of an uncomfortable or ego-deflating situation. When your child has a pattern of these types of complaints, you may need to be aware that this "signal" may be a symptom of a more serious problem.

9. **Exhibits "spotlight" behaviors**. "Spotlight" behaviors are any behaviors that bring the focus of attention to your child: For instance, calling out, laughing out loud, getting up out of seat, annoying other children. When this occurs it is usually a release of tension. Some children use "spotlight" behaviors to alleviate the tension of academic inadequacy and may even hope to get into trouble to leave the room. In this way they will not have to deal with possible academic failure. Another reason for "spotlight" behaviors is control. However, keep in mind that the more controlling your child is, the more out of control they may feel. The third reason for "spotlight" behaviors is for the sole purpose of gaining the teacher's attention. However in this way your child is determining when he/she gets attention, not the teacher. It is better for the teacher to spontaneously and randomly pay attention to your child when he/she is not expecting it. In this way you may reduce your child's impulsive need for seeking attention.

How Problems May Affect Your Child's Behavior and Ability to Learn

We feel that as a parent it is very important that you learn to recognize the difference between symptoms and problems. Many times, parents will mistakenly try to correct symptoms thinking that they might be the problem: for instance, stubbornness, procrastination, daydreaming. When a serious problem exists within your child, the problem creates tension. This tension needs to be released so it is turned into symptomatic behavior. Symptoms reduce the tension created by a conflict or a problem. If you treat the symptom you will miss the problem. However symptoms, like signals, allow us the opportunity to become aware that a serious problem exists. Negative symptomatic behavior only results from serious conflicts or problems. Positive symptomatic behavior will only result when your child is free from serious conflicts or problems. Therefore, it is crucial that you understand both types of symptoms and what they represent so that you can be able to deal with a potential problem as soon as possible.

If your child is experiencing many conflicts, problems, and insecurities, there will be an increase in the number, types, and degree of negative symptoms. Therefore, the greater the frequency, duration, and intensity of the symptoms, the greater the energy drain on the part of the child. All conflicts require energy and the greater the number of conflicts or the more serious the conflict the greater expense of energy required. Since everyone has a certain amount of available energy, the energy required to deal with these conflicts must come from somewhere. Therefore conflicts tend to drain energy away from other processes such as concentration, memory, attention, and so on. Since these processes are so necessary for success in school, the child will begin to suffer.

Normal Development—Division of Energy

Everyone has a certain amount of psychic energy to use in dealing with the everyday stresses of life. In normal development there is a certain amount of stress but because of an absence of major conflicts which tend to drain energy, the individual has more than enough to keep things in perspective. Consequently, the division of energy and the positive symptoms that result (more often than not) when a child is relatively "conflict-free" may take on a certain pattern.

For instance, in school your child will exhibit (more often than not) behaviors that include good concentration, being responsible with school work, consistency, age-appropriate attention span, flexibility, appropriate memory, high frustration tolerance, appropriate peer interaction, organization, and an appropriate ability to focus on tasks. You will hear these comments from teachers and notice many at home when your child is involved with homework. It is also important that you keep in mind that not every child who is conflict-free will exhibit these symptoms all the time. Only become concerned if you notice patterns of behaviors that may reflect a potential problem.

If your child is conflict free, you will also notice certain positive behavior patterns at home. These will include (more often than not), normal strivings for parental approval, resiliency, willingness to reason, willingness to try, appropriate judgment, and normal responses to discipline. Again keep in mind that these patterns may vary to some degree during adolescence and still be within "normal" limits.

If your child is not experiencing any major problems, he/she will usually have little difficulty falling asleep. While they may have problems waking up, as many of us do, it will not interfere in their ability to get to school. A problem like this is only serious when it affects one's ability to function. Such would be the case if a child could not get up every morning and was consistently late to school. This type of symptomatic behavior might be a signal of a more serious problem.

Socially, your child will (more often than not) maintain social interactions, show a willingness to try new social experiences, and treat his/her peers appropriately.

High Tension Level—Division of Energy

However, when serious conflicts arise, the available energy must be "pulled" to deal with the conflicts like white blood cells to an infection. Since energy must be drained away, there is less available energy to keep things in perspective. In this case the resulting symptoms and behaviors take on a different look.

When a parent or teacher observes a pattern of behaviors similar to these, he/she should automatically become aware that some serious problem may exist. These symptoms are not the *problems*, but an *outgrowth* of a serious problem. It is therefore very important for the parent to try to identify what the problem or problems are so that treatment can take place.

If you suspect some difficulty as a result of a negative symptomatic pattern, do not hesitate to contact the school psychologist or contact a local therapist for a consultation. Like an "infection," waiting too long will only aggravate the situation.

Serious problems may arise for many reasons. The following are examples of some of the causes of serious problems which might result in negative symptomatic behavior:

1. **Intellectual Reasons.**

   Limited intelligence/slow learner

   Retardation

2. **Social Reasons.**

   Peer pressure

   Peer rejection

3. **Emotional Reasons.**

   Consistent school failure

   Traumatic emotional development

   Separation or divorce

High parental expectations

Sibling performance

Health-related problems

Change in environment as a result of moving

Abuse

Dysfunctional family situation

Parental loss of job

Death in the family

4. Academic Reasons.

Learning disabilities

Poor academic skills (math, reading)

Style of teacher versus style of student

Language difficulties

Falling behind in school because of an imbalance in other areas (for example, too social)

Consequently, when such serious problems or conflicts arise, they will drain off energy normally used for home and school. As this energy is drained away to deal with these serious issues, negative symptomatic behavior patterns will develop. Such symptoms should indicate to you that a problem exists and needs to be defined as soon as possible. These negative behavior patterns, indicating the presence of conflicts, will be observed in many areas of the child's life.

For instance, at school your child may now exhibit negative symptoms like inability to focus on task, procrastination, disorganization, denial, irresponsibility, inflexibility, projecting the reasons for problems on everyone and everything else, selected forgetting, daydreaming, and so on.

At home you may observe oversensitivity, overreactions, forgetfulness, unwillingness to venture out, unwillingness to reason, stubbornness, lying, exaggeration, and possible somatic complaints such as stomachaches, headaches, and so forth. You may even begin to notice changes in your child's sleeping patterns. He/she may have great difficulty falling asleep since tension interferes with relaxation, and may even begin to sleepwalk or exhibit other signs of restless sleep. In the morning you may find extreme resistance in getting up, which may result in lateness or absence. More frequent nightmares may also be a signal of some unresolved inner conflicts.

Socially, you may observe your child withdrawing from social situations, constantly finding fault with peers, being unwilling to try new social experiences, or expressing social fears or beliefs that no one likes him/her.

Remember that such symptoms occur only as a result of a deeper undefined problem. Once the problem is identified and resolved, the negative symptomatic behavior will dissipate since the tension will be alleviated. If caught early, most of these issues can be resolved in a relatively quick period of time. However, also be aware that even though the problem may be identified, many months or years may have passed and will result in a longer treatment period.

If therapy is required be aware that it can be a long-term process, especially if the problems have been around for a long period of time. However, you can tell if your child is making progress in therapy by the reduction of the negative symptomatic behavior patterns. As a child begins to verbalize the issues and finds better ways of coping, the tension becomes diminished. As the tension is reduced the need for symptomatic behavior is also reduced. Usually a reduction in the frequency, duration, and intensity of negative symptoms will mean that your child is getting stronger and may be on the right track.

chapter five
PRESCHOOL SPECIAL EDUCATION

Early Intervention—Preschool

As stated earlier, as a parent, you are your child's most important teacher. Your child's future will be guided by these early years as you help your child to grow. When your child has a disability or a developmental delay, life will seem more complicated than you had hoped. In order to help you and your child, there are many different types of services available. We hope that this chapter will help you through these times so that the goals you have for your child may become a reality.

When Should You Be Concerned?

When one or more of the following is reflective of your child: Is your child not rolling, walking, or moving like other children the same age? Does your child talk differently than other children? Is your child not talking? Does your child have problems seeing or hearing, or other health problems? Is child too active, or not active enough? Does your child have difficulty sucking or swallowing?

If you answered yes to any of these questions, you may want to think about having your child evaluated. You can contact your county's early intervention office. A service coordinator will explain this program more fully to you. Your service coordinator can provide you with the names of persons or organizations that are approved to evaluate your child for free. From this list, you will be able to choose the evaluator. This evaluation will help you in deciding if your child is eligible for early intervention services and what types of services may be needed. Just remember, only you can decide to have your child evaluated.

Why Parents Are Important

You are your child's best advocate. You are the person who can help your family through the many decisions that will need to be made and the special services to be sought. You are the person who knows what is helpful and what is not; knows about other evaluations that professionals have written or said about your child; knows what your child does not like; knows what interests your child, and *knows your child*. In a world filled with professional titles, consider yourself a *family specialist*!

Referral of Your Child

You or someone else (for example, your child's doctor or other health-care provider) will call the early intervention official to refer your child for early intervention services.

Talking With Your Service Coordinator

You will talk with your service coordinator about the Early Intervention Program.

Evaluation

You will choose whether or not to have your child evaluated; you will choose who will do the evaluation and to give written permission to have your child evaluated.

Individualized Family Service Plan

You will decide if you want to participate in an Individualized Family Service Plan meeting; you and other persons on the Individualized Family Service Plan team will identify the services your child and family will receive; you will give your consent for any early intervention services to be provided to your child and family.

Review of the Individualized Family Service Plan

You will help review your child's Individualized Family Service Plan at least every six months or at more frequent times if you request.

Transition

You will help plan for changing services or programs when your child turns three.

As a parent you are the most important person in your child's life. Early Intervention Program directors will look to you for your advice on what your child and family needs. Here are some simple points to remember to help you be an effective advocate:

- View yourself as an equal member of early intervention teams.
- Know your rights and stand up for your rights. To do that, you need to find out about parent support groups and advocacy groups in your area. Do not hesitate to call them early for advice, support, or help.
- Resolve problems early but be willing to file a complaint if you cannot find a solution with which you are happy.
- Keep copies of letters you write and notes about conversations you have with your service coordinator and service providers.
- Ask professionals why they are recommending certain services.
- Ask questions of your service coordinator and the evaluator if anything is not clear to you.
- Be involved in every step of planning for and providing early intervention services.

What Is the Early Intervention Program?

An Early Intervention Program is a statewide program that provides a wide variety of services to eligible infants and toddlers with disabilities, and their families. The program will help you and your family to meet the special needs of your child. You can help choose the services and the places where they will be provided depending on your child's needs. Whenever possible, these services can be provided in your home or in a community setting such as a daycare center. The services that should be available to you and your child include, but are not limited to:

1. Medical services for diagnostic and evaluation purposes.
2. Early identification, screening, and assessment services.
3. Service coordination services.
4. Special instruction.
5. Speech pathology and audiology.
6. Occupational therapy.
7. Physical therapy.
8. Psychological services.
9. Social-work services.
10. Vision services.
11. Health services necessary for the child to benefit from Early Intervention.
12. Nursing services.
13. Family training, counseling, home visits, parent support groups.

14. Transportation.
15. Technology devices and services.

In addition to these early intervention services, *respite services* (services that are provided when a student needs in-home or out-of-home care) may be provided to you. These services may include in-home or out-of-home respite. You will have an important role in planning how these services, if needed, can be provided.

If your child is found to be eligible and you wish to have your child receive services, an Individualized Preschool Service Plan (IPSP) will be developed. This plan will describe the early intervention services your child will receive, and how often and where the services can be provided. When deciding on where your child will receive services, the Early Intervention Program can, when appropriate for your child, have these services provided in a natural environment. A natural environment could be your home, daycare setting, or other place that normally serves children without disabilities. Remember, only the services you consent to should be provided to your child and family. Your child has the right to receive those early intervention services included in the Individualized Preschool Service Plan, so make certain that this plan addresses their concerns.

What Determines Your Child's Eligibility for Services?

The individual evaluation of a preschool child who is suspected of having a disability must include information pertaining to functional areas related to cognitive, language and communicative, adaptive, social-emotional or motor development in order to determine the child's individual needs as expressed on the Individualized Education Program (IEP). Information must be obtained from a physical examination, an individual psychological evaluation, a social history, a parent interview, a structured observation of the child's performance and behavior, and other assessment procedures as necessary to ascertain specific factors contributing to the suspected disability. These procedures may include, but are not limited to, norm-referenced tests, criterion-referenced instruments, developmental checklists, teacher reports, and other test results of the child. The amended regulations require that such evaluation must be administered individually, provided in the child's dominant language, not be dependent on a single procedure, administered by a multidisciplinary team, and be consistent with all other requirements. All available information about the child must be reviewed and considered in comparison to accepted milestones of child development.

What Is the Criteria Used in Determining Eligibility?

A determination of a disability should be made when a child exhibits a significant delay or disorder in one or more of the functional areas of development which adversely affects the preschool child's ability to learn. A significant delay or disorder must be documented by the results of an individual evaluation and should indicate the following:

- A 12-month delay in one or more functional areas.

- A 33-percent delay in one functional area, or a 25-percent delay in each of two functional areas.

- If standardized instruments are administered individually in the evaluation process, a score of 2.0 standard deviations below the mean in one functional area, or a score of 1.5 standard deviations below the mean in each of two functional areas.

- Meet the criteria of autistic, deaf, deaf-blind, hard of hearing, orthopedically impaired, other health-impaired, traumatic brain-injured, or visually impaired.

Under Individuals with Disabilities Education Act (IDEA), special education must be made available to every eligible preschool child with a disability at no cost to the parent, and regular education at no cost, to the extent it is available to children who do not have disabilities. Every Individualized Education Program (IEP) must define the extent to which the preschool student will participate in programs in the least-restrictive environment (for instance, opportunities for interaction with peers who do not have disabilities).

Further, while specialized instruction and related services must be made available as part of a state's free appropriate public education requirements under Federal law, it does not require the municipality to make regular education available at no cost, if the state law expressly prohibits or does not authorize the expenditure of public funds to provide education to children who do not have disabilities in that age group. Law does not provide a free universal system of preschool education for three- and four-year-olds. A Committee on Preschool Special Education is only authorized to place a child in a preschool setting that is approved by the State to provide special education or provide special-education-itinerant-teacher services or related services in the child's natural environment which could include the early childhood setting where the parent has arranged for the child to attend. An early childhood setting means a regular preschool program or daycare program in which a child under the age of five attends, including a school district's prekindergarten program.

Most states provide for special education through the schools beginning at age three. Prior to age three parents can receive services through the family courts and local county governments. Contact your local school district for guidance regarding your early concerns. Do not delay if you suspect there is a problem. If your local district is not helpful, contact your State Education Department, the Department of Health or the Council for Exceptional Children at: 1920 Association Drive, Reston, VA 22091 (703-620-3660).

Special-education programs and services are available to preschool children with disabilities. Agencies, organizations, and some school districts provide special-education services to preschool children. Infants and toddlers receive special-education services. Currently, children from birth through age two with disabilities access the service delivery system when their parents petition the Family Court in their county of residence for special-education and transportation services. Three- and four-year-old children also receive special-education services. Three- and four-year-old children who are suspected of having a disability may be referred to a Committee on Preschool

Special Education (CPSE) in their school district of residence. The district will arrange for an evaluation of the child at an SED approved program of your choice, at no cost to the family. Following a review of the evaluation report by the CPSE, if a child is determined to be educationally disabled, the Board of Education will make a recommendation for special-education programs and services. Parents can find out about programs and services available to preschool children with disabilities. Early Childhood Direction Centers coordinated by the Education Departments, are sound resources for parents. They provide information about preschool special-education programs and help parents obtain services for their children. To be eligible for services, children ages birth to five who may have physical, mental, or emotional disabilities and may be in need of services are eligible. State Education Department professional staff provides information about:

- Preschool programs
- Transportation
- Medical, educational, and social services
- Evaluation and assessment services
- Funding
- Petitioning the Family Court
- Parent-education programs and resources
- Daycare

Services that will be provided include:

- Matching the needs of children with available services
- Referral to agencies providing direct services
- Assisting parents in obtaining services
- Assisting parents in petitioning the Family Court
- Following up to ensure that children receive services
- Coordination of services

Who may use the services?

- Parents or guardians of children with disabilities
- Ages birth to five
- Local school districts
- Hospital programs
- Agencies and organizations
- Head Start programs

Remember, early identification is the key to success.

chapter six

THE SPECIAL-EDUCATION PROCESS

The Referral Process—Step 1

A referral is nothing more than a form starting the special-education process in a formal manner. A referral can be submitted by any number of staff, or parents such as yourself, or judiciary as follows. A referral for evaluation and possible special-education services is initiated through a written request by any one of the following individuals:

- You as your child's parent and advocate, or person in parental relationship.
- A classroom teacher.
- Any professional staff member of your public or private school district.
- A judicial officer.
- A student on his/her own behalf if he/she is 18 years of age or older, or an emancipated minor.
- The Chief School Officer of the State or designee responsible for welfare, education, or health of children.

Contents of a Referral

A referral should be in written form and should be dated. This makes it official and gives you a start date since there are timelines involved. A referral from you as the parent should include the reason for the referral and any details describing the problems your child may be having. The same should hold true for a judicial officer and student referrals. It is important to be clear as to why you are referring your child. This will let the district know you know you have done your homework and are concerned about your child's progress.

A referral from a professional staff member, a physician, or the Commissioner of Education should include documentation as to why a possible disability exists, descriptions of attempts to remediate the child's behaviors, or performance prior to the referral. All of the above is important, especially what attempts have been made prior to the referral. Remember the district members should try to keep your child in the mainstream and the documentation they provide at this step in the process should ensure you and your child that they have done everything possible to circumvent the referral process; that they have provided services in the mainstream such as remedial reading, math, Chapter 1 services, (federal dollars for remediation), E.S.L. services, speech improvement, and so on.

Referrals can be sent either to the building administrator or to the CSE chairperson. In either case the referral should be shared with the other party as soon as possible. If the referral is not from you, the district must inform you in writing immediately that your child has been referred. The referral indicates that the person submitting believes your child may have a disability that adversely affects educational performance. A referral to the CSE does not necessarily mean that your child has a disability. It signals that your child is having learning difficulties and that the person making the referral is concerned that the problem may be due to a disability. When you get the referral, begin a file and note the thirty school days to evaluate your child from this date, if you agree to our evaluation.

Parental Guarantees in the Referral Process

You are now into the CSE Special-Education Process and have due-process rights under IDEA. When your child is referred to the Committee on Special Education, you should be notified in writing as previously stated. The notice should include the following rights:

1. Attend meetings of the CSE that pertain to your child. As a parent you should always attend all CSE meetings and ask to cancel if you cannot make them.

2. Your child remains in the current educational placement during formal due-process proceedings, unless you and the district agree otherwise.

3. Any relevant information from the district about your child's proposed evaluation and how the CSE may use the information; what skills will be tested.

4. Submit any outside testing information done on your child for the CSE's consideration.

5. Review your child's school files, records, and reports and make copies. These copies may require a nominal fee; you should have reviewed the screening mate-

rial by now. When the evaluation is complete, you should review those materials with the school, staff, or an outside professional.

6. Request a physician's attendance at the CSE meeting; this is very important if there are medical issues involved or if there are legal questions you may have.

7. Bring others to the meeting if you are not confident about all the professional jargon that may be used.

8. Obtain an independent evaluation as you see necessary. Remember this can be at district expense.

9. Obtain an impartial hearing if all else fails; "if all else fails" is the key phrase.

10. Appeal the decision from the impartial hearing officer to the State Review Officer of the State Education Department.

11. Receive free or low-cost legal services and a listing of such services from the district.

12. Be informed that that you may be awarded reimbursement for attorney's fees if you prevail in administrative proceedings or litigation, or court appearances.

In addition to the above rights, if this is the first time your child is being referred to special education, the notice should also inform you of your right to withhold consent for the initial evaluation or placement of your child if you so desire. If you are not comfortable, you can refuse the evaluation. If the district will want to proceed, they will have to call for an impartial hearing at this point. The notification should also inform you that during an impartial hearing or appeal to the State Review Officer, your child will not be evaluated unless you and the Board of Education agree to do so. The notice should request your consent to the proposed evaluation which is necessary to proceed in the process; unless you have good reasons, you should immediately sign the consent. It should also inform you that your child will stay in his/her current placement (pendency) during an impartial hearing or appeal unless you and the Board of Education agree to another placement.

If your child has a suspected disability and is being admitted to public school for the first time, then he/she will be placed in the public school program until all CSE proceedings are completed. All notices must describe other options considered by the district. This is an important concept because the district must show their attempts to maintain your child in the least-restrictive environment. If you have any difficulty understanding the content of the notice, contact your CSE chairperson or ask for a list of child advocates in your area. If your child received special-education services before entering school, he/she should continue to receive a program similar to the one prescribed in the IFSP. Remember this is a legal document that protects you and your child.

Suggestions for Parent Participation in the Referral Process

Your participation in the referral process can only benefit your child and reduce misconceptions, fears, and misunderstandings. Your right to know and be involved every step of the way is a right you should exercise. This is the time you should be very involved, be in contact with your child's teachers, review the files, and stay informed.

In order to ensure that your participation in the referral process results in the best interests of your child, you will need to be aware of several things. As a parent, you will need to stay informed about your child's progress in school. You should contact the teachers and be aware of any difficulties and discuss them with your child, specialists, and administration. If you suspect your child has a disability, immediately write a letter of referral to the school principal or CSE chairperson. Never be afraid to ask questions about the reasons for the referral and the types of tests that will be needed. Request to see the written referral or contact the referring person for further information and clarification. If you are notified of a referral to the CSE, contact the Committee chairperson to begin planning for the CSE meeting. Unless you disagree with the need for evaluation, return the consent form as soon as possible with your signature.

You may want to speak with a parent who has gone through this process. If this is the case, ask the Committee chairperson or the principal to put you in touch with the parent member of the CSE or with other parents who have expressed an interest in sharing their experiences, or with a member of the Special Education Parent Teacher Association.

Review the rights that are included in the Notice of Referral. Ask questions if you are in need of more information. Gather any materials that may be useful during the evaluation and recommendation process. This may include medical information, school records or family history, your child's activities, interests, and experiences. Keep copies of your child's work and tests. These will be important documentation later if you need to prove your case.

Record-Keeping Ideas During the Referral Process

Ask your district for a copy of the referral once you have received notice. Make a record of the date of the notice and save a copy. Ensure that you as a parent follow the appropriate timelines. If you are unsure of these timelines, contact your CSE chairperson.

Initial Referral to CSE From School Staff

This form is used to alert the CSE that your child may have a suspected disability and may be coming up for a review depending upon the outcome of evaluations. This occurs when the school suspects a disability. This form is forwarded with or without a signed consent for evaluation from you. If it is not sent with your signed evaluation, the CSE chairperson will send one out to you requesting it be signed and returned. Again local policy may differ and many schools will try to have you sign this consent when you meet to discuss the initial reasons for the referral.

EXAMPLE OF A PARENT REFERRAL LETTER TO THE CSE

Date _____

Dear _____

Building Administrator and/or CSE Chairperson

I am writing to refer my child, _____,
(date of birth) _____ to the Committee on Special Education.
I request that you conduct an individual evaluation to determine whether an educational disability is present that would make my child eligible for special-education services.

I am concerned about my child's educational difficulties in the following areas:

_____

Please contact me as soon as possible to discuss my referral.

Sincerely,

_____
Parent/Guardian

_____
Address

_____
City, State, Zip

_____
Phone

REFERRAL TO THE CSE FROM SCHOOL STAFF

From: _____ School _____ **Date** _____
       Name/ Title

The following student is being referred to the CSE for suspicion of a disability.

Student Name _____ Grade _____

Parent/Guardian Name _____

Address _____

_____ State _____ Zip _____

Telephone (   ) _____ Date of Birth _____

Current Program Placement _____

Teacher (Elementary) _____

Guidance Counselor (Secondary) _____

Is there an attendance problem? Yes ___ No ___ Language spoken at home? _____

Did student repeat a grade? Yes ___ No ___ If yes, when? _____

Is an interpreter needed? Yes ___ No ___ Deaf _____

TEST SCORES WITHIN LAST YEAR (Standardized Achievement, Regents)

TEST	**PERCENTILE SCORE**	**COMMENT**

Prior Parent Contact: _____

Reasons for Referral: Describe the specific reason and/or situations that indicate that a referral to the CSE is needed. Also, indicate attempts to resolve problems within the current educational program.

SPECIFIC REASONS FOR REFERRAL	ATTEMPTS TO RESOLVE
_____	_____
_____	_____
_____	_____

Principal's signature _____ **Date** _____

Date forwarded to CSE Chairperson _____

Referral Forms Used by Local Schools

It is very important for you to become educated in the process involved in local school procedures. The more informed you are the better decisions you will be able to make. This section will take you through typical local school procedures and sample forms that may be used to determine a suspected disability. In many cases these forms, filled out by classroom teachers, become the first sign of a potential problem.

Usually the first time a psychologist, special-education teacher, or pupil personnel team becomes aware that your child may have a potential problem is when the classroom teacher fills out a referral form. The major purpose of such a form is to alert other school professionals that your child is exhibiting difficulties in the classroom that may require further attention. These referral forms usually appear in two forms: *open-ended referral form* and *structured referral form*. An open-ended referral form my look like the following:

OPEN-ENDED REFERRAL FORM

Name _____ **Date of Referral** _____

Grade _____

Teacher _____

Why are you referring this child?

Has parent been notified of this referral? Yes _____ **No** _____

Administrator's signature _____ **Date** _____

This type of referral form allows the teacher to fill in what he/she considers the most important issues about your child. However the information given to the team may not be the type of information necessary for an overall indication of severity, history, and nature of the symptoms presented.

A structured referral form on the other hand, may look like the following.

Name _____ **Date of Referral** _____

Grade _____

Teacher _____

Please answer the following questions using behavioral terms:

What symptoms is the child exhibiting that are of concern at this time?

What have you tried that has worked?

What have you tried that does not seem to work towards alleviating these symptoms?

What are the child's present academic levels of functioning?

What is the child's social behavior like?

Have the parents been contacted? Yes _____ No _____ If no, why not?

Further comments?

As you can see from this type of form, the teacher is guided through a series of questions that define the specific areas determined as important by the Pupil Personnel Team. Room is also given at the end for any further comments that the teacher feels are necessary to the understanding of the child.

Regardless of the type of form used, the special-education teacher will then begin to look for signals in the symptoms being presented and may ask him/herself the following questions at the time of the referral:

1. What are the comments from past teachers?
2. What is going on at home?
3. What are the achievement test scores and what patterns do they reflect?
4. What does the developmental history look like?
5. When was the last time both vision and hearing were checked?

Rating Scales

There may be times when a school needs to refine the information received on a referral form into something more objective. This can be accomplished through the use of a personal interview with the teacher or a *rating scale*. Rating Scales are useful tools when schools wish to quantify a behavior or characteristic. Having a teacher answer yes or no to "Is the child overly active?" means very little. Having that same teacher rate the child's activity level across a 5-point scale allows for a better measure of the problem. Classroom teachers have the best long-term observational opportunities and will provide an excellent view of a child's status if given the right tool. However, since the terms presented may be open to interpretation—for instance, impulsivity may be defined by various people very differently—some members of the Pupil Personnel Team may sit with the teacher first and discuss the behaviors to be observed. This will operationalize the scale and provide a more consistent interpretative tool. It is also sometimes helpful for the PPT member to sit with the classroom teacher and fill out the scale together. This will allow the team to ask pertinent questions and may enhance the interpretative quality of the tool.

It should also be noted that the purpose of the rating scale is to help identify the source of the problem and not to be used as an indication of inferior ability, potential, or unwillingness to learn. If the teacher fully understands the nature of symptoms, these misinterpretations can be avoided.

Keep in mind that if the rating scale is too short, it will not provide an adequate overall picture of your child. And if it is too long, it may be seen as a burden by the teacher. The rating scale is an excellent tool in the case-study procedure and can begin to narrow down the specific areas of concern. There are many types of rating scales that focus on different academic, behavioral, social, self-help, developmental, and perceptual areas. If your school uses such tools do not hesitate to ask to see one.

The following is an example of how a rating scale can be used to qualify a series of observations by the classroom teacher and shed some light on the severity of the symptoms exhibited by your child.

The Evaluation Process—Step 2

What Is an Evaluation?

At the conclusion of the referral process to the CSE, an individual evaluation of your child will take place. This can only occur if you have given your written permission. This evaluation will include formal tests, observations, and assessments. This will help the school determine whether your child has a possible disability and whether special services are required. The evaluation will also attempt to determine if factors unrelated to the disability are affecting your child in school. The results of the evaluation will be used as a guide to develop your child's educational program. It will determine whether adjustments will have to be made to your child's educational program.

SAMPLE A
STUDENT RATING SCALE

	Always	Most of the time	Sometimes	Seldom	Never
Academic Behavior					
1. Has trouble comprehending what he/she reads.	____	____	____	____	____
2. Uses adequate word attack skills.	____	____	____	____	____
3. Loses his/her place while reading.	____	____	____	____	____
4. Slows down when reading aloud.	____	____	____	____	____
5. Exhibits good sight word vocabulary.	____	____	____	____	____
6. Shows adequate math computational skills.	____	____	____	____	____
7. Understands word problems.	____	____	____	____	____
8. Applies mathematical skills in solving problems.	____	____	____	____	____
9. Exhibits appropriate handwriting for age.	____	____	____	____	____
10. Exhibits adequate spelling skills for age.	____	____	____	____	____
Classroom Behavior					
1. Exhibits impulsivity.	____	____	____	____	____
2. Exhibits distractibility.	____	____	____	____	____
3. Gets along with peers.	____	____	____	____	____
4. Follows rules of a game.	____	____	____	____	____
5. Willing to reason.	____	____	____	____	____
6. Conforms to boundaries and rules in the classroom.	____	____	____	____	____
7. Attends to task.	____	____	____	____	____
8. Completes homework.	____	____	____	____	____
9. Completes classwork in allotted time.	____	____	____	____	____
10. Listens carefully.	____	____	____	____	____
11. Becomes easily frustrated.	____	____	____	____	____
12. Cooperates with others.	____	____	____	____	____
Language Behavior					
1. Exhibits adequate vocabulary.	____	____	____	____	____
2. Exhibits limited verbal fluency.	____	____	____	____	____
3. Exhibits faulty articulation.	____	____	____	____	____

SAMPLE B
PUPIL BEHAVIOR RATING SCALE

Please rate the following behaviors according to the following scale:

Rating

1. The behavior does not apply to this child and is never observed.
2. The behavior is rarely exhibited.
3. The behavior occurs some of the time.
4. The behavior occurs most of the time.
5. The behavior always occurs.

_____	Anxious	_____	Tires easily
_____	Disruptive	_____	Defies authority
_____	Fights frequently	_____	Fears criticism
_____	Unhappy	_____	Critical to others
_____	Withdrawn	_____	Controlling
_____	Moody	_____	Painfully shy
_____	Distractible	_____	Slow starter
_____	Impulsive	_____	Inconsistent
_____	Does not complete work	_____	Hyperactive
_____	Short attention span	_____	Hypoactive
_____	Daydreams	_____	Fearful of new situations
_____	Argumentative	_____	Procrastinates
_____	Disorganized	_____	Rarely takes chances
_____	Easily confused	_____	Overreactive
_____	Poor speller	_____	Problems with writing
_____	Poor reader	_____	Problems with math
_____	Limited reading comprehension	_____	Poor vocabulary usage
_____	Faulty articulation	_____	Poor expressive language ability
_____	Poor grammar	_____	Inadequate word-attack skills
_____	Problems judging time	_____	Poor balance and coordination
_____	Poor fine motor skills	_____	Poor gross motor skills
_____	Slow in completing tasks	_____	Tracing and drawing difficulties
_____	Poor logical reasoning and thinking	_____	Difficulty with abstract concepts
_____	Poor number concepts	_____	Problems with auditory memory tasks.

Components of a Thorough Evaluation

Before an evaluation is completed, speak to the staff regarding the dates and procedures for the evaluation. An evaluation should be conducted on an individual basis. It should be a comprehensive assessment of your child's abilities. The evaluation should include the following:

1. An individual psychological evaluation (when determined necessary by the multidisciplinary team) including general intelligence, instructional needs, learning strengths and weaknesses, social emotional dynamics. This will be completed by a licensed school psychologist.

2. A social history either taken by a social worker or a school psychologist.

3. A physical examination including specific assessments that relate to vision, hearing, and health, done either by the school physician or your own doctor.

4. An observation of the student in his/her current educational setting. This is an observation done in the classroom usually by another teacher, most likely a resource-room or special education teacher.

5. Appropriate educational evaluation specifically pinpointing the areas of deficit or suspected disability including but not limited to educational achievement, academic needs, learning strengths and weaknesses, vocational assessments.

6. Vocational evaluation to assess work-related skills and interests to be completed by any of the following professional vocational or rehabilitation counselors, work-study evaluators, or your guidance counselors.

7. A bilingual assessment should be included for students with limited English proficiency. The evaluation should be in the child's native language.

These evaluations may lead to the development of an individual educational plan if your child needs special-education services.

You as a parent should work closely with the school to ensure that the evaluation is comprehensive and beneficial in determining your child's future educational needs. However, you may decide that evaluations recommended and/or completed by the school are not appropriate or sufficient. In this case you may not be satisfied with the results. If this occurs, you have the right to obtain an independent evaluation at the expense of the district unless the district initiates an impartial hearing showing that the district's evaluation was sufficient. If the impartial hearing officer determines that the district's evaluation was appropriate, you may still wish to obtain an independent evaluation, understanding that the district will not be responsible for the expense.

Parental Consent for Evaluation

The district by law needs your consent for an evaluation. A request for an evaluation should not be misinterpreted as an automatic decision indicating your child has a disability. When the district asks for your consent, it is a means of assuring that you have full knowledge of school actions. It is involving you in the decision-making process.

You need to fully understand the reasons for an individual evaluation. It is important that you feel comfortable with the decisions you make.

You have the right to request an informal conference if you have any questions about the purpose or type of evaluation proposed or if you do not want your child evaluated. This conference may be held with the committee chairperson, building principal, or any other professional who will be part of the evaluation team, or you may even contact your Board of Education. You or the school may withdraw the CSE referral at any time if you and the referring party agree to another plan that better suits your child's needs. However, if agreement regarding your child's evaluation is not reached, your child's school is required to initiate an impartial hearing. At this point a hearing officer will need to be called by the district to determine whether to waive parental consent and proceed to an evaluation.

How Parents Should Deal With School Intakes and Interviews

The next step in the process used by the school may involve a complete social history which can be regarded as a description of the family-life situation. In some cases this part of the process may not be possible to obtain because of a number of variables such as parents' work restrictions, inability to obtain coverage for younger siblings, and so on.

While the intake in many schools is done by the social worker or psychologist, it is important that you understand the process in case you are called upon to provide this information. There are several things to consider before the meeting:

1. Try not to view the school as an adversary even if you have experienced a series of negative school meetings over the years. Keep in mind that you have due-process rights and no major decisions can be made without your input or permission.

2. Be sure to ask the teacher the purpose of the meeting and the steps involved in the referral process. Keep in mind that no recommendation should be made without your input and permission.

3. Request to know the purpose of testing and what you hope to gain from the process.

4. Make sure the staff member discusses and explains the procedures involved if the testing reveals a significant discrepancy between ability and achievement and the case needs to be reviewed by the CSE. This is an important piece of information since it involves your right to due process.

5. Go over the release form and ask each test and its purpose. The more information parents have, the less fearful they will be. Remember that your signature requires that the testing be completed 30 days from the date signed and will not take months before you are made aware of the findings.

6. Ask for a pad or paper and a pen so that you can write down information, terms, or notes on the meeting.

PARENT CONSENT FOR EVALUATION

To the Parent/Guardian of _____ **Birthdate** _____

School _____ **Grade** _____

We would like to inform you that your child _____ is being referred for individual testing which will help us in his/her educational planning. Referral was made for the following reasons:

_____

_____

Testing results will help us in determining your child's educational needs and in planning the most appropriate program. The evaluation procedures and/or tests may include the following:

Intelligence
Communication/Language/Speech
Physical
Behavior/Emotional
Academic
Vocational
Other

It is necessary that the School District CSE have your written permission to evaluate your child. You have had the opportunity to discuss the need for this testing and the possibilities for special educational services with the school principal/designee. The evaluation(s) will be conducted by the multidisciplinary team who will share the results of said evaluation with you at a building level meeting. Both this meeting and a CSE meeting will be held within 30 school days of receipt of this notice.

I grant permission for the evaluation(s) mentioned above _____

I do not grant permission for the evaluation(s) mentioned above _____

Date _____ **Parent's signature** _____

Date _____ **Administrator/Designee** _____

7. Ask about the confidentiality of the information gathered. Inquire about which individuals on the team will be seeing the information and the purpose for their review of the facts.

How to Examine Your Child's School Records

The school usually has a wealth of information about your child distributed among a number of people and a number of records. The *Freedom of Information Law* guarantees a parent's rights to look at, and make copies of any or all information on your child that is available within the school. In order to accomplish this, you need to inform the principal verbally and at times in writing that you wish to look at *all* the records available on your child. Be specific and tell the school which records and materials you would like to see when you come to the meeting. Gathering this information may increase your own awareness of your child's needs, reduce the need for testing, and provide a very thorough picture of your child and his/her abilities and patterns. School records usually exist in several files within a school. These may include:

- Permanent record folder usually filed in the main office.
- Guidance counselor's file on a secondary level usually filed in the guidance office.
- Psychological records including results of evaluations usually filed in a locked cabinet in the psychologist's office.
- Health records usually filed in the nurse's office.
- Disciplinary records usually filed in the principal's office.
- Special-education records including copies of IEPs, evaluation results and so on usually filed either in the special education teacher's files or at central administration with the Director of Pupil Personnel Services.
- Attendance records are usually found in the main office or attendance office at the secondary level.

All of these files will include a variety of information. Investigating the following areas will contribute to the overall "picture" of your child:

Prior teacher reports. Comments written on report cards may provide a different view of your child under a different style of teaching. Successful years with positive comments may be a clue to your child's learning style and may provide you with information about the conditions under which your child responds best. This is usually found in the permanent record folder.

Reports of prior parent-teacher interviews. Notes may exist in the permanent record folder or psychologist's folder on prior conferences between you and previous teachers. This may provide you with information that may be important in understanding your child's patterns and history.

Cumulative school record. This particular file may contain information from standardized achievement test results, group IQ results, teacher comments dating back to kindergarten, records from previous schools, and individual reading test results. There is usually no set rule on what must be kept in this folder.

Group IQ test information. This information is usually found in the permanent record folder. Many schools administer this type of test, such as Otis Lennon and Henmon Nelson in grades 3, 6, and 9 so look carefully. Within the past year or so the term *School Abilities Index* has replaced the term "IQ" or Intelligence Quotient.

Report card grades. These materials can be reviewed for comments, and patterns of productive and difficult years. Copies of these reports are usually placed in the permanent record folder.

Attendance records. These records should be reviewed to determine the accuracy of patterns of lateness or absence. If such patterns exist then the reasons should be reviewed by you to rule out medical causes (hospital stays, illness), psychological causes (dysfunctional family patterns, school phobia), or social causes (peer rejection or isolation).

Prior teacher referrals. Investigate school records for prior referrals from teachers. There are times when a teacher will refer but no action may have been taken due to time of year, delay in evaluation procedures, oversight, bureaucracy, and so on. These referrals may still be on file and may reveal information that can be useful.

Medical history in the school nurse's office. Investigate these records for indications of visual or hearing difficulties, and to assess what the school may or may not have on file. It may not have important information on illness, medication, allergies, medical emergencies, and so forth.

Teacher anecdotal records. These personal notes may be kept by teachers without your awareness. While this is legal, you do have a right to see these if they exist. Ask the school if any such records exist and make arrangements to see them.

In addition to the above factors you should also:

Speak to other parents who have children in similar placements. If possible, obtain opinions on the placement, the pros, the cons. How are their children doing? What skills does the child need to be successful in the program? If you can, build a network of parents who can provide useful information about various placement opportunities.

Try to visit possible placements yourself. When you arrive try to speak to as many different staff members who will be involved with your child. Keep the following in mind:

- Ask questions regarding the needs of the program.
- What skills are required for success in this program?
- Who has been successful? Why? Who has not? Why?

- Try to get a feel for the atmosphere of the setting.

- Observe the style of the staff members and the ease with which the children approach the staff and note their reactions.

Prior to any possible placement or CSE meeting, make an appointment to confer with the Director of Special Education or the Committee on Special Education Chairperson. The person who will have the greatest input on your child's placement is the person who sits in one of those chairs. It may, and usually is, the same person. You can gain great insight into the CSE or special-education process by a one-on-one meeting with the chairperson. You may possibly settle any issue regarding placement (or any other problems for that fact) prior to the CSE.

Remember when meeting with school staff the more knowledge you bring with you to this meeting, the better your chances of successfully pleading your case. It is also much easier to work with the school staff and administration, than to be adversaries.

Whatever the situation, you as a parent of a child with a suspected disability should review available school records. Keep in mind that the school can request a fee for copying the materials. This is well worth the cost if it enhances your understanding of your child. The school will give you the important information when attending a case conference with a teacher, annual review, an initial referral to the CSE, or an impartial hearing.

Social and Developmental Intakes

A necessary part of the evaluation process involves a parent intake to gather relevant information, past and present, that might have an impact on the child's present situation. This intake may be conducted by any member of the Child Study Team or Pupil Personnel Team. At the time of the intake many questions may be asked about family history, developmental history, academic history, social history, and so on. If at any time you feel uncomfortable with the question just indicate that you would rather not discuss the issue. A parent-intake form should contain necessary but not intrusive questions. The questions should be specific enough to help in the diagnosis of the problem, but not be so specific as to place you in a vulnerable and defensive position. An example of a completed form follows:

Example of an Intake Form Used by Schools

Identifying Data

Name of Client: Matthew Jones
Address: 12 Court Street
Phone: 675–7863
Date of Birth: 3/4/82
Age: 9
Siblings: (names and ages) Brian 15, Karen 4

Mother's Name: Jill
Father's Name: Ben
Mother's Occupation: Medical Technician
Father's Occupation: Accountant
Referred by: Teacher
Grade: 4
School: Holland Avenue

Developmental History

Length of Pregnancy: Full term—22-hour labor
Type of Delivery: Forceps
Complications: Apgar score 7, jaundice at birth
Long Hospital Stays: None

Falls or Injuries: None

Allergies: Early food allergies, none recently
Medication: none at present
Early Milestones (walking, talking, toilet training): According to parent, Matthew was late in walking and talking in comparison to brother. He was toilet-trained at 3. Parent added that he seemed to be slower than usual in learning things.

Traumatic Experiences: None
Previous Psychological Evaluations or Treatment (Please explain reasons and dates): None. However parent indicated that it was suggested by first-grade teacher but the teacher never followed through.

Any Previous Psychiatric Hospitalizations? No
Sleep Disturbances: Trouble falling asleep, somnambulism at age 5 but only lasted a few weeks. Talks a great deal in his sleep lately.
Eating Disturbances: Picky eater, likes sweets

Last Vision and Hearing Exams and Results: Last eye test in school indicated 20/30. Last hearing test in school was inconclusive. Parent has not followed through on nurse's request for an outside evaluation.

Excessively High Fevers: No
Childhood Illnesses: Normal ones

Academic History

Nursery School Experience: Matthew had difficulty adjusting to nursery school. The teacher considered him very immature and his skills were well below those of his peers. He struggled through the year.

Kindergarten Experience (adjustment, comments): Matthew's difficulties increased. According to the parent he had problems with reading and social difficulties. His gross and fine motor skills were immature.

First Grade Through Sixth Grade (teacher's comments, traumatic experiences, strength areas, comments): According to past teachers Matthew struggled through the years. He was a nice boy and polite and at times tried hard. But in the later grades 2 and 3 his behavior and academics began to falter. Teachers always considered referral but felt he might grow out of it.

Subjects Which Presented the Most Difficulty: Reading, math, spelling
Subjects Which Were the Least Difficult: Science
Most Recent Report-Card Grades (if applicable): Matthew has received mostly NEEDS TO IMPROVE on his report card

Social History

Groups or Organizations: Tried Boy Scouts but dropped out. Started Little League but became frustrated.
Social Involvement as Perceived by Parent: Inconsistent. He does not seem to reach out to kids and lately he spends a great deal of time alone.
Hobbies or Interests: Baseball cards, science

Observation Scales

Observing your child in different settings is also a necessary part of the screening and referral process used by schools. This part of the process offers another perception of your child. If your child is referred, he/she needs to be observed in a variety of settings, including the classroom, playground, gym, and lunchroom.

Basic behaviors need to be observed such as attention, focus, aggressiveness, compliance, flexibility, rigidity, oppositional behavior, shyness, controlling behavior, distractibility, impulsivity, social interaction, and so on.

Questions That May Be Considered by the PPT

1. **Is there a difference between the nature of your child's behaviors in a structured setting (classroom) and an unstructured setting (playground)?**

   This factor may shed light on your child's need for a more structured environment in which to learn. Children who do not have well-developed internal control systems need a highly structured environment to maintain focus and appropriate behavior. Some children cannot shift between structured and unstructured and back again. They may not possess the internal monitor which regulates conformity and logical attendance to rules. These children may be more successful in a structured play setting set up by teachers during the lunch hour.

2. **Does your child seem to respond to external boundaries?**

This factor is important to the teacher since it is a monitor of potential learning style. If a child who lacks internal controls does conform to external boundaries such as time out and teacher proximity during worktime, then this factor needs to be taken into consideration when prescribing classroom-management techniques. When the child conforms to such boundaries, then his/her behavior is a message for what works for him/her.

3. What is your child's attention span during academic tasks?

Attention span at different ages is measured normally in minutes or hours. You should become aware of the normal attention span for children of all ages and compare your child over several activities and days to see if a pattern of inattention is present. If the attention span is very short for someone of his/her age then discuss with the teacher some modifications to work load (for instance, shorter but more frequent assignments may have to be included).

4. Does your child require constant teacher supervision or assistance?

A child who requires constant teacher supervision or assistance is a child who may be exhibiting a wide variety of possible symptomatic behavior which may be resulting from but not be limited to attention deficit disorder, processing problems, emotional difficulties involving need for attention, need for control, high anxiety, internal stress, limited intellectual capacity, hearing problems, and so on. All these areas need to be checked out and a good evaluation should determine the root of such behavior. However the key is always the frequency, intensity, and duration of such symptoms as discussed previously.

5. Does your child interact appropriately with peers?

Observing children at play can tell us a great deal about self-esteem, tension levels, social maturity, physical development, and many other factors. Social interaction is more common in children over the age of 6 or 7 while parallel play is still common in younger children. Appropriate social interaction gives us insight into the child's own internal boundaries and organization. A child who always needs to control may really be masking high levels of tension. The more controlling a child is, the more out of control they are feeling. A child who can appropriately conform to group rules, delay his/her needs for the good of the team, conform to rules and various changes or inconsistencies in rules, may be a child who is very self-assured and has low anxiety levels. The opposite is most always typical of children at risk. However, one should always consider developmental stages since certain behaviors, such as control, may be more typical at early ages.

6. Is your child a high- or low-status child?

Observing a child in different settings allows both you and the teacher the opportunity to see the social status of your child and its impact on his behavior. Low-status children are often children with learning disabilities, are more apt to feel insignificant, and fail to receive positive social cues which help reinforce feelings of self-esteem. Having the psychologist begin a counseling group of five or six low-status children may enable them to feel empowered with feelings of connection.

The following is an example of a classroom observation checklist. Since there is no required form for this procedure, it will vary from school district to school district.

CLASSROOM OBSERVATION REPORT FORM

Student's Name/ID # _____

Date of Birth _____ **Dominant Language** _____

Dates of Observation _____ **Length of Observation** _____

Observer _____ **Position** _____

Classroom Observed _____ **Location** _____

Teacher's Name _____

Subject area being taught _____

Task–Individual

A. When assigned task, the student:

1. Initiates task without need for teacher's verbal encouragement.
2. Requests help in order to start task.
3. Complains before getting started on a task.
4. Demands help in order to start on a task.
5. Actively refuses to do task despite teacher's encouragement.
6. Passively retreats from task despite teacher's encouragement.

B. While working on task, the student:

7. Works independently.
8. Performs assigned task without complaints.
9. Needs teacher's verbal encouragement to keep working.
10. Needs teacher in close proximity to keep working.
11. Needs physical contact from teacher to keep working.
12. Seeks constant reassurance to keep working.
13. Is reluctant to have work inspected.
14. Belittles own work.

C. At the end of assigned time, the student:

15. Completes task.
16. Takes pride in completed task.
17. Goes on to next task.
18. Refuses to complete task.

Social Interaction

20. Establishes a relationship to one or two peers.
21. Shares materials with peers.
22. Respects property of peers.
23. Gives help to peers when needed.
24. Accepts help from peers when needed.
25. Establishes a relationship with most peers.
26. Teases or ridicules peers.
27. Expresses prejudiced attitudes toward peers.
28. Physically provokes peers.
29. Physically hurts peers.
30. Seeks to be attacked by peers.
31. Participates appropriately in group activities.
32. Postpones own needs for group objectives.
33. Withdraws from group.
34. Overly assertive in group.
35. Disrupts group activities (calling out, provocative language).
36. Exhibits aggressive behavior within group; not amenable to teacher intervention.

Relationship to Teacher

37. Tries to meet teacher's expectations.
38. Functions adequately without constant teacher encouragement.
39. Interacts with teacher in nondemanding manner.
40. Responds to teacher without haggling.
41. Tests limits, tries to see how much teacher will allow.
42. Seeks special treatment from teacher.
43. Responds to teacher's criticism without fear.
44. Responds to teacher's criticism without verbal anger.
45. Responds to teacher's criticism without physical outbursts (temper tantrums).

46. Defies teacher's requirement.

47. Scorns or ridicules teacher's support.

48. Responds with anger when demands are thwarted by teacher.

49. Blames and accuses teacher ("not helping," "not liking me").

50. Abuses teacher verbally (no apparent cause).

51. Abuses teacher physically (no apparent cause).

52. Requires close and constant supervision because behavioral controls are so limited.

Comments: _____

_____

_____

Due-Process Guarantees During the Evaluation Phase

- It is your guarantee that more than one evaluation be involved in assessing your child's suspected disability.

- Evaluations should be administered in the child's dominant language.

- A complete evaluation and recommendation within 30 school days from the time of your consent, or within 40 days of the referral, whichever is earlier. This timeline may vary.

- A list of resources where independent evaluations can be obtained.

- If your dominant language is other than English, all information provided must be in your dominant language.

- You have a right to an independent evaluation at any time and may request that it be conducted at district expense.

- The evaluations should include individual psychological and physical exams. The determination for each should be made by the appropriate professional personnel.

- Your child must be observed in his/her classroom by someone other than his/her classroom teacher.

- You should receive a notice regarding the evaluation and your due-process rights. You must consent to the evaluation.

- If you feel it is necessary to have an independent evaluation completed by an outside evaluator, it is your right.

- You may give consent or withhold consent, or request a conference regarding an initial evaluation.

- You should be given a description of the proposed evaluation and its intended purpose prior to testing.
- You are entitled to receive information on your child's areas of educational need.
- You should have the opportunity to provide information to assist in the completion of the evaluation.
- Your child's confidential records are protected by Federal law protecting the rights of students.
- Under the Freedom of Information Act, you have the right to review your child's records and make copies at a reasonable cost at any time.
- You should receive a copy of the due-process rights provided to you by your Sate Education Department. This material should include your due-process rights, right to obtain a hearing, right to appeal the decision, right to obtain free or low-cost legal assistance, right to have your child stay in the current placement, and the right to obtain attorney's fees for special-education disputes in which you prevail.

The evaluation should include more than one specialist or other specialists with knowledge in the area of your child's suspected disability.

There are personnel within your district who are trained and appropriate for analyzing the suspected problem through the administration of tests. These professionals will also use the appropriate methods for assessing various skills. The method of assessment should not interfere with your child's ability to demonstrate skills or knowledge.

Selected Tests for Special Education

There are numerous tests that can be used by professionals in the evaluation process. All the tests used to evaluate your child's suspected disability should be administered on an individual basis. For a comprehensive list of all types of tests refer to Chapter 13, Appendices.

Types of Tests

Most tests are either *norm-referenced* or *criterion-referenced*. Norm-referenced tests are those which are standardized on groups of individuals. Such tests measure a student's performance relative to the performance of a group of individuals with similar characteristics. Tests which are administered at the district, state, or national level are usually norm-referenced.

Criterion-referenced tests measure a student's achievement or development relative to a specific standard. Such tests are especially useful for planning instruction or measuring curriculum-content mastery because they can correspond closely to curriculum content and classroom instruction. Tests which are selected or developed and administered by the classroom teacher are generally criterion-referenced.

Recommendation—Step 3

What Is a Recommendation?

Once the evaluation process is completed, the CSE will arrange to meet with you to discuss the results of the evaluations. Normally, the results of the evaluations are discussed by the individuals who have completed each evaluation. However, this is an informal process and will depend on district policy. Formally, you will receive a notice indicating the time and date of a CSE meeting. In that notice the following individuals will be addressed:

- A parent of a disabled child in the district.
- A physician (may be required only under prior parent request).
- A school psychologist.
- A district representative who may provide, supervise, or administrate special education.
- Your child's teacher in most circumstances.
- The names and/or titles of additional persons in attendance. Depending on the State requirements, the required members may include an administrator of special education, psychologist, parent of a special-education student residing within the district, and any other professionals deemed necessary by the Board of Education. Other professionals might include a guidance counselor, social worker, or a special-education teacher.

You as a parent have the right to bring persons of your choice, such as lawyer, advocate, friends, clergy, therapist, and so on.

The CSE: What Is It?

A recommendation is a statement developed by the Committee on Special Education (CSE) that addresses the individual educational needs of your child. As a parent, you are by law invited to CSE meetings and encouraged to participate in developing the recommendation with the CSE. Based on the evaluations completed by your designees and the district evaluators, a decision will need to be made at the CSE whether or not your child meets handicapping criteria and is entitled to special-education services.

If your child does not require special education, the CSE will forward copies of the recommendation to you, the building administrator, and the Board of Education. It will state the CSE's findings and should recommend that other educational services, such as speech and language improvement services, be considered. The building administrator should determine what, if any, educationally related support services should be provided to your child.

If your child requires special education, the recommendation will need to specify the disability, describe your child's strengths and areas of need, list goals that your child should reach in the year's time, and include short-term instructional objectives which represent a series of specific skills to be mastered. The recommendation will lead toward reaching the annual goals, and identify the types of programs and services, including regular education, that your child will receive. This information will be included on your child's IEP. A copy of the recommendation will be sent to the Board of Education for approval. You will also be sent a copy of the IEP for your records. See Chapter 7 for more specific information concerning IEPs.

How Recommendations Are Made by the CSE

In developing recommendations, the CSE, you, and others present will discuss the evaluations presented and any other pertinent information on your child. The first thing decided will be whether or not your child has an educational disability that adversely affects his/her educational performance. If in fact it is found that this is the case, your child will be classified. There are a number of classifications from which the committee draws. They include, but are not limited to (depending on your state), the following:

Autistic. This disorder is characterized by a difficulty in the child's ability to respond to people, events, and objects. Responses to sensations of light, sound, and feeling may be exaggerated and delayed speech and language skills may be associated features. The onset of this condition is usually observed before age 2 1/2.

Deaf. The individual classified as deaf has a loss of hearing so severe, usually above an 80 decibel loss (as evaluated by a medical doctor or an audiologist) that it hinders effective use of the sense of hearing. This disability usually necessitates the use of specialized services or equipment in order for the child to communicate.

Emotionally Disabled. Students classified with this disability have behavior disorders over a long period of time and to such a degree that they are unable to do well in school. These disturbances may interfere in developing meaningful relationships, result in physical symptoms or irrational fears, and limit the individual's overall production.

Hard of Hearing. A student in this category has a hearing loss which may or may not be permanent, and has some sense of hearing with or without an aid. However, this student still requires specialized instruction and special-education assistance.

Learning Disabled. These students have a disability in receiving, organizing, or expressing information. They are of average intelligence but have difficulty listening, thinking, speaking, reading, writing, or doing arithmetic and this results in a significant discrepancy between ability and school achievement. This is not the result of emotional, mental, physical, environmental, or cultural factors.

Mentally Disabled. These students have a developmental delay that causes them to learn at a slower pace. They also exhibit a significantly lower level of intelligence and marked impairment in social-competency skills. This category includes Educable Mentally Disabled, IQ usually between 55 and approximately 80, and Trainable Mentally Disabled, IQ below 55.

Multiply Handicapped. This category is set aside for children who are disabled in more than one category, such as deafness and blindness.

Orthopedically Impaired. These students are physically disabled and their educational performance is directly affected by this condition. Such conditions as cerebral palsy and amputation fall into this category.

Other Health Impaired. Students who are classified in this category have limited strength, vitality, or alertness to chronic or acute health problems. Conditions which fall into this area include heart conditions, asthma, Tourettes Syndrome, Attention Deficit Hyperactive Disorder, diabetes, and so on.

Partially Sighted. Children classified in this area have some functional sight, usually 20/70 or better with best correction. This student may be able to learn to read regular print with glasses or to read special books that are printed with large type.

Speech Impairment. These students have a communication disorder. They are unable to correctly produce speech sounds, have difficulty in understanding or using words or sentences, or exhibit stuttering or some other voice impairment.

Visually Impaired. The child who is classified as blind exhibits vision that requires special Braille equipment and reading materials. The condition is so severe that they do not have what is considered functional sight.

Conditions of Public Law 504

During the CSE process, it may be determined that your child's suspected disability is not severe enough to warrant classification and services under Individuals with Disabilities Education Act (IDEA). However, another alternative that may be available to you and your child involves services under Public Law 504. The following will give you an overview of the conditions of PL 504:

1. **Coverage**. Persons who have, have a record of having, or are regarded as having a physical or mental impairment substantially limiting one or more major life activity but not severe enough to warrant classification under Individuals with Disability Education Act (IDEA).

2. **Entitlement**. Regular or special education and related services.

3. **Students covered under Section 504 but not covered under IDEA**. Do not have one of the 13 disabilities under IDEA (Note: children with ADD may have a health impairment under IDEA). Also do not need special education but need related services or accommodations to benefit from an education.

4. **Students covered under IDEA but not covered under Section 504**. Have the right to placements in private state-approved schools when the local educational agency has made available (not denied) to a child a free, appropriate public education.

5. **Funding.** No federal funds are available specifically for Section 504. All agencies receiving any Federal funds must comply with section 504.

6. **Procedural requirements similar to IDEA.** Even though your child may not be classified as disabled under IDEA, if he/she meets the requirements for PL 504 then he/she is entitled to the following services:

   - Free education

   - Evaluation

   - Least-restrictive environment

   - Procedural due process

   - 504 Individual Educational Plan. This plan is much shorter than an IEP but lists the student's special services and is open to a yearly review as is IEP.

7. **Equal educational opportunity issues pertinent solely to Section 504.** This includes access to magnet (schools that may have similar types of services, such as vocational schools) schools, program accessibility (your child has the right to equally participate in programs offered within your school district and the buildings should be accessible to all disabled staff and students and community members), and access to parents/community members with disabilities to school activities (parent conferences, board meetings and so on).

8. **Enforcement**. Office for Civil Rights, U.S. Department of Education.

CSE Procedures

As previously stated, the CSE makes decisions based on information provided by a multidisciplinary team whose purpose is to determine from a wide variety of sources whether there is a suspected disability. Every state will have its own criteria to determine what a disability is. It is your job as a parent, to know what those criteria are for your particular state.

The members of the Committee on Special Education will vary from state to state, but generally include a representative from the district who qualifies as someone who can supervise or administer special education, the student's teacher or teachers, a school psychologist, a school physician (usually on call if necessary), and a parent who has a child with a disability, and who may reside in the school district.

Besides the usual mandated members, the district may include other staff or specialists who may be helpful to the team process as designated by the Board of Education. These may include speech therapists, occupational therapists, physical therapists, school administrators, audiologists, and vocational rehabilitation staff. This is not all-inclusive; there may be others who could prove helpful.

You as a parent are invited to bring anyone you feel would be helpful to accompany you to the meeting. A district, particularly a large district, may have more than one CSE.

As you can see, the CSE is very important in the special-education process. Get to know members of this team starting with your child's teacher and any specialist working with your child. Listen carefully to what they report concerning your child's functioning in school.

Become familiar with the CSE chairperson; he or she will have a lot to say about the final disposition of your child's case. Join the Special Education PTA (SEPTA) if there is one. Meet the parent representatives to the CSE. Speak with them regarding the CSE process in your district. Find out their usual procedures and the criteria they go by for classifications and placements. Build a positive rapport with these people to ensure your credibility when dealing with them. Compare what you know about your child with the district profiles, understand how your child is functioning and where that places him or her in the district's education plan. You need to plan a positive strategy from what you know about your child and what you know about your district.

Another important group that will contribute in educating your child are the district administrative team, starting with the building level administrators. The building principals, assistant principals and other administrators, coordinators, and chairpersons oftentimes can offer direct support and advice regarding the day-to-day, nitty-gritty information about what is happening in a particular school. They can tell you the nuts and bolts about how your child can function in their particular building. They can answer questions related to the day-to-day operation and instruction. They can also be a tremendous support for you and your child. If you have a good relationship with building administration, it can be instrumental in creating a positive outcome in the special-education process. Take the time to meet with your building administrators at school and at social functions.

Central office administrators, particularly directors and assistant superintendents for special education are usually the people who will either chair your CSE or supervise the person who does. These people are crucial to the special-education process. It is one of your main functions to know this person. He or she can and usually is the most important individual in the CSE process. It is his or her job to ensure the team functions well, that all appropriate t's are crossed and i's are dotted. On the one hand and on the other it is his or her job to provide the least restrictive appropriate education to your child and report such to his or her superiors and the Board of Education. The person in this position then can be very important in the decision-making process. Learn to work with this person, and help him or her to understand the needs of your child in your role as the child's best advocate.

The final authority at the administrative level is the superintendent of schools. The superintendent recommends policy to the Board of Education, including special-education policies. The superintendent is also responsible to assure that Board policies and procedures are implemented.

Specific Responsibilities of the Committee on Special Education (CSE)

Some of the responsibilities of your district's Committee on Special Education are as follows:

- Review and evaluate all relevant information that may appear on each disabled student.
- Determine the least-restrictive educational setting for any child classified as having a disability.

- Follow appropriate procedures and take appropriate action on any child referred as having a suspected disability.

- Determine the suitable classification for a child with a suspected disability.

- Review, at least annually, the status of each disabled child residing within the district.

- Evaluate the adequacy of programs, services, and facilities for the disabled children in the district.

- Maintain ongoing communication in writing to parents with regard to planning, modifying, changing, reviewing, placing, or evaluating the program, classification, or educational plan for a disabled child.

- Advise the Board of Education as to the status and recommendations for all disabled children in the district.

Most Committees on Special Education try to remain as informal as possible to reduce the anxiety of the situation. This is a crucial issue since you may feel overwhelmed or intimidated.

The parent member usually serves as a liaison and advocate for you, establishing contact prior to the meeting to reduce anxiety and alleviate any concerns that you may have. School personnel should also be in contact with you prior to the meeting to go over the process, your rights, and what may take place at the meeting. At no time should anyone in contact with you prior to the meeting give you false hope, make promises, or second-guess the CSE. What needs to be communicated are procedural issues and options, and the awareness that it is the CSE that will make the recommendation, not one individual. Further, you must be made aware of their rights and understand your right to due process if you do not agree with the CSE recommendation.

The process of identifying and finding an appropriate educational placement for a disabled child should be a joint process between the district and the family. When both work in the best interests of the child, the process can be very positive and rewarding. However, there can be times when the district and the family disagree. When this occurs, the parents or the school has the right to due process. This procedure protects the rights of both the school and the family and allows another avenue for resolution.

Classifications help the CSE determine if a student is eligible for special-education services under IDEA. If the CSE determines that your child is not eligible for special education, it may mean that your child's educational difficulties may not be the result of an educational disability that adversely affects his/her educational performance. For example, if your family is recently going through a separation or divorce and as a result your child is experiencing academic problems, he/she may not be classified since there is no long-term history and there is identified and consistent academic success prior to the onset of this particular family issue. In this case the CSE will send the evaluation results and recommendations to your school's principal. This information should be used to coordinate other appropriate interventions within the regular educational program. The CSE will formally notify you and the board of education of their results.

If the CSE determines that your child is eligible for special education, the recommendations will describe your child's special and regular educational program in detail. At this point you will be requested to give consent before the program begins. Again, you have the right to agree or disagree with the recommendation. Any recommendation cannot be instituted without your approval if this is the first time your child is being placed in special education. If you do not agree, the disagreement will be resolved through formal or informal meetings (later described in the section on due-process rights).

Individual Educational Program Development

If your child is found to have a disability and is classified, the next step is extremely important. It is the development of the Individual Educational Plan (IEP) that will be the basis for his/her instruction and educational program. The IEP is used to:

- Document and review progress of your child.
- Summarize your child's current abilities.
- Establish educational goals and objectives on a yearly basis.
- Describe the programs designed to meet your child's goals.
- List ways to periodically check your child's progress.

An in-depth discussion of IEP can be found in Chapter 7.

Continuum of Services

Least-Restrictive Educational Services

The concept of *least-restrictive education (LRE)* applies to the placement of disabled students in the most advantageous educational placement suitable for their needs. Contrary to the belief of many teachers and parents, LRE does not mean every disabled student will be placed in a regular classroom.

The placement of disabled students is the responsibility of the Committee on Special Education with the input of staff and consent of parents. The CSE must analyze all the available information and determine the best "starting placement" for the child that will ensure success and provide the child with the highest level of stimulation and experience for his/her specific disability and profile of strengths and weaknesses.

In order to accomplish this task the CSE has a variety of placements from which to choose. These placements range in levels of restriction, including class size, student-teacher ratio, length of program, and degree of mainstreaming.

In the normal course of events it is hoped that children should only be placed in a more restrictive environment if it is to their educational advantage. However, they should be moved to a less-restrictive setting as soon as they are capable of being educated in that environment.

The placements that follow offer a path from least restrictive to most restrictive.

1. **Regular class placement**. This placement is the least-restrictive placement for all nondisabled children. This placement alone without some type of special education supportive services is not suitable for a disabled child and is usually not considered suitable by the CSE.

2. **Regular class placement with consulting teacher assistance**. A consultant teacher model is used when supportive special-education services are required but the CSE feels that the child will be better served while remaining in the classroom rather than being pulled out for services. Since the child remains within the class, even though he/she is receiving services, this placement is considered the next LRE setting.

3. **Regular class placement with some supportive services**. This placement may be used with mildly disabled students who require supportive services but can remain in the regular class for the majority of the day. The services that may be applied to this level include adaptive physical education, speech and language therapy, in-school individual or group counseling, physical therapy, and occupational therapy.

4. **Regular class placement with itinerant specialist assistance/itinerant services** (services subcontracted by the district and provided by outside agencies). These services are usually provided for students when the disability is such that the district wishes to maintain the child in the district but there are not a sufficient number of students with that disability to warrant hiring a teacher. Examples of this may be a hard-of-hearing child who can maintain a regular class placement as long as supportive itinerant services by a teacher specializing in hearing impairments are provided.

5. **Regular class placement with resource-room assistance**. This placement is usually provided for students who need supportive services but can successfully remain within the regular classroom for the majority of the day. This type of program is a "pull out" program and the services are usually provided in a separate room. The student-teacher ratio with this type of service is usually 5:1 and the amount of time spent within the resource room cannot exceed 50 percent of the child's day.

6. **Special class placement with part time in regular class**. This placement is for students who need a more restrictive setting for learning, behavioral, or intellectual reasons, and who cannot be successful in a full-time regular class or with a "pull out" supportive service but can be successfully mainstreamed (part-time participation in a regular classroom setting) for a part of the school day. The nature of the mainstream is determined by the special-education teacher.

7. **Full-time special class in a regular school**. This placement is viewed as the LRE setting for students whose disability does not permit successful participation in any type of regular class setting, even for part of the day. These are students who usually require a very structured, closely monitored program on a daily basis but not so restrictive as to warrant an out-of-district placement. These students can handle the rules and structure of a regular school building, but not the freedom or style of a less-restrictive setting within the school.

8. **Special day school outside the school district**. This type of restrictive educational setting is a desirable placement for students whose disability is so severe that they may require a more totally therapeutic environment and closer monitoring by specially trained special-education teachers or staff members. The child is transported by district expense to the placement and many State policies try to discourage travel time on the bus to more than one hour.

   These types of programs may have student-teacher-aide ratios of 6:1:1, 6:1:2, 9:1:1, 9:1:2, 12:1:1, or 15:1:1 depending upon the severity of the child's disability. The more severe the disability the lower the number of student-teacher ratio. These programs can run ten or twelve months, again depending upon the severity of the disability and the individual needs of the child.

9. **Residential school**. Residential placements are considered the next most-restrictive placement. Not only does the disabled student receive his/her education within this setting but usually resides there for the school term. The nature and length of home visits depend upon several factors that are usually determined by the residential school staff after evaluation and observation. For some students, home visits may not take place at all, while others may go home every weekend.

   Some students are placed in residential placements by the court. In this case, the child's local school district is only responsible to provide the costs of the educational portion including related services if needed.

10. **Homebound instruction**. This very restrictive setting is usually provided for students who are in the process of transition between programs and have yet to be placed. It should never be used as a long-term placement because of the social restriction and limitations.

    This option is also used when a child is restricted to his/her house because of an illness or injury, and this option remains the only realistic educational service until the child recovers. Home-bound instruction requires an adult at home when the teacher arrives or can be held at a community center, library, or some other site deemed appropriate by the CSE.

11. **Hospital or institution**. The most-restrictive setting used is a hospital or institutional setting. While this is the most-restrictive setting, it may be the LRE setting for certain students, such as attempted suicide by an adolescent, pervasive clinical depression, severe or profound retardation.

    In conclusion, the least-restrictive educational setting is not something that is etched in concrete. It is something that is normally reviewed every year at the annual review and changes are made in either direction if the situation requires such change.

Facts About Inclusion

As parents you should understand the concept of *inclusion*. Inclusion is a crucial concern being addressed by many school districts. Inclusion stems from early recognition of the need for least-restrictive environment as provided for in the laws. In general, inclusion means maintaining disabled students in mainstreamed setting through the use of collaborative efforts within the school, including the following:

- Classroom teacher
- Special-education teachers
- Resource-room teachers
- Psychologists
- Social workers
- Speech and language teachers
- ESL teachers
- Physical therapists
- Occupational therapists
- Remedial teachers
- Adaptive physical-education teachers
- Parents
- Administrators

Inclusion Is:

- All children learning in the same school environment helped by supportive services so that they can be successful in their adjustment and performance.
- Having each student's specific needs addressed in the integrated environment of a regular school setting.
- All children participating equally in all aspects/functions available within the school.
- Educating and providing support for regular classroom teachers who will have special children in their classroom.
- Educating children to be tolerant of and to respect the differences in each other.
- Creating a comfortable environment within which students with and without disabilities can develop healthy social interactions and relationships.
- Educating and supporting parents in their concerns.
- Allowing parents to participate in the team process responsible for inclusion.
- Arranging for appropriate work and educational experiences for disabled children within the community environments.
- Using new delivery systems for special-education programs that emphasize collaboration between special-education staff and the classroom teachers.
- All children learning together in the same environment even though their educational needs and prescribed goals may differ.
- Making sure that each child has an appropriate individualized educational program.

Inclusion Is Not:

- Dumping children with challenging needs into regular classes without proper supports and services necessary to be successful.
- Trading the quality of a child's education or the intensive support services the child needs for integration.
- Ignoring each child's unique needs.
- Sacrificing the education of typical children so that children with challenging needs can be integrated.
- All children having to learn the same thing, at the same time, in the same way.
- Doing away with or cutting back special-education services.
- Expecting regular-education teachers to teach children who have challenging needs without the support they need to teach all children effectively.
- Locating special-education classes in separate wings at regular schools.
- Ignoring parents' needs.
- Maintaining separate schedules for students in special and regular education.
- Students with disabilities receiving their education and job training in facilities outside their communities.

Recommended Placements

Individualized Education Programs may be implemented in a number of placements. A placement is the location where the educational program will be provided. The following are some examples of types of placements that you may consider, listed in order of educational restriction.

Local School District. Your child's home school, depending on the severity of the disability, will generally provide the types of services required by your child. This is preferential for many reasons, as discussed previously. Maintaining the child in his/her home school should be your, and the district's goal. This, of course, is not always possible. If not, the next step is another school in the district.

Neighboring School District. Due to the nature of special-education programs, all special-education services are not offered within every district. Your local school may arrange for participation in necessary programs and services in surrounding districts if they cannot be provided within your home district.

Cooperative Educational Services. Cooperative service agencies usually may be set up by your State to assist the student population, or specific services in one or more of the districts.

Home/Hospital Settings. There may be times when you may need temporary instruction at home or in a hospital setting due to severe illness or special circumstances indicated on the IEP. The key term here is temporary. The instruction should approximate what is offered in school within reasonable limits. Home and hospital instruction is highly restrictive; the continuing need for such services should be assessed frequently and this service should be seen as temporary. State laws may vary on the minimum amount of educational time allotted to children involved in these services. A general guide should be two hours per day of individual instruction for a secondary student and one hour per day for an elementary grade student.

Private Approved Schools. School districts may place students in private schools, special-act schools (schools set up by the State to provide services for disabled children) or residential placements approved by your State Education Department. These schools may be located in or out of state. Students placed in such facilities have such diverse needs that the home school district may not be able to service them due to the severity of their medical, physical, mental, or emotional needs.

State Operated Schools for the Deaf, Blind, and Severely Emotionally Disturbed. These schools are examples of such schools that are available for students with educational needs that require a school with a special focus.

It is the responsibility of the CSE to provide programs based on the least-restrictive environment concept. Remember, it is important to provide programs that are in close proximity to the child's home (some states limit this to one hour on a bus). Your child should have involvement with his/her nondisabled peers. Finally, the program should be based on the student's needs.

At times the CSE may recommend placements in schools that use psychotropic drugs. Psychotropic medications are those drugs intended to modify behavior. If this occurs, that school must have a written policy pertaining to the use of the drugs and it should be shared with you.

When considering any of the above placements, you must keep in mind that your interest is providing the best possible placement for your child in the least-restrictive environment. Your school district on the other hand, needs only to provide an appropriate placement, not the best placement in a program that is appropriate to your child's needs, as close to home as possible.

Recommendations Made by the CSE

Be aware that the laws require your district's Committee on Special Education to make a recommendation to the Board of Education within thirty days after initial consent for evaluation is received or forty school days from the receipt of referral, whichever is earlier.

Parental Guarantees During the Recommendation Phase

Throughout the recommendation process, your involvement continues to be of the utmost importance. You are always guaranteed of involvement in the process. Your school district may choose to notify you of the date, time, location, and persons expected to attend a CSE meeting, at the same time it sends you the notice. The notice of the meeting will include all of the due-process guarantees explained earlier in this chapter.

Following the CSE meeting you will receive another notice describing the CSE recommendation to the Board of Education. It will state the recommendation of the CSE concerning classification and placement. This will indicate if your child has been recommended to receive special education and you will receive a copy of your child's IEP, other information about the tests, reports, and other contributing factors used to make the recommendation. If no recommendation is made, you will be sent back to the building level as stated previously.

Board of Education is usually required to provide an appropriate education program within thirty days of the Committee's recommendation.

Suggestions for Your Participation

- Inform the CSE if you are planning to attend committee meetings.
- Arrange for meetings to be rescheduled at a mutually convenient time if you are unable to attend as scheduled.
- Present pertinent information to the CSE that is related to the topic of discussion.
- Ensure you and the CSE have considered factors related to the least-restrictive environment. Are the programs and services appropriate to your child's needs and abilities? Is there sufficient interaction with nondisabled peers? Are programs close to your home or is there a distance factor with which to contend?

Record-Keeping Ideas During the Recommendation Phase

During this phase of the special-education process you may want to record CSE meeting dates and who was present. Try to maintain a file for notices or information sent to you regarding the meetings. If your child is recommended for special education, ask for a copy of the IEP, and any published information about the recommended program. It is important that you retain materials that may be sent out by the school (information about future parent-training programs, calendars of Board meetings, PTA meetings, after-school activities, events sponsored by community groups).

Procedures for Changing a Student's Classification or Placement

The Parent

There may be times when you feel that your child's present classification or placement needs to be reviewed and perhaps changed. When this occurs you should follow these procedures:

1. While a request for a change of classification or placement can always be made by you, there should be some basis for such a request. These may include lack of growth on the part of your child, new diagnostic evaluations indicating anoth-

er possible cause for the disability, distance from the house if an out-of-district placement, some danger to your child's safety either in transit or at the site, disagreements with the school's educational program, lack of services, and so on.

2. Once you feel that such a meeting is necessary you should document your reasons carefully. The presentation to the committee is crucial especially when you keep in mind that professionals with a great deal of documentation may be present at the same meeting. Try to keep anecdotal records, papers, works samples, incident reports, calls to administration asking for assistance and any other records that will present a basis for such a request.

3. Once you have developed a packet of information, call the director of the CSE and request a special meeting to discuss your concerns about your child's classification or placement.

4. The director may ask you some questions over the phone but if this occurs, I would recommend that you ask for a preliminary meeting with him/her. Many times a compromise or solution may be obtained by such a meeting. If this does not happen ask for a meeting of the full committee. Keep in mind that even if the chairperson agrees with you any change in an IEP requires a full meeting of the CSE.

5. If the CSE does not agree with your request you always have the option to ask for an impartial hearing which is part of your due-process rights. At this meeting an impartial officer, not an employee of the district, will hear both sides and offer a recommendation usually within ten days.

The School

There may be times when the school feels that your child's classification or placement needs to be changed. If this occurs, it should follow certain procedures:

1. The reasons for such a request may result from an improvement in your child's performance over a long period of time possibly indicating declassification, no longer requiring supportive services to maintain adequate school performance, severe difficulties with the present placement and a need for a more restrictive setting, the development of a secondary disability requiring a change to multiply disabled, inability to provide appropriate supportive services within the present placement, and so on.

2. Once the school feels that such a recommendation is necessary, it should contact the chairperson of the CSE and request a special meeting for the purposes of classification or placement review. This usually just requires filling out the necessary form.

3. The school should then call you in to discuss its concerns and request a review by the CSE. Hopefully, you have been involved along the way so that such a request will not come as a total surprise.

4. The school should then put together a packet of information including but not limited to teacher's comments, work samples, grades, any testing updates, out-

side evaluations, and so on. This packet should then be sent to the CSE with a cover letter indicating the request for such a meeting and the school's position. You also have a right to a copy of these materials prior to the meeting.

5. The chairperson will then schedule a full meeting of the CSE which is required for any possible change in an IEP and notify you in writing.

6. At the meeting, the school should make a very thorough presentation for any change in classification and placement since this type of change constitutes a very serious modification due to the implications that follow.

7. If the school is recommending declassification then your child will still be able to receive transitional supportive services for one year. The school should be sure that such a recommendation is made on the basis of a historical pattern of success and not a short-term change. Declassifying and then having to reclassify a student can be traumatic.

8. If the review is based upon the school's feeling that a more therapeutic setting is required then documentation should indicate what has been tried and why the school feels that the present placement is unsuitable.

9. If you disagree, then the school also has the right to ask for an impartial hearing.

Implementation—Step 4

What Is Implementation?

Once recommendations are in place the district must implement the programs and services. It is the responsibility of the CSE and the school district to ensure that these arrangements are in place. If this is your child's first placement in special education, you will give your consent to implement the CSE recommendation. Requirement for consent will accompany the notice of recommendation sent by the CSE. Once you give consent and if the Board of Education approves the CSE recommendation, arrangements will be made to begin services indicated on the IEP. Arranging for programs and services may take awhile. However, it should be approximately a thirty-day process, and it shouldn't take longer. Your timely response will help move the process.

During implementation, the CSE and the district personnel will contact you concerning the coordination of schedules, transportation, assignments for staff and any special arrangements for your child's program. Any changes or additions to your child's program must be described by the CSE on the IEP (see Chapter 7).

What You Should Consider During the Implementation Phase

As a student is placed into the recommended program, the IEP becomes an instrument, or blueprint, for providing the education in the appropriate setting. The IEP is used as the plan of the program. To address a student's specific needs, certain factors within elementary and secondary education are important to consider during initial implementation and during continuation of your child's special-education program. It should be clarified to your satisfaction by the CSE. The following should be of assistance in understanding what needs to consider when implementing your child's IEP.

Educational Considerations

Grouping. Students need to be grouped together with similar social, academic, physical, and management needs as stated earlier.

Curriculum. Instruction in special education should be equivalent to the content within the mainstream.

Scheduling. Schedules that are changeable provide for individual student needs to be met. Programs should be coordinated with the mainstream and other services during the day. Scheduling should be coordinated so that your child's program does not become fragmented or uncoordinated. Sometimes pupils are pulled out so many times that they cannot meet the requirements of the regular program. Also, access to regular education areas such as art, music, and other subject areas must be available and is very important as it may be an area of strength for the student.

Testing. Every disabled child should have the same opportunity to participate in the testing programs, particularly those that identify achievement and performance levels necessary for minimum competency as required in some states. This is essential for preparing high-school students with disabilities. Modifications on your child's IEP may exempt him/her from certain testing situations such as tests which are used to screen children for special education.

Nonacademic Activities. Nonacademic and extracurricular activities are offered to support and supplement the basic program and are important especially for students with disabilities. Students with disabilities must be provided the opportunity to participate in all school-related activities. This may range from field trips and clubs to special events after school.

Alternative Testing Techniques. Test modifications are procedures that provide your child the opportunity to demonstrate his/her knowledge and skills without being limited by his/her disability. These modifications must be indicated on your child's IEP. When this occurs, it is a legal requirement that must be followed by any teacher providing instruction to your child. Refer to Chapter 7, IEP Development, for a complete explanation of test modifications.

Second Language Instruction. A student who has been determined to have a disability by the CSE may be exempted from these requirements if the student's IEP indicated that a second-language requirement is not appropriate to the student's special educational needs. An exemption should be carefully considered, based on the student's ability. If the student is capable, he/she should not be denied an appropriate opportunity for instruction.

Computers and Adaptations. Students in special classes are entitled to have the opportunity to acquire skills in computer use as are all students. Special devices and applications for students who are disabled should also be available, as recommended by the IEP.

Transportation. If necessary, transportation must be provided to all students with disabilities. Transportation recommendations indicated on the IEP are based on the specific needs of your disabled child and may include the assistance of a wheelchair lift or other adaptations.

Conduct and Discipline. Each school district should have a conduct and disciplinary policy for disabled children. This policy should address behaviors that are acceptable in the local school district. A disabled youngster should not be suspended from school for long periods due to infractions that are related to his/her disability. If your child is suspended, you have the right to a conference with the school authorities to determine the cause and outcome of the infraction. Your child should not be suspended for more than five days at one time. If your child is suspended for more than ten days in the course of the school term, he/she may be reviewed by the CSE for a change of placement.

High School Credentials. The different types of high-school diplomas may vary from state to state. Generally for the purposes of this book there are four types: the local academic diplomas, IEP diplomas, certificates of attendance, and GED (equivalency) Diplomas. Some of these diplomas require that students pass certain required tests and successfully complete specific approved, credit-bearing courses. These diplomas are discussed below.

Diploma Options and Requirements

Local Academic Diploma. Students obtaining this diploma must successfully complete approved, credit-bearing courses.

Individualized Education Program Diploma. Your child is eligible for this diploma if he/she is classified as disabled. Your child must have completed 12 years of school, not including kindergarten, and must have successfully completed the goals on his/her IEP during that year. Students will be provided with an IEP diploma if they meet their IEP goals and cannot meet the State requirements for graduation from a regular high school.

Local Certificate of Attendance. Your child with disabilities may be eligible for a local certificate of attendance. Some students are eligible after completing 13 years of school, excluding kindergarten. In some cases, students who function within the mentally retarded range may be awarded a certificate at age 16. The certificate is awarded if the child is unable to attain the goals and objectives of the IEP. The district may or may not award certificates, based on local policy. Students who receive a local certificate prior to age 21 are still eligible to attend school until age 21, or until receiving a local diploma.

High-School Equivalency Diploma. Your child may also receive diplomas through high-school equivalency preparation programs. These programs are designed to instruct students who are over the compulsory school age so that they may successfully complete the General Education (GED) tests which are required for a high-school equivalency diploma.

Occupational Education. If your child has an interest or ability in occupational areas, they may provide it to your child. It is very important that you consider, preferably early on in his/her high-school career, participation in such courses prior to your child's transition from school to work. Students with disabilities have the right to access all appropriate occupational education courses with all other courses. The key word is "appropriate."

Twelve-Month Special Service or Program. Your child may require a highly structured educational experience that may involve a twelve-month program in order to prevent substantial regression. If the CSE recommends and the Board of Education approves the recommendation, local districts are required to provide a twelve-month special service or program as specified on the pupil's IEP. The key is substantial regression. If you are interested in twelve-month programming, help your school to document the need for it by assessing past regressions.

Extended Time in High School. Your child may have the option of remaining in school until the age of 21 if he or she has not yet received a local high-school diploma. These additional years may help some students to attain a local diploma by allowing more time for preparation. It could also be used for vocational preparation.

Additional Parental Considerations

You know by now that if you disagree with a program you may request a CSE meeting to review the program. As a parent, you may challenge the recommendations by asking for a review, by reconsidering consent or by requesting an impartial hearing. You should ask yourself the following:

- When will my child be taking standardized competency tests, standardized achievement tests, or State testing of any type?
- Will my child need alternative testing techniques to be able to truly exhibit knowledge and demonstrate skills?
- If my child fails the required State tests when will the tests be given again? How can my child prepare for the next test? What type of remediation will be provided?
- What type of credit is my child receiving?
- In my state, how many credits are needed for a diploma?
- Will my child need to stay in school until age 21 to receive a diploma?
- How can I assist my child for future employment opportunities?
- What are my child's options if my child cannot achieve a local diploma?

Arranging for Implementation: Your Suggestions for Participation

- Review the notice carefully and make sure that it fully describes your child's anticipated programs, services, and placement during implementation.

- Ask about initial classroom assessments that might be conducted. Ask about thirty-day goals—these are goals to assist students in the transition.

- Know who will be working directly with your child.

- Express concerns with the recommendation as soon as possible so that your child's needs are addressed without delay.

- Prepare your child for changes in his/her programs, such as new schools, new classrooms and activities, change in transportation arrangements, new teachers, and so on.

- Try to bring your child for a visit to observe the agreed-upon program.

- Contact your CSE chairperson and be prepared to discuss questions or problems.

Record-Keeping Ideas During the Implementation Phase

You should maintain on file a copy of the IEP and save any pertinent correspondence from teachers, administrators, and CSE members. Keep a calendar of your child's projected daily/weekly schedule. Record the date your child begins the recommended program.

Annual Review—Step 5

What Is the Annual Review?

Each year the CSE is required to review your child's existing program. During this process the CSE will make recommendations upon review of records that will continue, change, revise, or end your child's special-education program. Based on these findings, the CSE will make adjustments to the IEP and recommendations to your Board of Education.

The annual review occurs within a year of initial placement and yearly thereafter. The date of the annual review should be part of your child's IEP. A CSE review may be requested by you, your child's teacher, or a school administrator, at any time, to determine if a change or modification is needed. If this occurs, the next review must be conducted within one year.

As a parent you will be notified of the date, time, location, and individuals expected to attend your child's meeting. You will also be given a statement about your right to bring other people to the meeting. As stated earlier, you have the same rights as the initial CSE meeting. You will also be notified that if you cannot attend the meeting, you will have the opportunity to participate in other ways such as through telephone calls or written reports of the annual review meeting. If necessary, you will be able to have an interpreter provided to you at no cost. Your child's notice of the annual review will include your right to have information about the planned review. You may at any time inspect your child's school files, records, and reports and make copies at a reasonable cost. Such records can be very helpful at the meeting. If medication or a physical condition is part of your child's disability you may request that a physician attend the meeting. You may also request an independent evaluation, impartial hearing, or appeal the decision from the impartial hearing to the State Review Office of the State Education Department.

You are also entitled to receive free or low-cost legal services and a listing where those services can be obtained. You are so entitled to *pendency*, having your child stay in the current educational placement during formal due-process proceedings, unless both parties agree otherwise. As parents, you may be able to obtain reimbursement for attorney's fees in special-education disputes in which you prevail.

After the annual review, you will receive another notice regarding the recommendation which has been made to the Board of Education. A copy of your child's IEP will be sent to you if he/she has been recommended to continue to receive special education. The notice will also explain all factors used to make the recommendation. Again, the notice will describe your due-process rights.

Suggestions for Your Participation in the Annual Review

- Suggest ways to meet your child's proposed goals and objectives as specified in the IEP.

- Discuss changes or additions for your child's upcoming program and services. Talk about what worked and what needs adjustment from your point of view.

- Ensure that the IEP was developed at the CSE meeting in order to determine the effectiveness of the program throughout the year as you see it. Make members of the CSE aware of the areas in which your child showed success and significant progress.

- Discuss high-school diploma and credential options.

- Discuss need for a referral to an adult service provider such as state vocational rehabilitation coordinator, for services your child may need as an adult.

- Review problems that you or your child have experienced or encountered throughout the year with the CSE and staff.

- Ask questions about your child's proposed goals in the IEP and request more information, as needed. Usually this component is not reviewed at CSE. It's important!

- By age 13, you should begin to consider plans for occupational education and transition services.

Record-Keeping Ideas During the Annual Review

You should save copies of the current IEP, report cards, samples of your child's work, and teacher-conference reports. You should also save copies of all notices or correspondence with the school and the CSE during the year. Save a copy of your child's IEP developed at the Annual Review meeting.

PARENT'S PREPARATION CHECKLIST FOR ANNUAL REVIEW
RECORDS TO KEEP THROUGHOUT THE YEAR

Item:_____ **Date:** _____

Comments: _____

Classroom Information

Test Results   _____

Teacher Reports   _____

Student's Schedule   _____

Attendance Records   _____

Samples of Classwork   _____

Copy of IEP   _____

Report Card   _____

School Correspondence

From Teacher   _____

Phone Contacts   _____

School Calendar   _____

Parent Meetings Attended   _____

School Notices   _____

CSE Notices   _____

Additional Reports

Other Independent Evaluations _____

From Other Agencies   _____

Additional Health Records   _____

The Triennial Evaluation—Step 6

What Is the Triennial Evaluation?

Your child will have a triennial evaluation which occurs every three years to provide current assessment information to help determine his/her continued placement in special education. At this triennial evaluation, updated information is provided through reexamining many of the areas previously tested in the initial evaluation. The results of this evaluation which is usually conducted by school officials must be discussed at a CSE meeting.

Parental Guarantees During the Triennial Evaluation

The triennial evaluation must assure:

- The right to disagree with the evaluation because you feel it is inappropriate.
- The opportunity for you, the parent, to provide information for the triennial evaluation.
- Information is provided to you in your dominant language or mode of communication. An interpreter must be provided if you need one.
- Appropriate evaluative measures for assessing your child's various skills are used. These tests should also be modified to meet your child's needs if he/she has impaired sensory, manual, or speaking skills. The method of testing should not interfere with demonstrating skills or knowledge.
- More than one specialist was involved in the evaluation.
- Comprehensive evaluations are conducted in all areas related to the suspected disability.
- Nonbiased tests are administered in the child's dominant language or other mode of communication.
- Tests are administered by trained personnel and are appropriate for analyzing the suspected problem.
- Your child's confidential records are maintained. School districts must follow the requirements mandated by the Federal law protecting the privacy rights of both you and your child.
- You have the right to review your child's records and make copies at a reasonable cost.
- The right to initiate an independent evaluation on your own, or to request it from the school district.
- At least one teacher or other specialist with knowledge in the areas of the suspected disability was involved.

Suggestions for Your Participation in the Triennial Evaluation

You should check your records at home to make sure an evaluation is scheduled every three years. When you are notified of the triennial evaluation, you may want to request additional evaluations which may provide you with a more comprehensive assessment of your child's needs. If you have questions about new tests, call the CSE for information. Prior to the meeting, you should ask to review evaluative results and write down any questions you may have regarding reports.

Record-Keeping Ideas During the Triennial Evaluation Phase

Try to record the names of tests that are given and keep an ongoing record of test results from the triennial evaluation.

Due Process—Step 7

Due process is a crucial part of the special-education process and is there to fully protect your rights as a parent of a disabled child. The due-process rights afforded to parents also apply to your child. It is most important that you understand your due-process rights as they are presented in this chapter. You need to know that under IDEA (Individuals with Disabilities Education Act) your rights are extensive and you have due process through every stage of the special-education process. How you use these rights and how you communicate with your district will determine how smoothly the process proceeds.

Overall Summary of Due-Process Assurances

The due-process guarantees discussed in previous sections are summarized below. They include:

Consent. You have a right to give or withhold consent under certain situations. First, you may give or withhold consent for the school to test prior to the initial evaluation of your child. Second, prior to placement of your child in special education for the first time. Third, prior to an initial placement of your child in a twelve-month special service or program. Lastly, you may give or withhold consent prior to a referral for adult services.

Your Right to Notification of Actions. You as a parent or guardian must be fully informed of your rights regarding any proposed action by the school district. You also have the right to be adequately notified of any changes in classification, placement, or services in your dominant language. You also have the right to examine and obtain copies of your child's school records at any time. Some districts may charge a fee for copying.

Your Right to Participate. You have the right to participate in any decisions affecting your child through attendance at meetings and through your ongoing involvement in your child's education. This will ensure consideration of your point of view.

Your Right to File a Complaint. If you feel that your child's rights have been violated you have a right to file a written complaint to your State Education Department (SED).

It is important to note that resolution is required at all other levels before you can initiate this written complaint. The State should resolve your complaint within 60 days. If the district has acted in violation of law or regulation the State will monitor until the complaint is fully resolved. Where the district has violated a law or regulation, the corrective action required must correct the problem not only for your child, but for all children. Once the investigation is complete, you will receive a written response from the SED.

Your Right to an Independent Evaluation. If you disagree with the evaluation performed or obtained by the school district, you have the right to an independent educational evaluation of your child at district expense. If the district feels that its evaluation is appropriate, it may initiate a hearing. If the hearing officer agrees with the district you may still have an independent evaluation but at your own expense.

Your Right to Challenge. You as a parent have the right to challenge your school district's decisions regarding your child. If you do, you have the right to request an impartial hearing regarding the school's decision. You may bring an attorney or other knowledgeable individuals with an understanding of special education to represent you at the hearing. You may also be entitled to free or low-cost legal services. The school district must provide you with a list of individuals or agencies. If you prevail, you may also be reimbursed for your attorney's fees.

In some areas of the country, school districts provide special-education mediation at no cost. *Mediation* is a process involving a third party assisting the district and yourself to come to an amicable resolution. The hope of mediation is to open up communication between you and the district. To determine whether special-education mediation is available in your school district, contact your child's CSE.

Your Right to Appeal. The right to appeal is always an option if you disagree with any decision by the CSE or an impartial hearing officer. You also may appeal to a state review officer and if you disagree with his/her decision you can appeal for judicial review. If you wish you can go as far as the United States Supreme Court.

What Is an Impartial Hearing?

At times a formal procedure is required to resolve disagreements between parents and school districts. This process is called an impartial hearing. Most parents and school districts attempt to resolve their differences prior to an impartial hearing for two reasons. First, they are timely. Once initiated they may take up to forty-five days. Second, it can be costly to both the parent and the district. Similarly, in order to fulfill its responsibility to provide your child with a free appropriate public education, the school district must initiate due-process-hearing procedures under certain circumstances. The impartial hearing has been established as a mechanism to hear both sides of the issues and resolve the dispute fairly through a third party.

When either you or the school make a request for an impartial hearing, the board of education must arrange for the location of the hearing and appoint the hearing officer from the list of State certified hearing officers. Impartial hearing officers cannot be employees of the district and may not have any personal or professional interest that could conflict with his or her objectivity.

Try not to be concerned about the formal nature of the impartial hearing. Most school districts try to keep it relaxed even though it is an administrative proceeding. However, there may be times when you may feel like an adversary of the school district. The hearing can be conducted in an open or closed session. This decision is up to you.

The impartial hearing process includes the calling of witnesses by both school district and you to provide information and to respond to questions on the issue. Any documentation needs to be presented to the hearing officer five days in advance of the meeting. The school district will call witnesses first. However, you will have the opportunity to question each of their witnesses. You will then have an opportunity to call your witnesses and the district will have its opportunity to question. You have the right to ask the hearing officer to issue subpoenas to compel witnesses to attend or produce documentation that you are not able to obtain voluntarily. If a hearing officer feels that the interests of parents are inconsistent with those of the child he/she may appoint a guardian for the child. The hearing officer must inform you that your due-process rights will be preserved throughout the hearing. At the meeting an electronic or written record of the proceeding will be taken and a written record will be provided to you. A provision is made for an interpreter for the deaf or a translator. An impartial hearing provides you as a parent and the school district with the opportunity to present each case to an impartial officer for a fair resolution of the matter that is consistent with the law. The hearing officer should refer to Federal and State laws and regulations as well as the most recent court decisions regarding dealing with special-education issues. The hearing officer must declare impartiality informing both parties at the onset of the hearing of any possible conflicts of interest. You will have the right, as will the district, to object to the continuance of the hearing officer with the case if you feel that there may be a possible conflict of interest. You may then ask that he/she step down and allow the board of education to appoint another hearing officer.

Your child has the right to attend the hearing if he or she is over the age of 18. You as a parent or the school district may also deem it necessary that he/she attend if under 18.

At the conclusion of your case, you and the district will have an opportunity to make closing statements to the hearing officer. You should refer to any evidence that has been introduced or statements made by witnesses in your closing arguments. You should explain to the hearing officer exactly what you would like his/her decision to be.

After the hearing a copy of the decision must be mailed to the board of education within forty-five days of the written request of the hearing. The hearing officer's decision may only be based on evidence presented at the meeting. It includes the reasons and the basis for the decision. The hearing officer's decision is final unless you or the district appeals the decision to a state review officer. If a decision is appealed to the state review officer, the decision is final unless taken to a court of law. Information on how to appeal to the state review officer will be provided in the impartial hearing officer's decision. Your rights are protected throughout the special-education process from your initial referral straight through to the United States Supreme Court.

The IDEA authorizes the courts to award reasonable attorney's fees to parents to defray their costs if they prevail in an administrative proceeding. If you as a parent use the services of an attorney and you prevail in either an impartial hearing, a subsequent appeal, or a court of law, you may be eligible to recover a portion or all of the fees. This determination can only be made by the courts.

When Are Impartial Hearings Requested?

You can initiate an impartial hearing under the following conditions:

- When you disagree with your child's special-education program.
- When you disagree with the recommendation of the CSE or board of education.
- When the CSE fails to evaluate or make its recommendation within thirty school days of consent.
- When the board of education fails to review, at least annually, your child's program, or fails to reevaluate your child every three years.

The board of education must initiate an impartial hearing when:

- You do not consent to the initial evaluation and the referral has not been withdrawn by mutual agreement.
- When the school district wants to establish that its evaluation is appropriate, to avoid paying for an independent evaluation.
- When you withhold consent to the initial recommendation for special education.
- When you withdraw consent to an evaluation or to a proposed placement.

Record-Keeping Ideas During Due Process

Since any challenge or appeal may have a serious impact on your child's education, you will want to maintain copies of all documents (notices, consents, communications from the school, communications to the school, written agreements reached at mediation). Take very detailed notes during information conferences, meetings, and hearings.

Remember, it is always better to resolve conflicts at the building and CSE level whenever possible. Impartial hearings and court cases should only be used as a last resort.

chapter seven

INDIVIDUAL EDUCATIONAL PLANS

IEP Guidelines

Your child's Individual Educational Plan (IEP) is a very crucial document. It contains the district's plan for the education of your child. The IEP contains a great deal of information usually separated into many sections. While there are no specific guidelines in terms of the IEP format, there are requirements about what must be included. There are usually seven general sections to any IEP. They are:

1. **General Identifying Data**:

   Name

   Address

   Phone

   Date of Birth

   Parents' Names

   Dominant Language of Child

   Dominant Language Spoken at Home

   Date Child Entered Program (This is only filled in for previously classified students and basically informs the reader about when the child first started receiving special-education services.)

2. Current Placement Data:

Classification: (This is filled in if the child had been previously classified.)

Grade: Present grade

Current Placement: Regular class for an initial review by the CSE or present special-education setting if child has already been classified.

Class Size Ratio: (Only filled in for previously classified students.)

Length of Program: Ten- or twelve-month program

School: Present school

Teacher: Child's present teacher or guidance counselor if a secondary level student

Diploma: (This will either be a local diploma or an *IEP diploma*, (which can be given to classified students who may not meet the school requirements for graduation but have accomplished all the objectives on their IEP.)

Transportation: (This is filled in if the child is presently receiving special transportation arrangements.)

Physical Education: Present class type (regular, adaptive)

Annual Review Date: Usually April, May, or June of the school year

Triennial Review Date: Usually three years from the date of the last full evaluation.

Intelligence Test Results: Must be within one year of review by CSE and indicates Verbal, Performance, or Full-Scale IQ.

3. Recommendations by the CSE:

Classification: The child must fit the criteria for one of the state-defined classification categories, and the disability must significantly impede his/her ability to learn.

Grade: Projected grade for the coming year.

Placement: This depends upon the child's least-restrictive educational setting.

Class Size Ratio: Indicates the maximum student population allowed, the number of teachers required and the number of assistant teachers or aides required.

Length of Program: Some special-education programs maintain a ten-month calendar. Programs for more seriously disabled students may be twelve-months long.

School: Projected school for the coming year.

Teacher: Identifies the child's contact teacher for the coming year. When a child has several special-education teachers as in a departmentalized special-education high-school program, one teacher is assigned as the contact teacher. On the elementary and secondary levels this can also be the resource-room teacher, if the child is assigned there, or the child's self-contained special-education teacher if this more-restrictive program is used.

Program Initiation Date: Indicates when the special-education services will begin.

Transportation needs: Indicates whether or not your child has special transportation needs, as with a severely physically disabled child who may require door-to-door service with a special bus to allow easy access and departure.

Physical Education: Indicates whether your child is being recommended for regular physical education or *adaptive physical education* (means a specially designed program of developmental activities, games, sports and rhythms suited to the interests, capacities, and limitations of pupils with disabilities who may not safely or successfully engage in unrestricted participation in the activities of the regular physical-education program).

Related Services: Indicates other services that the child will be receiving that support the academic special-education process. Also noted in this section would be the number of sessions per week, minutes per session, maximum group size, start date and end date. Related services may include:

- In-school individual counseling
- In-school group counseling
- Resource room
- Speech/language therapy
- Physical therapy and occupational therapy
- Art therapy
- Adaptive physical education
- Music therapy

A more detailed explanation of related services can be found in Chapter 8.

Mainstreamed Courses: A listing must be included on the IEP if the child's disability allows for any mainstreamed class in which the student will participate.

Special Classes: This indicates the types of special-education classes the child will have in the coming year such as Math, Social Studies, Health.

Testing Information: This section reviews the academic test results including the tests administered, date administered, percentile, and/or age or grade equivalents.

Comments: This section is used to indicate any questions, reminders, reviews, parent concerns, identified areas of strengths and weakness, and progress to date.

4. Goals and Objectives:

Social Development: Means the degree and quality of the pupil's relationships with peers and adults, feelings about self, and social adjustment to school and community environments.

Physical Development: Means the degree or quality of the pupil's motor and sensory development, health, vitality, and physical skills or limitations which pertain to the learning process.

Academic Characteristics: Means the levels of knowledge and development in subject and skill areas, including activities of daily living, level of intellectual functioning, adaptive behavior, expected rate of progress in acquiring skills, and information and learning style.

Management Needs: Means the nature and degree to which environmental modifications and human material resources are required to enable the pupil to benefit from instruction.

The second part to this section deals with the specific academic goals and objectives that will be remediated. The basis for this area comes from the evaluation and the diagnosis of strengths and weaknesses. Also included in this section may be specific content-area goals such as science, social studies, math, and English, if the child is in a special-education setting for these subjects.

Examples of these types of goals and objectives are follows:

5. **Mastery Levels**:

When determining an objective, mastery levels need to be considered. A *mastery level* is a predetermined level of competency indicating a clear understanding of a particular skill. This is the teacher's way of validating a child's movement to the next objective.

Setting the mastery levels too low will increase the possibilities of luck or chance influencing success, while setting them too high may set the child up for constant frustration and failure because of careless mistakes or minute errors. Mastery levels can be indicated according the following standards:

- *Ratio-based mastery level*: John will be able to _____ 8 out of every 10 attempts.

- *Percent-based mastery level*: Mary will be able to _____ 75 percent of the time.

- *Time-based mastery level*: Ben will be able to _____ 12 responses within a 10-minute period.

There may be times when one general statement of mastery level can apply to all the objectives: *All objectives will be completed with 80 percent accuracy.*

6. **Evaluative Measures**:

An important part of the IEP includes the procedures and techniques the teacher will use to determine if your child has successfully accomplished the objectives set forth in his/her goals. There are many such tools available to teachers and some of them include:

- Student assignments and projects
- Informal conferences between student and teacher

- Student self-evaluation
- Textbook tests and quizzes
- Standardized tests
- Review of quarterly report cards
- Discussions with classroom teachers
- Parent-teacher conferences
- Record of attendance
- Stanford Diagnostic Test
- Teacher-made tests
- Teacher evaluation
- Homework assignments
- Criterion-referenced tests

7. **Alternate Testing Modifications**:

It is very important that you become aware of all the available modifications allowed by law. These modifications can play an important part in the academic and social life of your child. Keep in mind that every disabled child is not automatically entitled to every modification. The records, evaluations, observations, and so on must indicate a need for the inclusion of such an alternative. The following modifications are available if the need can be documented:

Alternate Testing Techniques Which Modify Manner of Presentation

FLEXIBLE SCHEDULING. This modification is usually applied for students who may have problems in the rate in which they process information, such as physical disabilities like motor or visual impairments. Examples of modifications which fall under this category include:

- Untimed tests
- Administration of a test in several sessions during the course of the day
- Administration of a test in several sessions over several days

FLEXIBLE SETTING. This modification allows disabled students to take a test in another setting other than the regular classroom. This may become necessary in cases where a child has health impairments and may be unable to leave home or the hospital, where a child's disability interferes with his/her remaining on task or is easily distracted. In other cases a disabled student may require special lighting or acoustics or a specially equipped room. Examples of flexible setting include:

- Individual administration of a test in a separate location
- Small group administration of a test in a separate location

- Provisions for special lighting
- Provisions for special acoustics
- Provisions for adaptive or special furniture
- Administration of test in a location with minimal distractions

REVISED TEST FORMAT. This modification is utilized by students whose disability may interfere with their ability to take a test using the standard test format (for instance, students with visual or perceptual disabilities may not be able to read regular size print). Examples include:

- Use of a large print edition
- Increased spacing between items
- Reduction in the number of items per page
- Use of a Braille edition
- Increase in size of answer bubbles on test answer forms
- Rearrangement of multiple-choice items with answer bubble right next to each choice

REVISED TEST DIRECTIONS. This modification allows students with certain disabilities a greater chance of understanding directions and thereby completing a test successfully.

- Ability to have directions read to child
- Ability to reread the directions for each page of questions
- Ability to simplify the language in the directions
- Ability to provide additional examples

USE OF AIDS. Some disabled students require the use of aids in order to interpret test items (for instance, hearing-impaired children). These may include:

- Auditory amplification devices
- Visual magnification devices
- Auditory tape of questions
- Marks or markers to maintain the student's place on a page
- Having questions read to the student
- Having questions signed to the student

Alternate Testing Techniques Which Modify Manner of Response

USE OF AIDS. These modifications allow a disabled student to record answers to examination questions. Techniques may include:

- Use of a tape recorder
- Use of a typewriter
- Use of a communication device
- Use of a word processor
- Use of a secretary

REVISED FORMAT. Some disabled students may be unable to record their responses to test questions on conventional answer forms and as a result require a change in the test format. This may include:

- Allowing the child to record answers in the test booklet directly
- Allowing the child to increase the spacing between questions or problems
- Allowing the child to increase the size of the answer blocks
- Allowing the child to provide cues (stop sign, arrows) directly on the answer form

Alternate Testing Techniques Which Modify Process Used to Derive Response

USE OF AIDS. Some students may possess the innate ability to process mathematical information, but may have a disability that prohibits them from using paper and pencil to solve computations. Other disabled students may not be able to memorize arithmetic facts but can solve difficult word problems. When these problems occur with disabled students, consider the following modifications:

- Use of a calculator
- Use of an abacus
- Use of arithmetic tables

Student Eligibility and Criteria for Testing Modifications

Alternate testing techniques are modifications that take into account the individual needs of a child having a disability and as a result modify testing procedures or formats. These modifications attempt to provide these students with equal opportunity to participate in testing situations.

These techniques, which must appear on the student's IEP, provide the opportunity to demonstrate a disabled student's mastery of skills without being unfairly restricted by the presence of that disability.

Student Eligibility for Use of Testing Techniques

Only students who have been identified as having a disability by the Committee on Special Education normally receive alternate testing techniques. However, there are three other possible avenues that can be taken to provide alternate testing techniques without classification.

1. The law usually allows the school principal the authority to approve a student's need for testing modification which does not alter the intended purpose of a test for a student who may have a disability, but not severe enough to warrant identification by the CSE. An example of this may be a student who has Attention Deficit Disorder (ADD) and as a result may have some mild problems but they do not constitute a severe discrepancy in his/her functioning.

2. In cases of certain tests (for example, college entrance SAT), two pieces of documentation from outside professionals (not working in the same agency) indicating the need for alternate testing techniques (untimed tests) may allow the student these privileges even thought they have not been identified by the CSE.

3. Students receiving *transitional services* (services provided to students having been declassified by the CSE, entitling them to receive services and/or modifications up to one year after declassification).

Criteria for Allowing Use of Testing Techniques

The CSE tries to keep in mind that all students can benefit from alternate testing techniques and as a result a recommendation based just on potential to enhance performance may be inappropriate. The need for modifications must be substantiated in the evaluation results.

Alternate testing techniques are determined by the CSE for students identified as having a disability. The Committee takes into account several variables when making this determination:

1. The individual needs of the child as determined by evaluation, observation, background history, and other pertinent information presented at the CSE meeting.

2. The necessity for modification in light of the student's past academic and test performance without modifications.

3. The student's potential benefit from the modification.

Impact of Alternate Testing Modifications on Specific Tests

Scholastic Aptitude Test

Students with documented learning disabilities or visual, physical, or hearing handicaps are eligible for alternative testing techniques. Computational aids are prohibited. No items may be omitted.

General Equivalency Diploma

Each test must be completed on the day that it is started; all tests must be completed within two weeks. Candidates who are visually impaired or who have visual perceptual disabilities may use an audiocassette edition and an abacus. Reading of test questions is not allowed; use of a calculator is prohibited. Only test instructions may be signed to candidates who are hearing impaired or deaf.

In addition to the tests listed above, there are many other standardized tests which students may take during their schooling. The number and variety of these tests preclude their inclusion in this chart. In each case, the testing authority sets the guidelines for both standard and nonstandard administration. Procedures for test administration and descriptions of restrictions are included in most test manuals.

Roles and Responsibilities for Implementation

Many individuals are involved in the process which resulted in the use of alternative testing techniques by pupils with handicapping conditions. These include members of the Board of Education, the Committee on Special Education, the building principal, special- and regular-education teachers, and parents. The purpose of this section is to define the role of each and to provide suggestions for carrying out responsibilities.

Responsibilities of the Board of Education on Testing Modifications

Two important responsibilities of the Board of Education are the establishment and dissemination of school district policies and the review of recommendations made by the Committee on Special Education for students with handicapping conditions.

With regard to alternative testing techniques for students with handicapping conditions, members of the Board need to be familiar with the different types of alternative testing techniques and the manner by which these are matched to individual student needs. District policies can emphasize that the use of these techniques is consistent with the school district's responsibility to maintain educational standards, and does, in fact, enhance the school's ability to allow all students equal access to the full range of instructional and testing opportunities.

Procedures regarding the use of alternative testing techniques should be consistent for all schools within the district and should be fully understood by members of the CSE, building administrators, teachers, related-services personnel, other school staff, and parents. Because principals are responsible for ensuring implementation of CSE recommendations regarding alternative testing techniques, district policy should identify the procedure by which principals are informed of such recommendations. This might be done by including the principal among those who regularly receive copies of IEPs which include alternative testing techniques.

In reviewing recommendations from the Committee on Special Education, Board members decide on the appropriateness of alternative testing techniques as well as other recommended services. Appropriateness is determined by how closely the techniques are matched to both the individual needs of the students and the purpose of the test or tests to be administered.

Responsibilities of the Committee on Special Education on Testing Modifications

The Committee on Special Education is responsible for identifying and documenting the student's need for alternative testing techniques. This determination is made when a student is initially referred to the CSE, is reviewed annually for as long as the student receives special-education services, and is reviewed when the student is determined to no longer need special-education services.

In making its decision, the CSE reviews all available information regarding the student's individual needs. Such information might include recent evaluations, previous school records, IEPs, classroom observations, and the student's experience on previous tests. Information and suggestions from the student's teachers, related-service providers, and parents might also be sought.

Members of the Committee on Special Education should be knowledgeable of the types and varieties of testing modifications that may be used by students with handicapping conditions, the types of tests that are commonly administered and the purposes of each, and the specific alternative testing techniques which are prohibited for use on certain tests.

The CSE records its recommendations for alternative testing modifications of the IEP for review and approval by the Board of Education. Such recommendations will serve as a guideline for further IEP development and are documented in the objective criteria and evaluation procedures of the IEP.

Responsibilities of the School Principal on Testing Modifications

The principal in each school is responsible for implementing the district's policies which provide equal access to instructional and testing programs for all students. Principals have direct responsibility for authorizing the use of alternative testing techniques by students who have special testing needs but who are not educationally handicapped. In addition, principals ensure that students who have been identified by the CSE as educationally handicapped are provided the alternative testing techniques which have been recommended by the CSE and approved by the Board of Education. These are listed on a student's IEP. Principals, therefore, have responsibility for making sure that teachers and other appropriate school personnel receive information and training on the consistent and appropriate use of alternative testing techniques.

Responsibilities of the Special-Education Teacher on Testing Modifications

You should be aware that your child's special-education teacher is responsible for the implementation and monitoring of the modifications listed on the IEP. You should also be aware that if your child is mainstreamed, *all* teachers must abide by the alternate testing techniques listed. The modifications are legally binding and must be offered, if the child is entitled. This is accomplished in the following ways:

1. A special-education evaluator provides a clear understanding of a child's strength and weakness areas, learning style, and the affects of the child's disability upon academic performance. With this information in hand, the special-education teacher can analyze the need for specific modifications that can be substantiated by the results of the evaluation.

2. A special-education teacher in a self-contained special-education classroom comes in direct contact with the student in classroom instruction. This experience

provides a strong basis for recommending specific changes or additions to the modifications on a student's IEP.

3. The special-education teacher on the CSE provides background experience that can assist the committee in recommending appropriate test modifications that may become part of an initial referral IEP, change in an IEP during an annual review, or modification of alternate testing techniques as the result of a report from an outside agency.

4. The special-education teacher can also assist you as the parent of a special-education student in understanding alternate testing techniques and available options.

5. The special-education teacher may serve as a consultant to teachers, parents and administrators and offer advice on testing modifications to students.

6. The special-education teacher may monitor the implementation of assigned modifications for a particular student to ensure that the student's rights are being followed.

Responsibilities of the Regular-Education Teacher on Testing Modifications

The regular classroom teacher has an active and significant role in the use of alternative testing techniques for students with handicapping conditions. It is required that students with handicapping conditions have full access to programs and services. Teachers are expected to be able to work effectively with all students who are appropriately placed in their classes. In some instances, this will require that regular education teachers modify or adapt instruction and testing.

Alternative testing techniques which have been approved for use by a student must be used consistently in both special- and regular-education settings. Regular classroom teachers should be aware of possible alternative testing techniques and should be skilled in their implementation.

The regular educator may participate in the planning conference to develop the IEP for students who will be attending regular-education classes. In order for a student to have equal opportunity to demonstrate mastery of instructional objectives in all settings, regular- and special-education teachers plan together for use of alternative testing procedures.

You may have questions about the use of alternative testing techniques within the context of the regular-education setting. As the teacher providing instruction in a given subject area, regular-education teachers communicate with you regarding the nature and rationale of the techniques in use.

Responsibilities of the Parents on Testing Modifications

You are encouraged to exercise your right to participate in the development of recommendations for special-education programs and services for your child who has a handicapping condition. You, knowing the strengths and weaknesses of your son or daughter, should contribute to the discussion about the need for alternative testing techniques. This opportunity exists both at the CSE meeting and the planning conference. Providing such information to appropriate persons at these meetings, or at other times during the year, will help to ensure that an appropriate program is being provided. You should be aware of the purpose of testing modifications and understand the rationale for their existence.

If you believe that your disabled child is being denied appropriate use of alternative testing techniques, request a meeting with the CSE. You may also pursue the due-process procedures of an impartial hearing and subsequent appeal to the Commissioner.

You should have adequate information regarding the variety and use of alternative testing techniques. Such information may be obtained from members of the Committee on Special Education, the principal, and teaching staff.

chapter eight

RELATED SERVICES

Overview of Related Services

Related services are any other services that the child will be receiving that support the academic special-education process. Also noted in this section would be the number of sessions per week, minutes per session, maximum group size, start date and end date. Related services may include:

In-School Individual Counseling

When this service is recommended on an IEP it usually means that the child could benefit from a more intimate therapeutic situation with emphasis on control, insight, cause-and-effect awareness, special attention, and developing a trusting relationship with an authority figure. While some children only need individual counseling, others might move from individual to group to try out the insights and experiences learned from the individual experience.

In-School Group Counseling

When this service is recommended on an IEP it means that the child would benefit from a group situation that emphasizes interpersonal relations, social skills, cooperative play and interaction, interdependence, social delay of gratification, peer feedback and social connections. The group usually meets once or twice a week and many times may be combined with individual in-school counseling.

Speech/Language Therapy

This service is recommended when the CSE feels that the child's poor performance is directly related to disabilities in language or speech development. The emphasis on this service might include remediation in expressive or receptive language, articulation, voice disorders, fluency disorders, and so on. These services may be administered in small group or individual settings. This recommendation can also be made in conjunction with some other service such as resource room if indicated.

Physical and Occupational Therapy

This recommendation is usually made by the CSE when the child is suffering from some physical or motor impairment. Physical Therapists usually provide exercise therapy and special devices to improve the total physical functioning and strength of a disabled student. Generally Occupational Therapists will focus more on fine motor skills such as hand control, using the mouth to chew, and any other factor involved in daily living skills.

Art Therapy

This recommendation, while not as common as some other services, is usually recommended when the CSE feels that the production of art in its various forms would have beneficial qualities for exceptional students. Major factors involved in this recommendation include the opportunity for the disabled child to express creativity, to improve fine motor skills, and to develop appropriate leisure-time activities.

Adaptive Physical Education

This service is usually recommended when the CSE feels that the disabled child's general physical development is impaired or delayed. When these programs are instituted, they tend to have a therapeutic orientation. The teachers utilized for this service must have special training in the use of specialized equipment to improve muscle development and coordination.

Music Therapy

This recommendation may be made by the CSE when it feels that music can be used to prompt the development of various functional behaviors for disabled students such as motivation, improvement of speech, language, and communication skills through singing.

Itinerant Services for Hearing Impaired

This recommendation may be made by the CSE when it is determined that a student falls below the criteria level set by your state, is considered classifiable as hard of hearing, and thus will need services and equipment to ensure free and appropriate education in the least-restrictive environment.

Itinerant Services for Visually Impaired

This recommendation may be made by the CSE when it is determined that a student falls below the criteria level set by your state, is considered classifiable as visually impaired, and thus will need services and equipment to ensure free and appropriate education in the least-restrictive environment.

Sign Language Interpreter

This recommendation may be made by the CSE when it is determined that the student meets the criteria for being either deaf or hard of hearing within your state and would benefit from having an interpreter within the classroom to provide sign language to the student.

What You Need to Know About Physical and Occupational Therapy

Physical and occupational therapies are important components of the special-education process. This chapter will familiarize you with each of them. They are related therapies but are specific in their function. Occupational therapy focuses mainly on fine motor/upper body functions, where physical therapy concentrates on lower body/gross motor difficulties. The services are provided for disabled students who exhibit a range of disabilities such as: learning disabilities (fine and gross motor problems, perceptual problems), developmental delays, (mental retardation, vision, or hearing impairment), respiratory problems (cystic fibrosis or asthma), neuromuscular problems (muscular dystrophy, cerebral palsy), muscle skeletal problems (arthritis, orthopedic problems, postural deviations), traumatic accidents, amputations, brain injuries, burns. Physical and occupational therapists provide many services including evaluations, screenings, consultations, education, training, as well as provide therapy for students.

Guidelines for Occupational and Physical Therapy Evaluations

Occupational and physical therapy evaluations may be referred to the CSE by any number of school or medical professionals. You may also refer for occupational and physical therapy services. Your written consent is required for an evaluation. As with other evaluations, occupational and physical therapy evaluations need to be individualized, well documented, with specific assessments of your child. The evaluation will serve as a blueprint for the development of an IEP should one be necessary. The evaluation will identify your child's deficient areas of development in the physical realm. The purpose of the evaluation is to determine your child's current level of performance. These evaluations focus on what he or she needs to achieve the next level of function. The level of your child's performance relates to the demands of his/her educational setting. The process is subjective. In some districts if you can walk into a classroom, you would not be provided with physical therapy. If you can hold a pencil, you would not be provided with occupational therapy. The two previous examples are extreme, of course, but be aware of these limitations.

In general, for occupational therapy and physical therapy, assess the following. Common to both occupational therapy and physical therapy are:

- Range of motion
- Sensory integration
- Activities for daily living
- Developmental assessment
- Muscle testing
- Need for and uses of adaptive equipment

Assessments unique to physical therapy include:

- Posture
- Gait analysis
- Endurance
- Personal independence
- Joint abnormalities
- Wheelchair management
- Transportation needs
- Architectural barriers
- Prosthetic and orthotic equipment checks

Assessments unique to occupational therapy include:

- Neuromuscular functioning
- Sensory processing
- Manual dexterity
- Leisure-time abilities
- Physical facilities
- Prevocational skills
- Oral motor and feeding problems

Therapists should meet with all professionals who are involved with your child to fully explain the nature of the disability, train them to work with your child in the areas of dysfunction, and provide assistant devices or environmental aids to help the child be maintained in his/her least-restrictive environment. The therapists should also model remedial techniques that can be duplicated by other teaching professionals. All the above should be shared with you as a parent, to assist you while working with your child. Many of the activities provided for by occupational and physical therapists can be duplicated in the home. Many of the exercises are really activities for daily living, such as hopping, jumping, buttoning, and so on.

The consultation component of occupational and physical therapy is one of the most important parts of the service. Examples of this component include:

- Referring you and your family to appropriate sources for assistance.
- Helping you order adaptive or prosthetic equipment.
- Cultivating physical-education programs.
- Instructing you and your child about methods used in physical therapy.
- Teaching you media used in therapy.
- Long-range planning development for your child in school.
- Training school professionals with special equipment.
- Helping you deal with architectural barriers.

Your therapist should act as a liaison between the CSE, the teaching staff, medical professionals, outside agencies, and you as a parent. Many pupils in need of physical and occupational therapy have severe medical conditions. These conditions often require supervision of your family doctor. The therapist should help with the coordination between the school physician and your doctor. The therapists play an important role in severe cases. Many school districts now have occupational and physical therapists as part of their staff as full-time and part-time employees. In order to provide occupational and physical therapy the CSE must approve the services. It is the occupational and physical evaluations that guide CSE through its deliberations. The better the documentation the more appropriate the services will be. The therapists play a significant role in regard to the service provided. Occupational and physical therapy may be provided in individual or small groups. It may be also be provided as a consultant service.

Occupational and physical therapies are required when your child is new to a program, whether it be a preschool, home-bound, or school-age program where therapy is mandated by the CSE. Therapy is also required when your preschool child is moving into an elementary program. Finally, if your child has been receiving therapy at the preschool level, a formal evaluation should be forwarded to the CSE from the CPSE.

Types of problems requiring occupational therapy:

- Perceptual problem (eye-hand coordination).
- Sensory problems (sensitive to sound, sensitive to visual changes, sensitive to odors, sensitive to touch).

- Gross motor (trouble with balance, problems with coordination, problems with moving).
- Fine motor (with coordination, handwriting, using scissors).
- Daily living activities (cannot dress, feed, or care for own personal hygiene).
- Organizational problems (difficulties with memory, time, spatial concepts).
- Attention span difficulties (focusing on task, short attendance span).
- Interpersonal problems (difficulty with environmental and school-related social situations).

Guidelines for Occupational Therapy Evaluations

Occupational therapy evaluations include the following:

- Vision
- Abnormal Movement Patterns
- Range of Motion
- Skeletal and Joint Conditions
- Behavior
- Skin and Soft Tissue
- Fine Motor
- Perceptual
- Gross Motor
- Balance and Equilibrium
- Activities for daily living
- Equipment
- Background Information

Guidelines for Physical Therapy Evaluations

Physical therapy provides services that develop and improve sensory motor functions, relieve pain, minimize or prevent disabilities, control postural deviations, and establish maximum performances within the individual. In a school, physical therapy services are directed for the development and maintenance of your child's physical potential so that he/she be may be maintained in the least-restrictive environment and perform educationally related activities.

The following are general areas assessed by a physical therapist:

- Behavior (which interferes with program implementation or that affects student compliance, concentration, alertness).
- Communication (augmentative devices, communication board, expressive or receptive language deficits).

- Vision (tracking, focusing, visual acuity, and field deficits).
- Neuromuscular (muscle strength, motor planning, muscle tone, sensation, coordination).
- Range of Motion (motion and length of muscle, standardized joint range).
- Skeletal and Joint Condition (skeletal and joint condition that limits function).
- Pain (frequency, location, and onset).
- Skin and Soft Tissue (includes integrity, skin and tissue, lesions, rash, scars, discoloration, temperature, edema).
- Developmental (birth to three population, developmental milestones including gross, fine, motor, language, social, emotional, and cognitive).
- Balance and Equilibrium (walking, standing, sitting).
- Posture (prone sitting, standing alignment).
- Gait Pattern (weight bearing and assistant devices, walk).
- Endurance (time, speed, fatigue ability).
- Equipment (prosthesis, orthosis, assistant devices, wheelchairs).
- Functional Mobility (ability to negotiate ramps, buses, curb, stairs, wheelchair mobility)

Description of Service Delivery

Occupational and physical therapists provide for the following: ability for the student to participate in ancillary activities or programs. Adaptation of the classroom environment to improve the student's educational performance, provide for specific needs in a particular school setting, to provide adaptive equipment. They also support the student's ability to become independent within his or her classroom setting; your child should receive occupational and physical therapies in the least-restrictive environment such as classroom, school building, gym, in as natural location as possible. A brief description of the types of services you can expect for your child are as follows. Therapy will depend on your child's disability and performance. The therapist may utilize any of the following in his or her sessions:

1. **Education and Communication.** The therapy will coordinate with other personnel and programs when in the educational setting. A therapist will discuss the student's dysfunction and how it affects his or her performance during a normal school day. He or she may suggest changes in routine, classroom modifications, or barrier reductions in an effort to improve the student's ability to perform. The therapist will share this information with teachers, other specialists, classroom aids, the building administrator and the CSE. The therapist should also share this information with you. This is especially important for your child if he or she has cerebral palsy, spina bifida, muscular dystrophy, arthritis, or other progressive deformities.

2. **Direct therapeutic treatment**. The therapist will follow IEP goals and objectives to remediate specific dysfunctional areas. The treatment can be provided in

an integrated school day or in a separate environment. There are times when your child may benefit from therapy as part of the normal routine of his or her school day. The therapist may integrate into situations such as playground activities or during a physical-education class. He or she also may help and work with the student during art classes or other times when physical activities are involved. The student may also be seen in a separate environment especially with moderately or severely disabled youngsters who are highly distractible or have behavior problems.

3. **Assistant Devices**. These will be utilized if your child requires assistant devices for adaptive equipment. The therapist will be helpful in evaluating these for fit, modification, reevaluation, and for ordering any equipment or devices.

4. **Small Group Sessions**. Your student may receive his or her therapy within a small group if other children have similar needs. The therapist may model strategy that all students within the group can follow. This is not a usual service delivery and has to be orchestrated carefully. Most occupational and physical therapy sessions are consultative or individualized.

5. **Consultation**. We have covered the consultation model earlier, but in review the therapist will work together with other professionals to solve the problem your child may encounter within his or her educational program.

6. **Monitoring**. Once therapists establish therapy routines, classroom programs, or the use of specialized equipment they may periodically monitor and review what is in place for effectiveness. This is one step removed from the consultation model in that the therapist will check in periodically.

Legal Aspects

A physical therapist may not see or treat your child without receiving a referral from a licensed physician, podiatrist, or dentist, and only by following his or her prescription. An occupational therapist must receive a physician referral in order to provide therapy. A physical therapist in some states may evaluate a student without receiving a physician's referral, but cannot provide ongoing treatment without such referral. An occupational therapist cannot treat or evaluate without a physician's referral. A physician's referral should advise the therapist regarding any concerns or precautions incumbent in your child's medical history or diagnosis. The physician should be current regarding your child's medical history and condition. Professionals from both the medical and legal fields advise that medical referrals be updated at least once a year and more often if the medical condition changes within a school setting. Changes may include hospitalizations, seizure control, or surgery which may necessitate a change in the therapy that could be either temporary or permanent.

In conclusion, physical and occupational therapy provided in the schools must follow a medical referral and are provided to improve your child's ability so that he or she may be able to function within the least-restrictive environment. The therapies provided by the occupational and physical therapists must be related to school achievement. Remember occupational therapy concentrates on upper body and fine motor problems where physical therapy focuses on lower body and gross motor problems. Occupational and physical therapists provide essential educational services in today's schools.

What You Need to Know About In-School Counseling

When Is In-School Counseling Necessary?

In-school counseling is a free service to children enrolled in a public school district. A child may be referred for counseling by a teacher, guidance counselor, principal, parent, or even through self-referral by the student. In-school counseling can be voluntary or recommended as a related service which may be the case on an IEP. This related service becomes necessary when a general pattern exists in which the child exhibits:

- An inability to learn on a consistent basis which cannot be explained by intellectual capability, hearing and vision status, or physical health anomalies.
- An inability or unwillingness to develop or maintain satisfactory interpersonal relationships with peers, teachers, parents, or other adults.
- Extreme overreactions to minimally stressful situations over a prolonged period of time.
- A general pervasive mood of sadness or depression.
- A tendency to develop somatic complaints, pains, or excessive fears associated with home, school, or social situations.
- Absence of knowledge and skill acquisition in academic and social behaviors not attributed to intellectual capability, hearing and vision status, or physical health anomalies.
- Absence of positive, satisfying interpersonal relationships with adults and peers.
- Frequent instances of inappropriate behavior episodes which are surprising or unexpected for the conditions in which they occur.
- Observable periods of diminished verbal and other motor activity (moods of depression or unhappiness).
- Frequent complaints of a physical nature, such as stomachaches, or general fatigue.

The pattern of behaviors should be evaluated as to the frequency, duration, and intensity of the symptoms. Specific symptoms which might be indicative of the need for a consultation with the school psychologist and possible in-school counseling might involve patterns of behaviors including:

- academic underachievement
- social isolation or withdrawal
- excessive latenesses
- excessive absences

- frequent trips to the nurse
- negativism
- open defiance to authority or rules
- highly distractible
- poor social relationships
- feelings of hopelessness
- verbal aggression
- confrontational behavior
- inappropriate classroom behaviors
- impulsive behavior
- rigid behavior patterns
- anxious and worried, excessive fears and phobias
- easily frustrated even when confronted with a simple task
- resistance to change

Your best bet is to be safe. While you may not want to overreact, catching inappropriate and unhealthy patterns of behavior quickly can reduce the child's tension, anxiety, and reactions which might intensify the problem.

Questions You Should Ask About In-School Counseling

If your child is recommended for in-school counseling, take the time to get as much information as possible about this related service. Being informed can greatly reduce your misconceptions and resistance. Keep in mind that counseling has a better chance of working if the child sees that the parents are positive and supportive about the process. Before your child begins in-school counseling you should make an appointment with the counselor and find out the answers to the following:

- The qualifications of the counselor.
- The individual's experience with this age group.
- The individual's experience with the child's specific problem areas.
- The goals of the session or what the therapist hopes to accomplish.
- The length of the sessions.
- The classes he/she may have to miss to go to counseling.
- Whether or not the counselor feels that an outside referral to a private practitioner might also be necessary.
- Whether or not the parents will be involved in the sessions, either alone or conjointly with the child.
- Whether or not the parents will be contacted on a regular basis by the counselor.
- The rules of confidentiality.
- Whether any records will be kept of the sessions.

- Whether there will be any indication of counseling noted in the child's permanent record card or folder.

Also keep in mind that your child may be recommended for individual or group counseling. In some cases, the counselor might feel that your child could benefit from both orientations. Do not hesitate to ask the counselor how he or she assessed this.

What You Should and Should Not Expect

In any case, the process of counseling is just that—a process. While you should not expect overnight changes, you should expect to see a reduction of the frequency, duration, and intensity of the symptoms after a few months if your child is making progress. Keep in mind that symptoms are a means of reducing the tension built up by some unresolved problem, fear, conflict, and so on. The greater the problem, the greater the frequency, duration, and intensity of the symptoms. When a child begins to regain control, confidence, and perspective, you should see a reduction in the symptoms because the tension is lessened. As tension goes down, the frequency, duration, and intensity of the symptoms go down as well.

It is also important that you maintain realistic expectations about change, otherwise you may become frustrated easily when it does not happen right away and actually aggravate the situation by making unrealistic demands. Keep in touch with the therapist for support and guidance.

chapter nine

SPECIFIC DISABILITIES

The Learning-Disabled Child

Diagnosing the Learning-Disabled Child

Learning-disabled children account for approximately 3 to 6 percent of the student population. You should keep in mind that the LD population is a very specific population characterized by certain characteristics. There are a number of academic, intellectual, social, and emotional behaviors which describe a student with possible learning disabilities. However, many children may exhibit any number of these characteristic behaviors and may not be learning-disabled for a variety of reasons which we will discuss. In either case, a closer investigation is warranted and should be fully understood by you. Understanding the symptoms will help identify the child earlier and offer the appropriate help so that further frustration and secondary problems can be avoided.

Intellectual Criteria

The first criterion used in identifying a learning-disabled child is usually potential intellectual ability. Since one of the criteria for identification as LD is average intelligence, one needs to review your child's intellectual profile. The average range of intellectual ability falls within a score range on most IQ tests of between 90–109.

Approximately 50 percent of the population has an IQ within this range. However, there may be times when you will find your child scoring below this level who exhibits all the other criteria for classification. One needs to look at the profile of scores for the presence of what is called "scatter or variability." The key word with this factor is "potential average intelligence." You may find that your child scores below the 90 level but upon investigation you notice a great deal of fluctuation in his/her scores. Variability or scatter usually indicates that the resulting score should only be considered a minimal indication of your child's ability and the real level of potential is higher. So it is possible that your child may score an 83 on an IQ test and because of scatter or fluctuation in scores have the potential for at least an average IQ and therefore meet the intellectual criterion for learning disabilities. On the other hand, if your child scores an 83 but there are no indications of any greater potential and past tests show consistent results, then limited intellectual capacity may be the reason for low academic performance and not a true learning disability. The psychologist is usually the one who determines true intellectual potential but you should be aware of what procedures are used to determine this result.

Academic Criteria

A history of low academic performance is usually a key factor in the identification of a child with a learning disability. A learning disability does not occur in grade 5 with high levels of achievement in past grades. An LD child usually has a history of academic difficulties in one or several areas. Test scores may reflect this pattern and generally a deficit of six months to one year below grade level is considered mild, one to two years moderate, and a deficit of more than two years a severe academic deficiency.

Process Criteria

Many batteries of tests used to identify a learning disability will rely on perceptual tests to identify possible difficulties in the child's learning process. In general terms, the learning process involves receiving information, organizing and giving meaning to the information, and then expressing it in some way. The underlying assumption with all learning disabilities is that subtle neurological difficulties contribute to some breakdown or slowdown in this process and consequently difficulties in learning. These perceptual tests can tell us if a child's ability to receive, organize, memorize, and express information and other areas are intact or in need of remediation. This process factor usually sets the LD population off from the underachieving population whose main reason for lack of performance is usually based on emotional reasons rather than limitations in the learning process.

Exclusion Criteria

The identification of a learning-disabled child also includes certain other conditions that must be ruled out as primary factors contributing to the child's inability to learn. These include primary emotional factors, mental retardation, visual or hearing handicaps, poor teaching, cultural deprivation, inconsistent attendance, or other environmental factors such as abuse.

Background Criteria

While it is not mandatory for identification, many children with learning disabilities may come from families with a history of this condition. Also, the child's history indicates a pattern of problems in learning dating back to primary grades. Some behavioral indications during development (language delays, motor difficulties, problems listening) may be observed in the intake history.

Behavioral Criteria

Other "typical" behaviors are commonly exhibited by a number of LD children and may include:

1. *Variability in performance* and not succeeding in school in one or more of the following areas:
   - Basic reading skills (decoding)
   - Reading comprehension
   - Mathematics calculations
   - Mathematics reasoning
   - Written expression
   - Oral expression
   - Listening comprehension
2. *Attention problems*, such as inability to concentrate for even short periods of time, distractibility, attention to irrelevant details.
3. *Organization problems*, such as:
   - Poor organization of information
   - Poor organization of school materials such as notes, homework, and so on
   - Poor organization involving productive use of time
4. *Perceptual problems*: Many are confused by words or numbers that look or sound alike. They may have trouble differentiating similar sounds.
5. *Poor motivation/attitude* mainly because they have experienced repeated failure.
6. *Memory problems*:
   - Retrieving information or concepts
   - Short-term memory
   - Sequential memory
   - Long-term memory
7. *Language deficits* such as listening, speaking, vocabulary.
8. *Poor motor abilities* such as fine and gross motor coordination.

9. *Inappropriate social behavior* such as social perception, emotional behavior, establishing social relationships.

Who Is a Student With a Learning Disability?

A student with a learning disability is *not* a student whose learning problems are primarily due to:

1. Other handicapping conditions such as:
   - Mental retardation
   - Emotional disability
   - Visual or hearing loss
   - Motor handicaps
2. Limited learning opportunities because of:
   - Prolonged absences from school
   - Lack of consideration for language differences
   - Inadequate instructional practices
3. Limited learning potential in all areas (for instance, a slow learner whose achievement is commensurate with his/her potential).
4. Sociological causes, including environmental, cultural, or economic disadvantages, limited proficiency in English language, or other such conditions which may result in, but are not the result of, a learning problem.

Severe Learning Discrepancy

Many state definitions of learning disabilities may include a statement indicating that in order for a learning disability to exist there must be a severe discrepancy between achievement and intellectual ability. In the past, this had been interpreted to mean achievement which falls at or below fifty percent of an individual's expected achievement level when intellectual ability, age, and previous educational experiences are considered.

Initially, a formula was derived to determine this level, which appeared in PL 94–142 or the 1975 Federal guidelines for the education of the handicapped. The formula used was:

$$\text{C.A.} \frac{(IQ + .17) - 2.5}{300} = \text{severe discrepancy level}$$

This formula was an attempt to quantify the definition of learning disabilities, since a word definition, interpreted differently by various committees, may have caused greater numbers of identified students and resulted in more costs to State and Federal governments. However, this *formula* was soon dropped and did not appear in the State definitions. Yet, the *concept* of "severe discrepancy between ability (as measured by an individual intelligence test) and achievement (as measured by individual academic tests)" did remain and the interpretation was left up to the individual Committees on Special Education.

Characteristics of Children With Dyslexia

Many parents have questions about the condition known as *dyslexia*. Dyslexia is a very specific serious type of learning disability. Not all learning-disabled children are dyslexic, but all dyslexic children are learning disabled. It is very important that parents know the early warning signs so that professional intervention can begin at an early age. Allowing this condition to go undiagnosed will definitely lead to a variety of very serious secondary problems. With this in mind, let's take a look at the characteristics of this disorder.

Primary Characteristics for Early Detection

1. The child has poor ability to associate sounds with corresponding symbols.
2. The child ignores details of words and has difficulty retaining the words in his/her mind.
3. Frequent word guessing—the child won't look at the word but will seek pictorial clues.
4. The child has confused spatial orientation. He/she reverses words, letters, and numbers. Mirror reading and writing is frequently encountered.
5. The child has poor auditory discrimination.
6. The child exhibits confusion of left and right (referred to as mixed dominance).
7. The child frequently loses his/her place on a page, and frequently skips lines.
8. The child has difficulty working with jigsaw puzzles, holding a pencil, and walking straight on a chalk line.
9. Newly learned words are forgotten from day to day. Reading rhythm is usually poor and labored.

Secondary Characteristics

Sometimes there are secondary and less obvious characteristics exhibited by dyslexic children. While these may not be present in all dyslexic children, you should be aware that they may signal some concern. First of all, it should be understood that dyslexic children usually do not have a mental disability and their intelligence is measured as average to superior. The child may also exhibit general confusion in orientation, days, time, distance, size, and right and left directions. Furthermore, the child may display poor motor coordination, and a swaying gate and awkwardness when playing games. There may also be speech delays and difficulty in pronunciation. Such severe problems can only lead to feelings of inadequacy and low self-esteem if not identified early. You may also find that special tutoring with conventional reading methods won't work and that the child displays general irritability, aggressiveness, avoidance reactions, defensiveness, withdrawal, and behavioral problems.

Instructional Considerations for Children With Learning Disabilities

Instructional Techniques

You should be aware of the many strategies that are available to classroom teachers when dealing with your learning-disabled child in the classroom. The teacher should be aware that not all techniques will work with all students, but should try as many of them as possible to create a better learning environment for your child.

HOW TEACHERS CAN MAKE ADJUSTMENTS IN THE TYPE, DIFFICULTY, AMOUNT, AND SEQUENCE OF MATERIALS   Children with learning disabilities can learn. However the "normal" presentation of educational material may have to be modified in some way to ensure success. Teachers have many options to ensure success. For instance, if a learning-disabled child is overwhelmed by anxiety, or by a delayed ability to process information, the teacher may want to give shorter but more frequent assignments. Shortening the length and scope of the assignments allows the child a greater chance of success and feeling of accomplishment, therefore increasing his/her confidence. Without a feeling of accomplishment your child may begin to avoid or procrastinate doing schoolwork because of his/her fear of failure.

Children with learning disabilities also have difficulty with organization. Teachers should make sure that the child's desk is free from all unnecessary materials. As a parent, you should try to organize your child's room in somewhat the same manner. Place only a few toys, games, books, and so forth in his/her room so that when you ask him/her to clean up there is a better chance for success.

Some learning-disabled children may experience a great deal of frustration in school. Therefore they have difficulty in delaying gratification since their anxiety levels build rather quickly. As a result, the teacher may want to correct the student's work as soon as possible to allow for immediate gratification and feedback.

All children learn differently. Learning-disabled children usually possess certain areas of strength and certain areas of severe weakness. If a child is being asked to respond to assignments in writing when his/her ability to process this type of activity is greatly impaired, he/she may resist, avoid, or create some reason why he/she is unable to do the assignment because of fear of failure, fear of reaction, and loss of approval. Therefore, teachers should allow the student several alternatives in both obtaining and reporting information. Several alternatives may include the following:

Audiotape	Bulletin board
Community study	Computer
Debates	Demonstrations
Discovery	Discussion

Displays	Dramatizations
Field trips/research	Film loops
Films	Filmstrips
Flannel boards	Flipcharts
Games	Graphics
Investigation/reporting	Laboratory work
Large-group/small-group instruction	Library research
Listing and diagramming	Panel discussions
Models	Projects
Real objects	Resource persons
Role playing	Simulation
Slides	Video illustrations
Videotape	Writing

As you can see, many optional reporting techniques are available and should be used with the learning-disabled child to ensure success.

The teacher and you can help your child with homework by breaking assignments down to smaller units. Allow your child to do five problems at time, or five sentences, so that he/she can feel success. Give immediate feedback if he/she is doing the assignment incorrectly and direct his/her energy to more manageable tasks.

The teacher should also hold frequent, short conferences with the child to allow for questions, sources of confusion, sense of connection, and avoidance of isolation which often occurs if the work is too difficult.

At home you should make copies of chapters of textbooks so that your child can use a highlighter pen, to underline important facts and circle important vocabulary words, and to write notes in the margins. This type of multisensory input can only enhance your child's ability to remember what he/she is reading.

HOW TO ADJUST SPACE, WORKTIME, AND GROUPING   Teachers also have the opportunity to make modifications in your child's learning environment that may enhance his/her ability to learn. The teacher can permit your child to work in a quiet corner, using a study carrel when requested or necessary. This should not occur all the time since isolation may have negative consequences. This technique depends on the *specific learning style* (the conditions under which one learns best) of your child who may be less distracted by working under these conditions. If necessary, the teacher may at first want to place your child closer to her/him for more immediate feedback or try to separate him/her from students who may be distracting. Alternating between quiet and active time to maintain levels of interest and motivation may also work for your child.

Again, depending upon your child's learning style, the teacher may want to make up a work contract with specific times and assignments so that your child has a structured idea of his/her responsibilities. Some children thrive on this type of structure while others may find it too restrictive.

Trying to match your child with a peer helper to help with understanding assignments, reading important directions, using oral drills, summarizing important textbook passages, and working on long-range assignments is also a good option for teachers.

CONSIDER ADJUSTING PRESENTATION AND EVALUATION MODES   Some students learn better by seeing (visual learners), some by listening (auditory learners), some by feeling (tactile learners), and some by a combination of approaches. Adjustments should be made by the teacher to determine the best functional system of learning for your child. This will vary from child to child and is usually included in the child's evaluation.

If the child is primarily an *auditory learner*, the teacher can offer adjustments by giving verbal as well as written directions to assignments, placing assignment directions on tape so that your child can replay them when needed; giving your child oral rather than written tests; having your child drill on important information using tape recorder; reciting information into the recorder and playing it back, having your child drill aloud to him/herself or to other students; having your child close his/her eyes to try and hear words or information.

If your child is determined to be primarily a *visual learner*, the teacher can offer adjustment in the mode of presentation by using flash cards printed in bold bright colors, letting the child close his/her eyes and try to visualize words or information. The teacher can also provide visual clues on chalkboard for all verbal directions, and encourage your child to write down notes and memos concerning important words, concepts, and ideas.

Characteristics of Writing, Mathematical, and Reading Disorders

There are many times when you may be the first to notice certain behaviors that may signal more serious problems. You should be aware of symptoms that are exhibited by your child if he/she is experiencing some specific type of learning problem. These symptoms may signal serious difficulties in writing, spelling, reading, and math. The following symptoms may be exhibited by children with these types of deficits:

Writing Disorders

CHILDREN WHO ARE PHONETICALLY ACCURATE SPELLERS

- Make phonetically accurate errors
- Spell words exactly as they sound—"lite" for "light"
- Spell words with only a general similarity to the actual word—"word" for "work"
- Have difficulty associating verbal labels with pictorial information
- Have problems with advanced language expression such as vocabulary definitions

CHILDREN WHO ARE PHONETICALLY INACCURATE SPELLERS

- Demonstrate significant weaknesses in basic auditory skills

- Have difficulty breaking words into syllables
- Have difficulty retaining auditory information
- Do not process language effectively

CHILDREN WITH MECHANICAL WRITING DISORDERS

- Find writing a slow and labored process
- Usually have poorly developed fine motor coordination
- Typically lack finger dexterity
- May have had earlier problems with buttoning and tying
- May have difficulty with the spatial aspects of writing
- May form letters of varying sizes
- May leave gaps between letters of a word
- May run words together
- May exhibit directional confusion by reversing letters

Mathematical Disabilities

CHILDREN WITH MATHEMATICAL DISORDERS

- May not fully comprehend the rules of arithmetic because of problems in applying language
- May not grasp language-based facts for arithmetic
- Have difficulty remembering multiplication tables
- May have trouble understanding teacher's verbal explanations
- May have visual spatial problems
- Have difficulty keeping track of numbers in the same column
- May switch from one column to another as they add or subtract
- Have trouble with the concepts of borrowing and carrying

Reading Disabilities

CHILDREN WITH LANGUAGE-BASED DISORDERS

- Are slower at naming objects and pictures
- Have auditory receptive areas of the brain that react more slowly to auditory stimuli
- Have difficulty comprehending complicated verbal directions
- Have difficulty separating words into phonetic segments
- Have poor memory for sequential information
- Have difficulty decoding words

The Emotionally Disabled Child

Characteristics of Children With Emotional Disabilities

Your child may not be learning in school for many reasons. One reason may be that he/she is experiencing severe emotional tension caused by conflicts, experiences, or some environmental change such as death or divorce. Emotional disorders vary from mild to severe, but the one characteristic of all of them is that they will interfere with learning on some level. Understanding what your child may be going through and looking for solutions rather than blame is a healthy first step to resolving the problems. Keep in mind that problems create tension and tension necessitates symptomatic behavior. These behavior patterns tend to alleviate the tension but are not really the problem (see Chapter 4, *How You Can Observe Your Child for Suspected Disabilities*). Also remember that the more intense the symptoms the greater the underlying problem. So it is crucial that you address these issues as soon as possible or like an untreated infection, many secondary problems will arise.

Some common characteristics or symptoms of emotional disorders that may be observed by you or the teacher over a period of time include:

- Academic underachievement
- Social isolation or withdrawal
- Excessive latenesses
- Excessive absences
- Frequent trips to the nurse
- Negativism
- Open defiance to authority or rules
- Highly distractible
- Poor social relationships
- Feelings of hopelessness
- Verbal aggression
- Confrontational behavior
- Inappropriate classroom behaviors
- Impulsive behavior
- Rigid behavior patterns
- Anxious and worried, excessive fears and phobias
- Easily frustrated even when confronted with a simple task
- Resistant to change

Since the behavior of children with emotional disabilities can vary from withdrawal, in the case of depression, to aggressive tendencies, in the case of a conduct disorder, both you and the classroom teacher(s) need to be aware of techniques which can be utilized in a variety of situations. However, certain behaviors should be targeted as priorities when dealing with emotionally disabled children in the home and school environment. These target behaviors include:

- Attendance and tardiness
- Challenges to authority
- Inappropriate verbalizations and outbursts
- Incomplete classwork
- Difficulty remaining seated
- Social relationships
- Following directions and paying attention

Instructional Considerations

Dealing With Problems of Attendance and Tardiness

Changing behavior requires attempting to reinforce the positive while creating an uncomfortable consequence for the negative. Consequently, you and the teacher may want to reward your child for being on time. This reward can be extra free time, a token if a token economy is being used, a note home, a verbal compliment, and so on. Keep in contact and work with the teacher on rewarding on-time behavior. You may want to plan a breakfast or some reward for being prepared in the morning. Use a chart to visually project the pattern of punctuality and lateness for your child. This reduces your child's level of denial and may make him/her more aware of his/her behavior. In school, the teacher may encourage and assist your child to start or join a club in his/her area of greatest interest and make participation contingent upon his/her positive pattern of attendance. Use a point system for on-time attendance. These points may be later turned in for class or special home privileges.

You may want to set up a buddy system if your child walks to school, to encourage on-time behavior. Set up a nightly contract for your child listing all the things he/she needs to do to make the morning easier to manage. Try to accomplish as much at night as possible, leaving very little to do in the morning. Also make sure you check his/her homework and assignments to be sure that he/she is ready for the next day. Children tend to feel less resistant when they feel adequately prepared for school.

Dealing With Challenges to Authority, Inappropriate Verbalizations and Outbursts

At home you can arrange a time-out area. In this case, the time spent in the area is not as significant as you being able to begin the consequence and end it. Therefore, make the time-out period something you can control. Structure a time where your child is allowed to speak to you freely without an audience around. In this way, your child will have an opportunity to speak his concerns rather than act them out. It will also allow you to deflect any confrontations to that specific time. Approach your child as often as possible and ask if there is anything bothering him/her that he/she would like to speak about. Offering them the opportunity, even if they refuse, may reduce their need for "spotlight" behaviors. Offer an emotional vocabulary so that your child is more able to label feelings. Tension is expressed either verbally or behaviorally. Providing your child with the proper labels may reduce frustration.

In school, the teacher may want to move your child away from those who might set him/her off. Preempting his/her behavior by waiting outside before class and telling him/her in private what you expect during class is another good technique that teachers can use with your child. Also, the teacher may want to make your child aware of the rewards and consequences of his/her actions. Offering other options and indicating that any inappropriateness is his/her decision is also a viable technique for getting your child to become more aware of his/her behavior and the consequences involved. Making your child aware that behavior is his/her responsibility allows him/her to realize that not doing something inappropriate is also within their control. Establishing clear classroom rules, stating rewards and consequences, and praising your child for complying to rules and carrying out directions without verbal resistance should be explored.

Dealing With Incomplete Classwork and Homework

Try to work out a contract with your child where he/she can determine the rewards for completion. In school, giving shorter but more frequent assignments and not forcing your child to write if handwriting is beyond correction is highly suggested. Compensation in the area of handwriting may involve the use of a word processor or typewriter. Try to correct assignments as soon as possible and hand them back for immediate gratification. Reward your child for handing in neat, completed, and timely assignments.

In school, the teacher can help your child become organized by keeping very little in his/her desk, using a bound book for writing rather than a loose-leaf where pages can fall out and add to disorganization, using large folders to keep work in, and so on. Both you and the teacher may need to be very specific on what you mean by "neat," "organized," and so on. Abstract labels have different meanings to different children. Instead say, "Please be neat and by neat I mean. . . ."

Dealing With the Child's Difficulty in Remaining Seated in School

Teachers may experience difficulty in having your child remain in his/her seat for an extended period of time. While other possible reasons for this problem should always be explored first, (for instance, with attention deficit disorder the teacher may want to try to determine a pattern when your child gets up out of his/her seat), once this is determined the teacher can arrange to have him/her run an errand, come up to his/her desk, and so on. In this way the teacher will be channeling your child's tension and thereby remain in control.

The use of an external control like an egg timer as an anchor to control behavior is a highly motivating technique. Praising other students or handing out rewards for remaining in their seats and following the rules can positively affect your child at times. Try to work with the teacher in developing a written copy of the rules that will result in reward or positive feedback. In this way, you can review them with your child before going to school. However, also give him/her a list of the behaviors that will lead to consequences and try to explain and offer alternatives.

In school, close proximity of the teacher to your child will assist him/her in staying seated during a lesson.

Helping the Child Develop Social Relationships

Teachers may want to use role playing with your child and another student during private time so that your child can get feedback from a peer. Providing your child with a "toolbox" of responses and options for typical social situations is very helpful and something that can be reinforced at home. Do not hesitate to speak with the school psychologist about including him/her in a group. Arranging for a peer to guide him/her through social situations may result in your child becoming more willing to model peer behavior.

At home you may want to start your child in a small-group activity with only one child. Slowly increasing the size of the group as your child becomes more comfortable will ensure a greater chance for social success. Arrange for goal-oriented projects where your child and a neighbor's child must work together to accomplish a task. Sometimes your child may rise to the occasion when placed in a leadership role. If an occasion arises try out his/her skills in this position. Also praise your child as often as realistic when not exhibiting aggressive or inappropriate social behavior.

Helping the Child Follow Directions and Pay Attention

Try to use a cue before giving your child directions or important information. Give one direction at a time and make it as simple as possible. Have your child chart his/her own patterns of behavior in relation to attention and direction. Physical proximity may assist your child in focusing on your directions. Praise your child when he/she follows directions or pays attention. However, be aware that if your child has a hard time accepting praise, especially in front of a group, accomplish this in private.

In school the teacher may want to provide optional work areas that may have less distraction. Randomly questioning your child and trying to have him/her participate as often as possible may increase his/her interest in the lesson. Making sure the materials being presented are compatible with your child's learning levels is a crucial factor in shaping success and avoiding frustration. The teacher may also want to use a variety of visual and auditory techniques, (overhead projector, tape recorder, computer) to enhance the lesson and stimulate attention.

Warning Signs of a Potential Suicide Risk in Adolescents

We are all aware that adolescence is a very trying time for children. As adults we only have to recall our own experiences to determine how awkward and difficult a period of development this may be on our children. There are times when the adolescent period may be so stressful for children that more serious consequences may arise. When some adolescents become very depressed and overwhelmed, and are unable to vent or label their feelings, they may ponder a traumatic resolution to their predicament. Before this usually occurs, many adolescents give off "signals" that need to be identified as a high-risk situation as soon as possible. As parents, you should always be tuned in to your adolescent's patterns, behaviors, idiosyncrasies, and so on. When these change in certain ways they may signal concern.

Behavioral Indications

Sudden changes in behavior such as withdrawal, apathy, too much sleep, or too little sleep, dramatic drop in academic grades or performance, are possible signals for concern. When recent and traumatic losses such as divorce, separation from family members, loss of self-esteem, loss of a relationship (boyfriend, girlfriend), loss of status (exclusion from peer group, not making grades) occur, be aware of your adolescent's reactions. Adolescents go through "normal" periods of moody or irritable behavior, but excessive fighting or abusive behavior, changes in behavior lasting more than two weeks, overnight feelings of happiness after long bouts of depression (frequently exhibited by teenagers who have decided to kill themselves and are now feeling the calm or peace of mind that follows the decision to die) are areas of concern and should be explored immediately. If your child has been depressed and begins to give away personal possessions or shows a preoccupation with dying (questions about dying, life after death, poetry with morbid themes, statements like, "Everyone would be better off without me" or "I feel like killing myself") do not hesitate to have him/her seen immediately by the school psychologist, outside professional, or even a psychiatrist at the hospital emergency room.

You should also be aware of the criteria that could determine the lethality of the suicidal threat. Teenagers who plan suicide attempts in areas with little or no chance of interruption have the greatest chance of success. When a teenager reports this to someone, the risk should be considered very serious. Many suicide attempts are made with the knowledge of someone coming home and hopefully ensuring a rescue because of routine patterns. However, many deaths have occurred when such a plan has not materialized, such as a parent stopping off at a neighbor's house before coming home.

The chance of a suicide attempt increases dramatically whenever a teenager expresses the time he/she would "do it." According to statistics, most teenagers will attempt suicide in their homes between midafternoon and midnight.

Whenever a teenager is talking suicide and under the influence of drugs and/or alcohol, the suicide risk is very high. Such factors greatly reduce controls and add to the teenager's impulsivity.

Any teenager is a very high risk if he/she has made previous attempts. Teenagers who write a note to parents, friends, or others indicating the possibility and manner of hurting themselves, will have a greater likelihood of attempting suicide. When a chronic illness or long-term emotional stress is present, the teenager is more of a risk for suicide. The chances for suicide are greatest when teenagers have few peer support systems and/or little parental involvement or support.

Teenagers who threaten to hurt themselves a certain way, and have the availability of that method are at a higher risk (for instance, a plan to use a family gun).

In the case of adolescents, it is always better to be on the safe side when dealing with the risk of suicide. As parents, you should not play doctor and believe that they are just being dramatic or looking for attention. Let a professional evaluate the situation.

The Mentally Disabled Child

Residential Alternatives

As your disabled child gets older, you may find yourself in a situation that requires an alternative placement. It is very important that you become aware of the many options that exist since the proper environment can enhance your child's feelings of accomplishment and self-worth. These placements will depend on the severity of the disability and the age of your child. The alternatives listed range from least restrictive to most restrictive:

Regular Public Schools: Traditionally, the mildly disabled child was educated in a self-contained classroom. Regular public schools are now leaning towards the concept of inclusion for such students. Inclusion involves the education of mildly disabled students within the normal classroom supported by professionals and services that help them maintain their placement in such an educational setting.

Special Schools: These special schools offer an education and training curriculum specifically designed for their students, usually moderately (trainable) mentally disabled children. The children in these programs usually live at home with their families.

Sheltered Workshops: These types of facilities provide supervised employment for many teenagers and adults with mental disabilities. Employees generally perform piecework labor and are paid on either an hourly or performance-output basis.

Apartment Living: These types of alternatives include independent apartments with minimal supervision, to apartment clusters, to coresidence arrangements (a disabled resident and a nondisabled roommate).

Board and Care Homes: Board and care homes are less structured than group homes. Residents sleep and eat in the home, but the family or staff are not generally responsible for supervision of the residents. The responsibility for scheduling daytime activities and services falls on the resident or an outside case manager.

Group Homes: This type of facility usually consists of between six and twelve adolescents or adults living in a large, family-type dwelling in a residential neighborhood. Professional staff are responsible for supervision and overall programming for the residents. The residents often work at sheltered workshops and participate in social and recreational activities in the community.

Regional Facilities: These programs offer total-care, twenty-four-hour residential programs like large state institutions, but on a much smaller basis, serving only those persons in a given geographical area within the state. The reduced distance between this type of facility and the individual's family allows for more normalized and individualized treatment programs.

Institutions: These are large custodial institutions that offer severely and profoundly disabled persons twenty-four-hour care and supervision. The concern with institutions involves the level of humane treatment and the concept of normalization.

Instructional Considerations

You should always take an active role in your child's education. Sometimes you may feel uncomfortable in making inquiries or even suggesting things that relate to your child. This feeling of apprehension may exist because of a lack of awareness of educational options or a misunderstanding of educational procedures or concepts. Becoming aware of what options are available will help you feel more comfortable and secure when dealing with the school.

Helping the Child Attain Functional Academics

1. **General**. You should expect the school to design practice activities in any basic skill that may relate to your child's daily-life problems. Providing materials that are commensurate with your child's skill levels and providing activities that will reinforce independent work are basic. If the activity is too hard your child may become too dependent on teacher supervision.

2. **Reading**. Schools should provide activities that focus on reading for information and leisure. Offering activities that require your child to become more aware of his/her surrounding environment are good educational techniques. For instance, having your child list the names of all food stores in the community or of all hospitals will increase his/her familiarity with the surrounding environment.

   At home you can have your children collect food labels and compare the differences. Allowing them to look up the names of other children's families in the phone book by using a smaller local guide for this activity can also enhance independency. Developing activities that will allow them to become familiar with menus, bus and train schedules, movie and television timetables, or job advertisements are also highly suggested.

3. **Handwriting/Spelling**. Teachers may use several techniques in this area including having your child make a list of things to do for the day or having your child run a messenger service in the classroom so that he/she can write messages and deliver them from one student to another. You should also expect the school to provide activities for older children that incorporate daily writing skills necessary for independence, so that they may eventually be able to manage social security forms, driver's license applications, bank account applications, and so on.

4. **Math**. At home you can have your child make up a budget on how he or she plans to use allowance. Encourage your child to cook at home to become more familiar with measurements. Have your child record the daily temperature, time of sunrise and sunset and other activities that involve instruments of measurement. Providing activities that teach your child how to comparison shop are very motivating. For instance, give your child a make-believe amount of money and a toy catalog and have him/her purchase items and fill out the forms.

In school the teacher can involve your child in measuring the height of class-mates or have older children apply for a "pretend" loan or credit card.

Helping the Child Improve Work Habits

This particular area is composed of many skill areas that are necessary to allow the child success in the regular classroom. They include:

1. **Work Completion**. You should expect the teacher to make reward activities contingent upon successful completion of your child's work. Having the child maintain a performance chart in school on the number of tasks completed each day is an activity that can be shared with parents. It is crucial that you be aware that your child's teachers evaluate the length and level of an assignment to make sure it is within his/her ability level.

2. **Attendance and Punctuality**. Communicate to your child the importance of being on time to class. Let your child know your expectations in clear terms con-cerning attendance and punctuality. Have your child maintain a record of atten-dance and on-time behavior. Develop a make-believe time clock that the child has to punch in on when he or she leaves for school in the morning.

3. **Working With Others**. Provide your child with small-group activities that are geared to his/her ability levels. Utilize peer tutors for your child so that relation-ships can be established. Have your child participate in many activities that require sorting, pasting, addressing, folding, assembling, and so on. Provide your child with some simple job that requires other children to go to him/her.

   In school the teacher can place a child in charge of attendance and have him/her check off the children when they report in. The teacher may also want to help your child start a hobby and then start a hobby club involving other stu-dents. Being part of a team that takes care of the class pets or some other class activity is always a motivating activity for children. Calling it a team will make the child feel more connected and part of a group.

Characteristics of Down's Syndrome

Initially categorized by Langdon Down as a type of mental retardation in 1886, the term *mongolism* was used to describe this disorder for many years. This particular syn-drome's (a syndrome is a group of symptoms) deviation of growth begins at about the eighth week of gestation. The main abnormality is the extra chromosome in the num-ber 21 position. This results in a condition known as *trisomy*. This means that three normal chromosomes instead of two are formed, producing a total of forty-seven chro-mosomes per cell instead of forty-six. Further, there is a correlation of advanced mater-nal age and Down's Syndrome. Some of the characteristics exhibited by children with Down's Syndrome include:

1. At birth, a large anterior fontanel and open sutures are present.

2. A flat broad head develops.

3. The skin is rough and dry.

4. The child develops almond-shaped eyes.

5. The tongue may be too large for the oral cavity.

6. The neck is short.

7. The features appear compressed.

8. Convolutions of the ear seem unusual.

9. The palms of the hand have one fissure.

10. There is a large gap between the first and second toes.

11. The palate is high.

12. The tongue is fissured.

13. Voice pitch is not normal.

14. Sex organs may be malformed.

15. The hair may be coarse.

16. The fingerprint patterns are distinctive.

17. The iris may be speckled.

18. Teeth are malformed.

19. Teeth are prone to decay.

20. Circulation is poor.

21. Respiration is fragile.

22. High concentration of gamma globulin is found in the blood.

23. High incidence of spinal disorders.

24. There can be disorders of the pituitary, thyroid, and thymus.

The Physically Disabled Child

Causes of Physical Disabilities

There are many conditions which can result in a physical disability. Your education in this area should include an understanding of the various disorders that can affect your child so that you can be alert to symptoms that might require a further look by a medical doctor. We have included the more common disorders that lead to the classification of physically disabled.

Cerebral Palsy is a disorder of movement and posture due to damage to areas of the brain that control motor function. This condition becomes evident in infancy or early childhood and the incidence is around 3 per every 1,000 live births. The impairment may involve different parts of the body, including *hemiplegia*, which involves the arm, leg, and trunk on the same side, *paraplegia* which involves the legs only, *quadriplegia* which affects both arms and both legs as well as the trunk and neck, *diplegia* where the legs are more involved than the arms, and *double hemiplegia* where the arms are more involved than the legs and one side is usually more involved than the other.

Arthogyposis multiplex congenita is a condition of fixed stiffness and deformity of the limbs in any joint prior to birth. The condition is sometimes referred to as "fixed joint" disorder. In this disorder, the limb muscles are absent or much smaller and weaker than usual and as a result, the child has little or no joint motion. Curvature of the spine may also be present.

Hypertonia is a condition found in 60% of cerebral palsy victims which involves increased stiffness of the joints and muscles.

Athetosis is a condition affecting the central nervous system which results in involuntary movements of the arms, hands, and facial muscles. These areas are typically more involved than the legs. This condition is exhibited by about 20% of individuals with cerebral palsy. The individual has little or no control over his/her movements and attention deficit is exacerbated by a lack of head control. This may result in severe dependence in activities of daily living and locomotion.

Ataxia is a rare condition of cerebral palsy characterized by an inability to achieve coordination in balancing and hand use.

Hemophilia is often called the "bleeders disease." This condition is characterized by poor blood clotting ability due to the absence of the clotting factor in the blood.

Juvenile rheumatoid arthritis is considered a metabolic disorder caused by the body's inability to burn sugars and starches to create energy. When this occurs, adequate insulin is not produced by the pancreas.

Limb deficiency is a condition which is characterized by the absence of a limb. This condition may be congenital or acquired after birth. The acquisition of an artificial limb (prosthesis) can be important to the physical and psychological well-being of the individual.

Muscular dystrophy is a condition characterized by increasing weakness of skeletal muscles. Progressive muscle weakness, awkwardness, and slowness in movement eventually force the child to become confined to a wheelchair. Further characteristics include rapid deterioration with death usually occurring in the teen years, with increased fatigue as the disease progresses.

Osteogenesis imperfecta is a condition characterized by "brittle bones." It results from the defective development of both quality and quantity of bone tissue. The condition is further characterized by abnormal growth of bones in length and thickness, and bone development results in brittle composition.

Spina bifida is a congenital disease caused by a defect in the development of the vertebral column which results in spinal cord and nerve root damage. As a result, related neurological problems develop.

Other important facts may include the following:

- *Myelomeningocele*, the most severe form.
- Deficits in spina bifida ranging from minor sensory and ambulatory problems to paraplegia and lack of sensation.

- Orthopedic deformities.
- Incontinence may occur in the severe form.
- Urinary tract infections are common.
- Susceptibility to the development of hydrocephalus, which is an abnormal buildup of cerebrospinal fluids in the cranial cavity.

Spinal cord injury can result from automobile, bicycle, skiing, and other accidents causing traumatic injury to the spinal cord. The extent of the injury varies according to the level and type of lesion or injury to the spinal cord.

Traumatic brain injury results from an insult or damage to the brain caused by an external physical force resulting in an impairment of cognitive (mental) abilities or physical functioning.

Cystic fibrosis is a hereditary disorder characterized by chronic pulmonary involvement and pancreatic deficiency.

Infectious Diseases: Modes of Transmission

Infectious/Communicable Disease	Mode of Transmission
Chicken Pox	• Respiratory secretions (sneezing)
Cytomegalovirus	• Direct or indirect contact with respiratory secretions (blood, urine)
Gonorrhea	• Sexual contact involving the exchange of body fluids (blood or vaginal fluids)
Hepatitis A	• Fecal oral transmission, direct contact
Hepatitis B	• Direct contact with blood
Herpes I (Above waist)	• Direct contact with fluid Herpes
Herpes II (Below waist)	vesicle
HIV Infection/AIDS	• Direct contact with blood, contaminated needles, sexual contact involving the exchange of bodily fluids
Measles	• Respiratory secretions
Mononucleosis	• Direct contact with respiratory secretions (saliva)
Mumps	• Respiratory secretions (sneezing)
Respiratory Synctial Virus (RSV)	• Direct or indirect contact with respiratory secretions (nasal discharge)
Salmonella Bacteria	• Fecal-oral transmission

The Visually Disabled Child

Characteristics of Individuals With Visual Impairments

1. The lack of vision or reduced vision may result in delays or limitations in motor, cognitive, and social development.

2. Without visual input, an infant may not be motivated to reach and move toward interesting objects in the environment.

3. As soon as the infant with a visual impairment finds it exciting to hear sounds, he or she will begin to reach and move toward the objects in the environment that make sound. This does not occur until several months later, since hearing sounds does not motivate movement toward objects as soon as seeing objects does.

4. Cognitively, the child who has a visual impairment cannot perceive objects in the environment beyond his or her grasp, including those that are too large, too small, or are moving.

5. While use of other senses enables the child to obtain information about the environment, a cognitive limitation does exist in the range and variety of experiences.

6. Socially, a child with a visual impairment is limited in interaction with the environment. The child cannot see the facial expressions of parents, teachers, and peers; cannot model social behaviors through imitation; and sometimes is unaware of the presence of others unless a sound is made.

7. While touch provides direct information, it is often socially unacceptable. The older child is limited in the ability to orient to environmental cues and travel freely.

8. The unique curriculum for students who are blind includes reading and writing through the use of Braille, listening skills, personal-social and daily-living skills, orientation and mobility, career education, and instruction in the use of special aids and equipment.

9. In addition to these areas, students with low vision and visual limitations may need instruction in the efficient use of vision and in the use of optical aids and alternative learning materials.

10. A high proportion of students with visual impairments have additional disabilities and may require a curriculum that emphasizes functional living skills and communication skills.

11. Educational settings and services for children with visual impairments vary according to individual needs. Self-contained classrooms, residential schools, or regular classrooms with or without special assistance may be appropriate options for individual students.

What Is Meant by Visual Impairments?

As you become involved in the education, health, and welfare of your visually impaired child, you will be faced with a great deal of terminology and definitions. For legal and administrative purposes, you may need to be aware of the following definitions:

> **Legally Blind**: Central visual acuity of 20/200 or less in the better eye with correction, or, if greater than 20/200, a field of vision no greater than 20 degrees at the widest diameter.

> **Partially Sighted**: Central visual acuity between 20/70 and 20/200 in the better eye correction.

The emphasis in schools on disability terminology comes from the Federal and State laws. For functional educational purposes, these definitions are used:

> **Visually Handicapped**: Requires special educational provisions because of visual problems.

> **Blind**: Has either no vision or, at most, light perception. (Students learn through the use of Braille or related media without the use of vision.)

> **Low Vision**: Has severe visual impairment after correction but visual function can be increased through the use of optical and environmental aids. Students with low vision learn from vision and other senses. Functional vision will depend on factors such as lighting, use of optical aids and devices, tasks, and personal characteristics. Modifications in lighting, size of print or objects, and distance may be required.

Causes of Visual Impairments

The causes for visual impairments may result from a variety of conditions. Some of these conditions can be treated and with best correction your child may be able to function in a regular-education setting. Other conditions may require special schools or services. Some of the more common visual impairments include:

> **Myopia**. Referred to as nearsightedness, this condition occurs when the rays of light from distant objects are not focused on the retina. The individual with this condition is able to see objects more clearly close up.

> **Hyperopia**. Referred to as farsightedness, this condition occurs when the eye is too short and the rays of light from near objects are not focused on the retina. The individual with this condition is able to see objects more clearly at a distance.

> **Astigmatism**. Referred to as "blurred vision" caused by uneven curvature of the cornea or lens. This curvature prevents light rays from focusing on the retina. This condition can usually be helped through use of corrective or contact lenses.

The Braille Alphabet

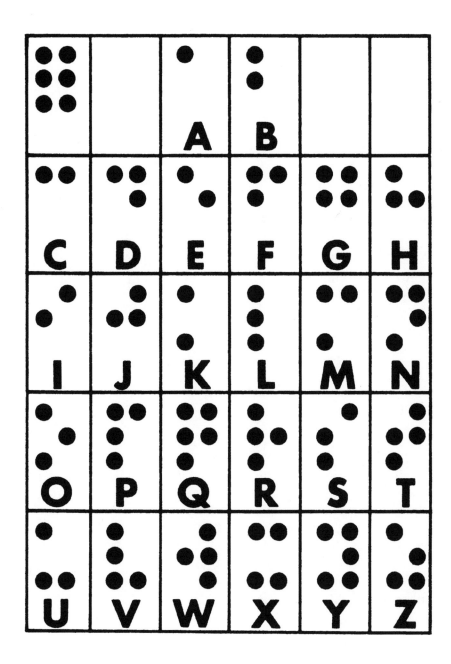

Cataracts. A cloudiness in the lens of the eye, which blocks the light necessary for seeing clearly. Vision may be blurred, distorted, or incomplete.

Glaucoma. This condition is caused by the failure of the aqueous fluid to circulate properly, which results in an elevation of pressure in the eye that may gradually destroy the optic nerve.

Diabetic Retinopathy. Children and adults with diabetes frequently have impaired vision due to hemorrhages and the growth of new blood vessels in the area of the retina. This results in a condition known as diabetic retinopathy. May be helped with laser surgery.

Retinitis Pigmentosa. An inherited disease that causes a gradual degeneration of the retina. This condition is not treatable.

Usher's Syndrome. Results from a combination of congenital deafness and retinitis pigmentosa.

Macular Degeneration. A fairly common disorder in which the central area of the retina gradually deteriorates. The individual usually retains peripheral vision but loses the ability to see clearly in the center of the visual field.

Retrolental Fibroplasia. This condition results from the use of too much oxygen in the incubation of premature babies.

The Hearing-Impaired Child

Causes of Hearing Impairments

Hearing impairments are the result of several different types of conditions. You should be aware of the factors that may lead to such a condition and make sure that the earliest possible detection techniques are employed if you suspect a problem.

Conductive Hearing Loss: Results from problems with the structures in the outer or middle ear, generally attributed to a blockage in the mechanical conduction of sound. In order to overcome this blockage, the sounds must be amplified. These conditions are usually temporary. The leading causes of this type of hearing loss are:

- Otitis Media (middle ear infection)
- Otosclerosis (formation of a spongy-boney growth around one of the three small bones in the ear which impedes its movement)
- Excessive earwax

Sensorineural Hearing Loss: Result from damage to the cochlea or the auditory nerve. This damage is caused by illness and disease not medically or surgically treatable. Causes of this hearing loss include:

- Viral diseases (rubella—German measles, meningitis)
- Rh incompatibility

- Ototoxic medications (medicines that destroy or damage hair cells in certain structures of the ear such as streptomycin) taken by pregnant mothers or very young children
- Hereditary factors
- Exposure to noise
- Aging

Mixed Hearing Loss: A hearing loss caused by both sensorineural and conductive problems.

Functional Hearing Loss: Those problems not organic in origin. Examples include:

- Psychosomatic causes (psychologically based disorders which cause the individual to believe that the condition exists even though no physical cause can be found for the hearing loss)
- Malingering (when someone feigns incapacity to avoid a situation)

Central Auditory Disorders: These disorders result in no measurable peripheral hearing loss. Children with this disorder have trouble learning and are often considered learning disabled. Causes include:

- Auditory comprehension problems
- Auditory discrimination problems
- Auditory learning difficulties
- Language development delays

Audiometric Evaluation Measures

As parents you should be informed of the evaluation techniques that may be used to determine whether or not your child is experiencing a hearing impairment. The use of the correct technique is crucial in determining your child's level of hearing loss. Many techniques are available including:

1. **Pure Tone Audiometric Screening**. Pure tone screening is often referred to as *sweep testing*, and is usually the child's first encounter with hearing testing. This type of testing which is common in schools presents the child with pure tones over a variety of frequencies ranges. The child is then asked to respond if he/she hears a tone, usually by some gesture. If a child is unable to hear sounds at two or more frequencies they are usually referred for further evaluation.

2. **Speech Audiometry**. This type of evaluation is used to determine a child's present ability to hear and understand speech through the presentation of words in a variety of loudness levels.

3. **Pure Tone Threshold Audiometry**. In this procedure, the child is asked to make a gesture or push a button each time he/she hears a tone. The child is presented with a variety of frequencies through earphones. This type of air conduction test reveals the presence of hearing loss.

Special Audiometric Tests

1. **Sound Field Audiometry**: This measure is used with very young children who cannot respond to manual responses or are unable or unwilling to wear headphones. The child is evaluated by observing the intensity levels at which he/she responds to different levels of sounds broadcast through speakers.

2. **Evoked Response Audiometry**: This measure which incorporates an electroencephalograph and a computer measures changes in brain wave activity to a variety of sound levels. This measure can be used with infants who are suspected of being deaf.

3. **Impedance Audiometry**: There are two major impedance audiometry tests. The first, *tympanometry*, measures the functioning level of the eardrum. The second, *stapedial reflex testing*, measures the reflex response of the stapedial muscle to pure tone signals. Since these tests do not require a response on the part of the child they can be used with very young children.

4. **Behavioral Play Audiometry**: This technique involves placing the child in a series of activities that reward him/her for responding appropriately to tone or speech.

Modes of Communication for the Deaf

There are many activities, techniques, and treatments that can enhance your child's communication skills. While your school may use a certain technique or approach, it is important as parents that you be aware of all options in case one approach is not working. Several modes of communication techniques include:

Oral-Aural Approach

This approach stresses the primary reception of language through the auditory channel, by the use of individually prescribed amplification. Examples include:

1. **Auditory Training**: The purpose of auditory training is to teach the hearing-impaired individual to use his/her residual hearing to the greatest extent possible. It is:
   - Usually provided by an audiologist or speech pathologist
   - Usually provided in individual or group-therapy sessions
   - Reinforced in the classroom and at home
   - Used to reinforce environmental cues in conversations
   - Used to help sharpen the child's ability to discriminate among sounds and words

2. **Cued Speech**: One method of supplementing oral communication:
   - Considered a visual/oral method of communication; carries no meaning without an accompanying speech signal

The Manual Alphabet

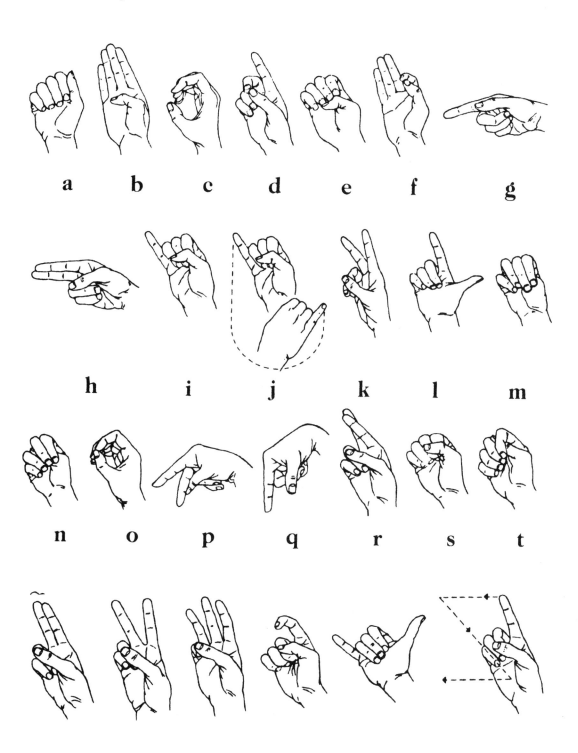

- Uses cues which consist of hand signals used near the lips
- Involves eight different hand shapes, used in four different positions

Manual Communication

This approach includes the following:

1. **Finger Spelling**: A series of finger positions to represent the individual letters of the alphabet, and to spell out words.
2. **American Sign Language**: A system of ideographic gestures representing words or concepts used by most deaf people.

Total Communication

This method combines the oral/aural and manual modes.

Technological Devices

1. **Teletypewriter Assistance for the Deaf**: Many people send and receive immediate written messages over telephone lines. To find out how to obtain this device contact your local telephone company or contact the National Association for the Deaf, 814 Thayer Ave., Silver Spring, MD 20910 or Alexander Graham Bell Association for the Deaf, Inc., 3417 Volta Place, NW Washington, D.C. 20007.
2. **Caption Decoder**: A device that allows deaf individuals to receive captions or subtitles on their television screen. To receive these services, contact your local cable company, the American Foundation for the Blind, 15 West 16th Street, New York, N.Y. 10011, or the Association for Education of the Visually Handicapped, 206 N. Washington Street, Alexandria, VA 22314.

Degrees of Hearing Impairment

Degree of Hearing Loss	Decibel Loss	Resulting Impairment
Slight	27–40dB	Difficulty hearing faint noises or distant conversation. The individual with a slight hearing loss will usually not have difficulties in the regular school setting.
Mild	41–55 dB	This individual may miss as much as 50 percent of classroom conversations. The individual may also exhibit limited vocabulary and speech difficulties.

Moderate	56–70 dB	The individual will only be able to hear loud conversation, may exhibit defective speech, vocabulary, and language difficulties.
Severe	71–90 dB	Hearing may be limited to a radius of 1 foot. May be able to discriminate between certain environmental sounds, shows defective speech and language ability, and has severe difficulty understanding consonant sounds.
Profound	91 dB or greater	The individual can sense but is unable to understand sounds and tones. Vision becomes the primary sense of communication, and speech and language are likely to deteriorate.

Examples of Typical Sound Intensities

Intensity in Decibels (dB)	Examples
140	Jet plane taking off about 100 ft. away
130	Industrial jackhammer
120	Rock and roll concert
110	Industrial punch press
105	Bulldozer and construction equipment
100	Chain saw
90	Heavy street noises, factory noises
85	Person shouting from 5–10 feet away
80	The noise from cars on an expressway at 60 mph
75	Noise in a restaurant
70	Window air conditioner
40–65	Typical conversational level, typewriter, small office machines, washing machine
35	Typical house noise
30	Radio station studio
20	Whisper at 5 feet, windy day

The Child With Attention-Deficit/ Hyperactivity Disorder

Defining Attention-Deficit/Hyperactivity Disorder (ADHD)

The disorder known as Attention-Deficit/Hyperactivity Disorder was previously referred to by a variety of names including: hyperactivity, hyperkinetic reaction to childhood, hyperkinetic syndrome, minimal brain dysfunction, hyperactive child syndrome, and others. The present disorder, abbreviated ADHD, has two subtypes: *Attention-Deficit/Hyperactivity Disorder* and *Undifferentiated Attention-Deficit Disorder* (without hyperactivity).

At the present time, Attention-Deficit/Hyperactivity Disorder affects approximately 3 to 5 percent of the elementary-aged population with 80 to 90 percent being boys. This disorder also accounts for the largest category of psychological referrals to clinics and other health-related facilities.

Diagnostic Criteria for ADD/ADHD

A child with this disorder will display for his or her mental and chronological age signs of developmentally inappropriate *inattention*, *impulsivity*, and/or *hyperactivity*. These signs are usually reported by teachers and parents and tend to worsen in situations requiring self-application, such as in a classroom setting. The following list of symptoms and conditions apply for children between the ages of 8 and 10, the peak age range for a referral of this type. In much younger children, the severity and quantity of symptoms increases. The opposite applies to older children.

Inattention—At Least Six of the Following:

1. Often fails to finish things he or she starts.
2. Often doesn't seem to listen.
3. Is easily distracted.
4. Has difficulty concentrating on schoolwork or other tasks requiring sustained attention.
5. Has difficulty sticking to a play activity.
6. Often has difficulty organizing tasks and activities.
7. Often loses things required for tasks or activities, such as books, homework.
8. Often is forgetful in daily activities.
9. Often fails to give close attention to details or makes careless mistakes in schoolwork.

Impulsivity/Hyperactivity—At Least Six of the Following:

IMPULSIVITY

1. Often acts before thinking.
2. Shifts excessively from one activity to another.
3. Has difficulty organizing work.
4. Needs a lot of supervision.
5. Frequently calls out in class.
6. Has difficulty awaiting turn in games or group situations.

HYPERACTIVITY

1. Runs about or climbs on things excessively.
2. Has difficulty sitting still or fidgets excessively.
3. Has difficulty staying seated.
4. Moves about excessively during sleep.
5. Is always "on the go" or acts as if "driven by a motor."

CHARACTERISTICS

- Onset before the age of 6
- Duration of at least 6 months
- Not due to schizophrenia, affective disorders (disturbance of mood) or profound retardation

You should be aware that many children with this disorder may experience severe academic problems, social difficulties, and problems adjusting to authority requests. This is not to say that all children with this disorder will exhibit such problems. However, if they should, action should be taken to avoid the appearance of secondary problems.

Since your child may have a greater chance of encountering difficulties, treatment should be instituted as quickly as possible. There are a variety of treatment plans and consultation with a professional should alleviate the confusion about which plan may be more appropriate for the child.

Treatment Plans for Children With ADD/ADHD

Help for your child must be individualized. It may include a variety of treatments including psychotherapy, medication, parental counseling, school management classroom modifications, special-education programs, and so on.

The most common treatment plan for children with this disorder includes pharmacological intervention (medication). The types of medication used may vary with age and severity, but the most common include psychostimulants like Ritalin®, Cylert®, and Dexedrine®. Such stimulants tend to heighten your child's awareness of the world around him/her and allow for greater selectiveness of behavior. Approximately fifty percent of children with this disorder will exhibit a decrease in inappropriate symptoms. Approximately ten percent of these children respond so positively to this intervention that their behavior reaches the normative range. Other reports indicate improvements in attention span, classroom behavior, and ability to think more clearly during academic tasks. Keep in mind that such medication does not "cure" Attention-Deficit/Hyperactive Disorder, it merely alleviates the primary symptoms.

Other studies have indicated adverse side effects such as reduction of weight, nausea, and loss of appetite. Usually such symptoms can be relieved by regulating the dosage. Since there are many issues to consider, parents should be sure they feel comfortable with this intervention.

One concern that may be raised by you involves the issue of drug dependency. There is no research or evidence that indicates stimulant drugs in children with ADHD results in drug abuse. In general, the effects of medication can be more easily monitored and regulated when given in the context of a therapeutic environment.

Another treatment alternative for your child with Attention-Deficit/Hyperactivity Disorder involves psychotherapy. This process will help your child increase self-esteem, vent feelings and conflicts that may give rise to other symptoms, and gain some control over impulsive actions. Some therapies may utilize a form of treatment called *behavior modification*. This is a process whereby your child, assisted by you and teachers, learns to modify unacceptable behavior through the use of a variety of management techniques including incentive systems, daily report cards, time out, selective attention, and so on. Some treatment plans will include a combination of both medication and psychotherapy. Family therapy is also suggested. This process will assist you in developing techniques that will reduce frustration at home in both your child and other family members.

Another approach used by some parents in treating children with this disorder involves the use of a special diet. Dr. Ben Feingold hypothesized that hyperactivity is a result of hypersensitivity to artificial colors, artificial flavorings, preservatives BHA and BHT, and naturally occurring substances called salicylates. He suggested that elimination of such substances from the child's diet would result in remission of their problems. However, there is a vast body of research that disputes the claims suggested by the Feingold theory. Dietary treatment of ADHD continues to raise a great deal of controversy and further research is needed in this area.

Any treatment plan must also include ongoing communication between the therapist/agency and the school and classroom teacher. Weekly updates and suggestions involving classroom management reduce frustration and feelings of helplessness on the part of your child and the teacher.

Classroom Management Techniques

As parents, you should be aware of how your child's classroom can adjust certain factors to accommodate your ADHD child's individual needs. There are many techniques and strategies that can provide a sound educational environment and result in feelings of success and accomplishment. The several areas that your child's teacher needs to focus on include social interaction, organizational ability, inattentiveness, impulsiveness, and academic skill areas.

In the area of social interaction your child's teachers may want to consider identifying appropriate social behavior for your child and reinforce it when exhibited. Sitting with your child and setting up a social contract which clearly outlines what goals he/she would like to accomplish is very helpful. Also, the teacher may consider including the behaviors that may be required to attain these goals. The use of verbal and written praise is a very important tool for children with ADHD since it provides them with immediate gratification. This type of praise gives your child the feedback necessary to understand his/her own behavior. Exposing your child to small group interactions at first provides more control and less social stimuli to distract him/her. Allowing the group to be goal oriented and interdependent so that they can accomplish some simple task and feel successful may be a major objective. The use of peer interaction and cooperative learning for certain academic tasks which do not require sitting for long periods of time is also a helpful tool that your child's teachers may want to consider. Identifying strengths in your child that can be publicly announced or praised is also helpful in changing his/her social perception by the other children. Teachers may want to role-play social situations with your child emphasizing the use of specific skills. In this way your child can develop a "toolbox" of skills that can be applied at a later time.

In the area of organization, your child's teachers may want to consider preparing a copy of the homework assignments and hand it to your child at the end of the day. This will alleviate a great deal of stress on the part of your child especially if he/she is disorganized and frequently forgets to copy the homework. The goal here is to create a comfortable and successful environment. In this case, having your child accomplish the homework is more important than the difficulty encountered in copying the assignment. You may also want to organize your child at night to avoid the stress and disorganization of the morning. Have him/her develop a checklist so that clothes, books, assignments, and so on are ready for the next morning. This will also make your child feel more secure when going to school. Avoiding numerous directions or assignments is another technique that can reduce frustration. Allowing your child to finish one assignment or direction at a time before going on to the next is highly suggested. Reinforcing word-processing skills, typing, spell checks on the computer, and use of the computer in general should be basic skills taught to your child to help in organizing his/her work. This device can be very motivating and the end product (typed report) will make your child feel very good about him/herself. Children with organizational problems will usually maintain very disorganized notes, notebooks, desks, and lockers. Work with your child's teachers and try to make it a weekly task of having your child organize these areas. Making it part of their contract and routine will also make them feel better about themselves.

If necessary, you may want to have your child finish all assignments in school. Work with the teacher on this issue so that time can be put aside to accomplish this task. There are times when your child may be so inattentive that sending work home to be accomplished may result in more stress. In school, the teacher can provide your child with extra time for completing assignments. Sometimes the time constraints set up by teachers are arbitrary and may not reflect the "real" time required by children with ADHD. Remember, confidence is repeated successful experiences and your child will have a greater chance of success with shorter assignments. If your child has problems listening and taking notes, have a "buddy" take notes using carbon paper. A copy will then be available for him/her and the stress of listening and writing will be reduced.

Try to be realistic about your expectations concerning your child's behavior. Choose your guidelines wisely. Try to ignore minor incidents and focus on the more intrusive or inappropriate ones. Shape appropriate behavior by reinforcing positive responses or actions. Do not hesitate to set up specific consequences for inappropriate actions. In this way your child will have to work at being more consciously aware of his/her behavior.

In school the teacher may want to consider building in periods of time when your child can leave his/her seat for some activity, such as collecting homework, getting some material for you from the closet, and so on. Trying to offer immediate gratification for appropriate behavior is always in your child's best interest when in school and home. Keep in mind that waiting too long to reward may lose the desired effect. The teacher may also want to assign a monitoring "buddy" to offer your child feedback and hints about appropriate and inappropriate behaviors. This may be especially helpful during recess and lunch. Having the teacher preempt your child's behavior especially during changes in the schedule, and informing your child about five minutes before the change, may reduce inappropriate responses.

Academic Skill Areas

There are many techniques that the school may want to consider when dealing with your child's academic skill areas. For instance, allowing your child to use graph paper while doing math will provide a structured environment in which to place numbers. Using very large graph paper so that your child has little difficulty placing one number in each box will keep him/her organized and focused. Further, the teacher many want to consider allowing him/her to use a calculator or basic math tables when doing his/her assignments. The goal here is for successful accomplishment of the assignment. If your child becomes frustrated because he/she can't recall the facts, they may give up. Providing other forms of reporting information is always a helpful tool for children with all types of learning problems.

When working with your ADHD child, the teacher should avoid using bubble sheets. Allowing your child to answer directly in the booklet or on the paper reduces the amount of movement during academic tasks. This tends to be more beneficial since ADHD children have difficulty refocusing. Using manipulative materials as often as possible is always a good technique for maintaining high levels of interest.

At home, you can tape-record a chapter so that your child can read and listen at the same time. Some children are overwhelmed by having too many problems on a page. Windowing out single math problems so that the child only sees one at a time during homework may increase success and accuracy. This can be accomplished by cutting out a square on a piece of paper that your child can move from one problem to the next. When he/she does this, all the other problems will be covered. If your child is older, allow him/her to have a sheet with the formulas already printed. Asking them to memorize may reduce their ability to accomplish the task. The less they have to worry about, the more they may be able to finish.

In the area of emotional support, try to become aware of your child's frustration "aura." Knowing when your ADHD child is about to lose focus may prevent inappropriate behavior and feelings of failure. Do not be afraid to discuss this with him/her so that both of you can identify the factors that lead to frustration.

Children With Communication Disorders

In determining whether or not your child has a communication disorder, teachers and other professionals can assist you in the diagnosis and remediation of the disorder. This type of information and the procedures to be considered by school personnel in providing appropriate general educational programs and services for your child with communication disorders, whether or not he/she may be educationally disabled, is the topic of discussion in this chapter. Furthermore, you will find out how schools need to provide your child with an appropriate special-education speech or language-development program.

The chapter is written for parents who may have varying degrees of understanding and awareness of the causes and effects of communication disorders among children in an educational setting. Therefore, the use of highly technical educational or medical terms associated with theories of speech and language development is avoided. If you are interested in more technical reading, you are invited to consult the references cited in the bibliography found in the Appendix.

The following statements provide basic definitions and underlying concepts, and may differ state to state:

1. A *speech-impaired child* is one who has been identified as educationally disabled by a Committee on Special Education because of a communication disorder, such as stuttering, impaired articulation, a language impairment or a voice impairment, which adversely affects the child's educational performance.

2. An *educationally disabled child* is a child whose educational performance is adversely affected by a learning disability, mental retardation, emotional disturbance, a visual, hearing, or motor handicap, or autism.

   Your child may have a *communication disorder* in one or more of the processes of speech, hearing, or language which interferes with his or her ability to speak, understand, or use language. Communication disorders may be the result of developmental or acquired factors. Further, this disorder may range from mild to severe and may or may not be associated with a disability.

   Your child's *educational performance* is an assessment of your child's current levels of academic or educational achievement, learning rate, social development, physical development, and his/her management needs in the learning situation.

There are two categories of children with communication disorders who may benefit from speech and language services:

- **Nondisabled children**. This category includes children whose academic performance is not adversely affected by a communication disorder but who could benefit from some form of speech or language service as part of their regular-education program.
- **Speech-impaired or otherwise disabled children**. This category involves children whose school performance is found to be significantly affected by a communication disorder and as a result, requires speech or language programs and services to function appropriately.

As a parent of a child with a communication disorder you will be exposed to many different professionals and terms that at times may confuse you. One such term is *speech pathology*. This is a speech/language program or service for the purpose of preventing, correcting, or remediating communication disorders. When this service is provided, it can include consultation, testing and evaluation, counseling, and instruction related to the development of communication skills. If your child has this service, it may be provided along with his/her regular-education program or in a special-education setting by a certified professional in this field.

What You Need to Know If Your Child Has a Communication Disorder

As a parent, you should be as involved as possible in your child's educational program and services. When it comes to communication disorders, you need to be aware of specific information that can be obtained through investigation, questioning, observation, and analyses of your child's situation. Some examples of the critical questions you should ask include:

- What is the quality of your child's voice?
- Does your child prolong or hesitate on words?
- Does your child understand the meaning implied by word endings?
- How is your child using skills in the area of expressive language?
- Does your child use sentences in a variety of grammatical forms appropriate for the age level?
- Does your child generate spontaneous phrases and sentences appropriate to the communication setting?
- Is there a discrepancy between oral and written language skills?
- Does your child exhibit negative and/or inappropriate classroom behaviors due to speech impairment, such as withdrawal from peer relationships and social interactions?
- Does your child have difficulty understanding age-appropriate vocabulary?
- Are your child's sentence formats sequenced correctly?
- Does your child use limited vocabulary?

- What are your child's auditory perceptual skills?
- Is your child having difficulty comprehending receptive language?
- What is the intelligibility of your child's speech?
- Is your child's articulation of sounds and words age-appropriate?
- Does your child use adequate intonation (pitch, inflection)?
- Does your child avoid using specific words?
- How do your child's language skills affect the educational performance?
- Is there a discrepancy between performance and verbal scores on IQ tests, with the performance score significantly higher than verbal?
- Does your child have difficulty receiving, processing, and expressing language, associating meanings of words and organizing proper sentences?

Keep in mind that many of the answers to these questions may require assistance from other professionals. Do not hesitate to be assertive.

Characteristics of Communication Disorders

There are several different types of communication disorders that you may see in your child, or which have been diagnosed by qualified professionals. These disorders of communication are varied and have distinctive characteristics. If you are a parent of a young child you should be familiar with the many characteristics that may signal some type of communication disorder. In this way, services can be provided as soon as possible.

Voice Disorders. Occurs when the quality, loudness, or pitch of the voice is inappropriate or abnormal. Problems include *hypernasality* (too many sounds come out through the air passages of the nose), and *denasality* (not enough resonance of the nasal passages). Voice disorders are far less common in children than adults. Examples of this condition include hoarseness, breathiness, and nasality. Problems may be the result of organic or functional causes.

Articulation Disorders. This disorder is most prevalent among school-aged children. If your child has an articulation disorder he/she may omit certain sounds, substitute one sound for another, and distort certain speech sounds, while attempting to produce them accurately. You may also notice that he/she may add extra sounds, which can impair comprehension. Maturity sometimes reduces this type of disorder. If your child suffers from a severe articulation disorder he/she will pronounce many sounds so poorly that his/her speech will be unintelligible most of the time.

Fluency Disorders. These disorders interrupt the natural, smooth flow of speech with inappropriate pauses, hesitations, or repetitions. One type of disorder is known as *cluttering*, a condition in which speech is very rapid and clipped to the point of unintelligibility. Another type is called *stuttering*, which is characterized by verbal blocks. While stuttering is not uncommon in every child's early language development, any long-term pattern needs to be investigated for a more serious situation.

Language Disorders. Two types of language disorders involve *receptive language disorder*, which interferes with the understanding of language, such as inability to comprehend spoken words, and *expressive language disorder,* which interferes with the production of language such as a limited vocabulary. These conditions may be caused by environmental deprivation, emotional factors, structural abnormalities, or retardation.

Summary of Normal Language Development

Birth to six months

- Vowel sounds are produced
- First form of communication is crying
- Babies also make sounds of comfort such as coos and gurgles
- Babbling soon follows as a form of communication
- No meaning is attached to the words heard from others

Six to twelve months

- Child may perform an action when asked
- The baby's voice begins to rise and fall while making sounds
- May respond appropriately to the word "no" or own name
- Child may repeat words said by others
- Child begins to understand certain words

Twelve to eighteen months

- Child is able to tell what he/she wants by pointing
- Child has learned to say several words with appropriate meaning
- Child responds to simple commands

Eighteen to twenty-four months

- Child begins to forms words into short sentences
- Great spurt in the acquisition and use of speech at this stage
- Child begins to combine words

Two to three years

- Child can tell simple stories
- Child can identify colors
- Child talks at this age

- Child will ask questions
- Child has vocabulary of about 900 words
- Child participates in conversation
- Child can use plurals
- Child begins to use some consonant sounds

Three to four years

- Child begins to speak more rapidly
- Child begins to ask questions to obtain information
- Sentences are longer and more varied

Four to five years

- Child is able to define words
- Child can modify speech
- Child can use conjunctions
- Child can recite poems and sing songs from memory
- Child has average vocabulary of over 1500 words
- Sentences average five words in length

Treatment and Remediation of Communication Disorders

You as a parent can become very involved in the remediation of your child's communication disorder even though he/she may be receiving professional assistance. There are several things you can do which will assist your child's progress. However, it is always better to first consult the speech therapist before doing any remediation at home so that you are working along with the therapist.

Articulation Disorders: In this area you may try to develop your child's ability to listen carefully and discriminate between similar sounds, and emphasize awareness and discrimination of sounds. Using a mirror so that your child can monitor his/her own speech production is very useful. Try to use a tape recorder to record his/her own speech and listen carefully for errors. You should always try to provide good language models and use positive reinforcement to encourage your child to talk.

Voice Disorders: In this area you may want to seek out a medical examination for possible organic cause. The doctor or speech therapist may recommend environmental modifications. The use of vocal rehabilitation to help your child gradually learn to produce more acceptable and efficient speech is helpful. Try to use exercises and activities to increase breathing capacity and use relaxation techniques to reduce tension. These techniques can be obtained from the school or from your private speech therapist.

Fluency Disorders: Because of the possible social ramifications of this disorder you may try to emphasize counseling or behavior modification with your child. Having a positive attitude about such services will only assist your child and offer him/her hope. You can also try to teach your child to manage his/her stuttering by prolonging certain sounds or by speaking more slowly. You can slowly increase his/her confidence by having your child speak in groups. Having your child monitor his/her own speech is a good technique. Teach him/her to speak to a rhythmic beat and use tape recorders for drills.

Language Disorders: In this area you can try to use precommunication activities which encourage the child to explore. Try to talk clearly to the child and use correct inflections when speaking. Providing a rich variety of words and sentences will help them learn proper usage. You may want to slowly expose your child to group interaction or emphasize the use of language through performing tasks. You can also assist your child in this area by using a variety of written and verbal labeling.

Determining the Presence of a Speech and Language Disability

To be eligible for speech and learning services under the special-education umbrella, your child must be classified as disabled as per Federal regulations. This entails a determination of the child's specific disability through evaluation and testing. As previously noted, speech services can be provided to both disabled and nondisabled children. The service is generally called speech improvement for nondisabled students, and speech impairment for disabled students. Not all children with communication disorders are disabled. The CSE in reviewing evaluation information will determine whether or not a communication disorder warrants classification. They may find that the speech or language disability does not adversely affect your child's education performance and this does not warrant identification as a disability.

In these cases, the disorder and/or its effect on your child's performance can be dealt with in the mainstream. In those cases the committee will notify you of its findings and then will notify the building administration and send the recommendation to the Board of Education. As with any CSE, you have the right to disagree and have due process. The CSE on the other hand may find the communication disorder to be a disability due to any number of conditions depending on the interpretation of the evaluation.

Speech and language instruction provides for formal testing and evaluation, counseling to parents, consultation to teachers, and individual or small-group instruction for the purpose of correcting speech and language disorders. A good speech and language program will have communication time built in for the speech and language teacher to meet with parents to review instruction, consult, and train so that you and the classroom teacher can provide the same or similar services in the classroom or at home. Small groups in school usually do not exceed five pupils.

Children who are found to be speech-impaired may require services with a combined resource-room program that will focus on curriculum. If the child's disability requires speech pathology, the program will supply supplemental help designed to correct the communication disorder and at the same time reinforce instruction in the child's educational program. In essence, he/she will have a resource room and speech-language teacher working together to remediate the child using both content area material and specific speech/language material. A speech/language teacher may see youngsters who are placed in self-contained special-education classes either individually or in small groups, as a pull-out, or within the classroom. Again this speech-language teacher will use a team approach, consult, and train special-education classroom teachers regarding the communication disorder.

In summary, speech, language, and communication disorders are a major factor in the educational process. Some students will be classified disabled and some will not. Early intervention is a key in dealing with communication disabilities. The CSE will provide the IEP recommendations; you as a parent need to communicate with the speech/language teacher to learn techniques that will benefit your child. The earlier, the better; the more repetition, the better.

The Autistic Child

Criteria Used to Diagnose Autistic Disorder

Throughout the years the diagnosis of autism has changed dramatically. At one time it was mistakenly diagnosed as childhood schizophrenia until several researchers and professionals in the field began to take a closer look. The term *autistic* was first described by L. Kanner in 1943. Kanner felt that several characteristics were typical of autistic children including the following:

- The child shows an inability to relate to people and exhibits extreme autistic aloneness.
- The child fails to assume an anticipatory posture in preparation to being picked up.
- The child exhibits speech problems such as delayed echolalia, repetition of personal pronouns, and mutism.
- The child shows an anxious, obsessive desire for the maintenance of sameness.
- The child shows a limitation in the variety of spontaneous activity.
- The child reacts to external intrusions such as food, loud noises, and moving objects.
- The child seems interested in objects and reaches to people as part objects.
- The child may show excellent rote memory.
- The child may appear to be physically normal.
- The child may come from a highly intelligent family.

As the field progressed, other researchers developed characteristics that were typical of children with autism. Another individual in the field, Rutter, observed autistic behavior patterns in children and came up with some other characteristics:

- The child exhibits profound and general failure to develop social relationships.
- The child exhibits language retardation with impaired comprehension, echolalia, and pronominal reversal.
- The child exhibits ritualistic or compulsive phenomena.
- The child may show repetitive movements.
- The child may exhibit a short attention span.
- The child may resort to frequent self-injury.
- The child may exhibit delayed bowel movements.

The most recent set of diagnostic criteria used to determine autism comes from the *Diagnostic and Statistical Manual–IV* which is used by all mental-health-care professionals. It is a manual of diagnostic characteristics of accepted mental-health disorders that may be identified by these professionals. The DSM-IV lists the following characteristics for autism:

- Marked lack of awareness of the existence or feelings of others.
- Abnormal or no seeking of comfort at times of distress.
- Impaired or no imitation.
- Abnormal or no social play.
- Gross impairment in ability to make peer friendships.
- No mode of communication, such as communicative babbling, facial expression, gesture, mime, or spoken language.
- Markedly abnormal nonverbal communication.
- Absence of imaginative activity.
- Marked abnormalities in the production of speech, including volume, pitch, stress, rate, rhythm, and intonation.
- Marked abnormalities in the form or content of speech, including stereotyped and repetitive use.
- Marked impairment in the ability to initiate or sustain a conversation with others, despite adequate speech.
- Stereotyped body movements.
- Persistent preoccupation with parts of objects.
- Marked distress over changes in trivial aspects of the environment.
- Unreasonable insistence on following routines in precise detail.
- Marked restricted range of interests and a preoccupation with one narrow interest.

Interdisciplinary Diagnosis of Autism

While certain characteristics are typical of autistic children, the diagnosis of the disorder is a multidisciplinary effort. A team of professionals should be involved in the diagnosis of this disorder because of its many unique characteristics and behaviors. You may want to initially seek out guidance from your pediatrician or a psychiatrist, psychologist or social worker. Each professional is responsible for a certain part of the evaluation. The *audiologist* is one member of the team that can assist you in the proper diagnosis. Your child may be evaluated by an audiologist either as part of a multidisciplinary assessment or as a referral from a pediatrician who wants to rule out a hearing loss as a possible cause for your child's lack of responsiveness, usually one of the first signals observed in autism. Specialized procedures and equipment for eliciting responses to sounds have been developed for other groups of people who are difficult to test and they can be applied to autistic children. Two such methods are: *Conditioned Orienting Reflex Audiometry* (CORA), a technique involving the pairing of an attractive visual object with a sound, and *Tangible Reinforcement Operant Conditioning Audiometry* (TROCA), is a technique that uses a machine that dispenses edible reinforcement (candy) when your child pushes a button in response to a sound.

The *social worker* is able to contribute to the diagnostic treatment process provided to your family when you suspect that your child may be autistic. The social worker provides the team with information on your family's dynamics, patterns of interaction among various family members, your family member's perception of your possible autistic child, parenting responsibilities, and your use of behavior-management techniques.

Different techniques are sometimes utilized by the *physician* when dealing with your autistic child. First, the medical history is obtained from records and from you without your child present. Second, your child is observed in the examination room with you present. The information gathered includes activity level, general state of physical health and development, and gross and fine motor coordination. Third, the general physical and neurological examinations are conducted with special attention directed toward looking for indicators of organic, not psychological dysfunction. A diagnosis of autism is not made by the pediatrician though it is possibly suggested in the conclusions.

The *psychiatrist* and the *psychologist* are responsible for the diagnosis of autism and the psychological evaluations involved in this process. When first encountered by you, psychiatrists and psychologists gather pertinent developmental history. This information coupled with clinical interviews, evaluations, and your intake information assist in the diagnosis of autism.

The *special-education teacher* may be involved on two separate levels. First, he/she may be involved in the diagnostic evaluation of your child suspected of a disability. Second, the special-education teacher will be responsible for carrying out the required services that will assist in the education of your child.

As parents of a potentially autistic child you may begin your search for diagnostic answers at a *speech/hearing clinic*, since your child is unresponsive to speech and has either no language or unusual patterns of communication. The speech and language pathologist will evaluate your child's movement and behavior, cognitive skills, expressive language, deviant language patterns, and receptive language.

As a parent. you want to make sure that you get the most professional and thorough evaluation possible. Do not hesitate to question the professional as to his/her experience in this field. If someone has little or no experience in the diagnosis of autism, seek out another professional.

Tourette's Syndrome

Tourette's Syndrome (TS) is a neurological disorder that appears to be genetically transmitted in most cases. It is one of a number of disorders classified as *tic disorders*. Tics are involuntary movements which present themselves through motor or sound.

The first tics or symptoms of Tourette's Syndrome are usually simple motor tics of the head, face, and neck area. *Simple motor tics* are usually rapid, apparently purposeless and repetitive movements of one muscle group. Examples of simple motor tics include the following:

Motor

- Eye blinking
- Shoulder shrugs
- Mouth opening
- Arm extending
- Facial grimaces
- Lip-licking
- Rolling eyes
- Squinting

Simple phonic (sound) tics are repetitive sounds that are not linguistically meaningful. They may include the following:

Sound (phonic)

- Throat clearing
- Grunting
- Yelling or screaming
- Sniffing
- Barking
- Snorting
- Coughing
- Spitting

- Squeaking
- Humming
- Whistling

Complex motor tics are involuntary movements that involve the coordinated sequence or activation of two or more muscle groups. Examples include:

- Pulling at clothes
- Touching people
- Touching objects
- Smelling fingers
- Jumping or skipping
- Poking or jabbing
- Punching
- Kicking
- Hopping
- Kissing self or others
- Flapping arms
- Twirling around
- Thrusting movements of groin or torso
- Walking on toes
- Copropraxia (sexually touching self or others, obscene gestures)
- Self-injurious behavior

Complex phonic tics represent involuntary, linguistically meaningful utterances or expressions, such as repetitive use of phrases. Examples include:

- Animal-like sounds
- Unusual changes in pitch or volume of voice
- Stuttering
- Coprolalia (socially taboo phrases or obscenities)
- Echoing one's own words or others

Diagnostic Criteria for Tic Disorders

There are several categories of tic disorders, Tourettes Syndrome being only one of these. While the different disorders may overlap in certain characteristics, there are differences which you may want to know in case your child is exhibiting certain symptoms. The first category involves *transient tic disorders* which are the most common of the tic disorders. The onset of this disorder usually occurs during early school years and affects five to twenty-four percent of all children. An important criteria for the diagnosis of this category must involve single or multiple motor and/or vocal tics which occur daily for at least two weeks but for no longer than one year. This disorder is three to four times more common in males than in females, and more common in the first-degree relatives of people who have transient tic disorders.

The second category involves *chronic motor/vocal tic disorders*. The onset of this disorder is usually before the age of 21. The tics usually persist unchanged throughout a period of more than one year and involve either motor or vocal tics. This condition is generally related to Tourette's Syndrome.

The third category is *Tourette's Syndrome*, and here also the onset is usually before age 21. Further, in this disorder the tics occur for more than one year but may be highly variable, changing over time in anatomic location, number, complexity, and frequency. There are usually associated problems which may include obsessive-compulsive disorder. The associated behavioral difficulties may include problems in attention, hyperactivity, and emotional ability. The symptoms of Tourette's Syndrome can be suppressed at school and at home only to have them emerge abruptly upon arriving in the safety of the home. About fifty to sixty percent of children with TS have Attention-Deficit/Hyperactivity Disorder.

Pharmacotherapy and Tourette's Syndrome

Pharmacotherapy has been reported to be the most widely used treatment for Tourette's Syndrome to date. The difficulty with this treatment is the attempt to balance the alleviation of symptoms with the side effects of many medications. The following is a brief overview of medications currently known to alleviate symptoms of TS:

Neuroleptics

- Decreases symptoms of Tourette's Syndrome in seventy to eighty percent of the patients.
- Side effects result in fifty percent of the patients discontinuing this medication.
- Side effects include Parkinsonian symptoms, sedation, weight gain, decreased concentration, impaired memory, depression, and personality changes.
- Usually used in patients whose symptoms cause significant impairment.
- Examples include Haldol®, Orap®, and Prolixin®.

Clonodine

- Reported to be effective in sixty percent of Tourette's patients.
- Less disturbing side effects.
- May require up to a twelve week trial to evaluate efficacy.
- Common side effects are sedation and dry mouth.

Antidepressants

- Generally used to treat associated ADHD (Attention-Deficit/Hyperactivity Disorder) and/or OCD (Obsessive-Compulsive Disorder) symptoms.
- Some patients report decrease in symptoms while others report increase.
- Side effects include dry mouth, sedation, low blood pressure, dizziness, and constipation.
- Examples include Tofranil®, Clomipramine®, and Prozac®.

Classroom Strategies for Children With Tourette's Syndrome

Many children with TS will have to face many pressures both at home and in school associated with tics, social concerns, reactions, and associated learning difficulties. Both your and the teacher's response to these conditions can make a critical difference. It is very important that everyone dealing with your child keep in mind that motor or vocal tics occur involuntarily and to try not to react with anger or annoyance.

There are many things the teacher may use to help your child if he/she has TS. He/she needs to be a role model for the other students on how to react to the Tourette symptoms exhibited by your child. The sensitivity shown by your child's teachers will be modeled by the other children in the class. The teacher may also want to provide your child with opportunities for short breaks out of the classroom to relieve some of the tension that normally builds up with this disorder. Ask the teacher to try to find a private place somewhere in the school where your child can "let out" the tics since he/she may try to suppress the tics for a period of time causing a buildup of tension. Allowing your child to take tests in a private room so that he/she does not waste energy suppressing the tics, which may interfere with concentration, increases the chances of success. The teacher may want to work with your child's classmates to help them understand the tics and reduce ridicule and teasing.

Try to secure materials such as audio-visuals and pamphlets, which may provide information for your child's classmates. Your child's teacher should also keep in mind that children with Tourette's Syndrome often have visual motor difficulties which may require a modification of written assignments by reducing the number of problems presented or required to copy.

Further, allowing your child to write the answers directly on a test paper or booklet rather than use computer scoring sheets reduces frustration. Other modifications that the teacher may use to assist your child include untimed tests to reduce stress, allowing another child to take notes for your child so that he/she can listen to the lecture without the added stress of copying notes, and not penalizing your child for spelling errors.

You as a parent should meet with your child's teachers as early as possible to explain his/her condition and offer information or suggestions. Never assume that all teachers know what to do when it comes to Tourette's Syndrome.

The Bilingual and Culturally Disadvantaged Child

Variables That May Influence an Exceptional Bilingual Child's Placement

Program placement should be the best fit between your child's needs and the available resources. Placement decisions for your bilingual exceptional child should reflect the type and nature of instruction to be provided, the language of instruction, the conveyor of instruction, the duration of instruction, and the student's learning needs and style. The following special-education variables and bilingual factors should be addressed in identifying placements for your child:

1. Student's age.
2. Type and degree of impairment or disability.
3. Age at which disability occurred.
4. Level of language involvement because of the disability.
5. Level of academic achievement.
6. Entry-level language skills (upon entering school).
7. Measured intellectual ability.
8. Method and language used in measuring academic achievement and intellectual ability.
9. Level of adaptive behavior.
10. Time spent in United States.
11. Current cultural home setting.
12. Social maturity.
13. Level of language proficiency in English and other language.
14. Amount and type of language input received in the home environment.
15. Speech and language capabilities in both languages.
16. Presence of multiple handicaps.
17. Ambulation or mobility.
18. Success in past and present placements.
19. Wishes of students and parents.

Basic Elements of an Individualized Education Program (IEP) for Exceptional Bilingual Children

Your involvement in the IEP process is crucial. This will be an opportunity for you to have input in your child's education and special services. The IEP conference should be attended by the professionals that will be involved with your child. You should always feel comfortable asking as many questions as it takes to clarify what you are hearing. However, if you are concerned about the IEP and feel uncomfortable discussing it at the meeting, consult with an outside professional and then request a special meeting to clarify your concerns with the IEP. The IEP for your exceptional bilingual child should include:

1. Your child's current educational placement, including all related services your child is receiving.

2. Goals, including adaptation to acculturation and growth in both the first and second language.

3. Your child's goals, which must be realistic considering your child's abilities, impairments, and available time in the educational setting.

4. The sequence of short-term instructional objectives leading up to each goal.

5. A list of instructional and service requirements including a balance between the first and second language, as well as delineation of who will assist with acculturation needs.

6. The amount of time your child will participate in mainstream classes.

7. The length of the program.

8. A schedule for evaluation of the IEP's effectiveness and goals.

9. A statement of the role of the parents.

Specific Requirements for Referral of Bilingual Students to the CSE

If you feel that your bilingual child should be reviewed by the Committee on Special Education for a suspected disability you will need to provide the school with certain information. This information along with the records, evaluations, and observations obtained by the school will represent the packet of materials presented at the CSE meeting. The more thorough the packet the greater the chances for classification and services. As a parent you can facilitate this process by gathering the following information:

- Identify the reason for your referral and include any test results in both languages as appropriate that may have already be done on your child.

- Include any records or reports upon which your referral is based.

- Attach a home language survey indicating the home language(s). You should be able to get this from the school. Your school may accomplish this section in some cases.

- Identify the length of residency of your child in the United States and his/her prior school experience in the native country and in an English-language school system.

The school must also provide information through a variety of methods and techniques. The information provided by the school includes:

- The specific level of language proficiency.

- The extent to which the LEP student has received native language instruction and/or ESL services prior to the referral.
- The experiential and/or enrichment services for your child.
- The school's efforts to involve you in meetings prior to the referral.
- The amount of time and extent of services in an academic program for your child if he/she has had little or no formal schooling.
- All attempts to remediate your child's performance prior to the referral, including any supplemental aids or support services provided for this purpose.

The Gifted Child

Evaluation Procedures

The determination of giftedness by schools may vary from district to district and from state to state. Since giftedness is considered an exceptionality but not a disability, it does not fall under the state laws governing IDEA. Therefore, the standards used are usually left up to the discretion of the local school district. One hopes that certain guidelines are the result of accepted research parameters. However, this is still a debatable point.

There are specific factors that should be taken into consideration when determining whether or not your child is gifted. Several evaluative tools are available and used by most districts. The first measure that may be instituted is the intelligence test. Some districts use group IQ tests (new term for IQ is now School Abilities Index or SAI) as a screening measure. If your child scores above the 98th percentile (50th percentile would be considered average), or 128 SAI they have met the first criteria. However, you may find that districts will lower this standard of 128 if they want more students in the program, or raise it to 130 or higher if they desire fewer students. Further, some districts may use national percentiles while others may use local percentiles. If you are in a very competitive district then you may find that while your child falls within the 98th percentile nationally, he/she may only be within the 70th percentile locally, thereby not meeting the local percentile standard used by some schools. In any case, try to become familiar with the test used and what the results mean. Some examples of intelligence tests used by districts include:

- Slosson Intelligence Test
- Otis-Lennon Mental Ability Test
- Stanford Binet Intelligence Test
- Lorge-Thorndike Intelligence Test
- Wechsler Intelligence Scales
- Short Form of Academic Aptitude

- California Test of Mental Maturity
- Peabody Picture Vocabulary Test

The second measure used by schools in the determination of giftedness is academic achievement levels. The standard may vary from school to school and from state to state, and again be aware of whether your child is being evaluated on national or local percentiles. Many school districts look for achievement performance over 90th percentile in math and reading. Examples of these tests include the Gates-MacGinitie Reading Tests, Metropolitan Readiness Test, Stanford Achievement Test, and the California Achievement Test.

Some school districts may use a test of creativity as part of their evaluation for giftedness. This is usually a timed test that measures the child's creative skills in a variety of areas. Such tests include the Torrance Test of Creative Thinking and the Creativity Assessment Packet (CAP).

There are some tests available that combine several characteristics exhibited by gifted children. These screening tests assess how your child compares to known characteristics of gifted children around the country. These tests include:

- Screening Assessment for Gifted Elementary Students–Primary (SAGES–P)
- Screening Assessment for Gifted Elementary Students (SAGES)
- Leadership Skills Inventory
- Process Skills Rating Scales

Other measures are available and utilized by school districts to get a global analysis of your child's performance as possibly gifted. Even though no school district uses all these measures, you still should be aware of all options available, especially if you feel your district's packet is too narrow.

- Parent Recommendation
- Teacher Checklist and Recommendation
- Behavioral Characteristics
- Renzuili-Hartman Scale for Rating Behavioral Characteristics of Superior Students
- Motor Development Tests
- Rating Scales (which offer a rating level of various skills)
- Anecdotal Records
- Personality Tests
- Interest Inventories
- Pupil Products and Work Samples
- Observation of Actual Performance
- Parental Interviews
- Peer Nomination Rating Scales
- Autobiography

Examples of Classroom Activities

It is not only important that your child receive the proper educational approach, but he/she should also be exposed to the best teaching methodology available for gifted children. Such methodology needs to cover a wide variety of skills to enhance the education of your child. These teaching skills involve different approaches to questioning, thinking, reporting, organizing, processing, and managing information. These higher-level skills will increase your gifted child's motivation and desire to learn. Examples of these classroom activities that your child's teacher may want to explore include:

Original Thinking

- Think of new ways to use a shoe-box.
- Write a new ending to a famous play.
- Design a new type of clothing.
- Design a mechanism to allow cars to park in narrow spaces.
- Design a school room of the future.

Fluent Thinking

- List various ways can you prevent air pollution.
- Describe the most useless, expensive thing imaginable.
- Devise a list of products that are the universal names for all products of that type (Brillo, Jello).
- List all the things you can fit through a hole the size of a dime.
- Name all the things that can be held up with scotch tape.

Flexible Thinking

- Discuss different ways you can use a rubber band.
- List how many items you can make from metal.
- List all the uses you can think of for a paper clip.
- Think of all the ways you can use items in your garbage can to reduce pollution.
- Discuss how life would be different if the wheel were not discovered.

Elaborative Thinking

- Decorate your jean jacket with some original creation.
- Draw a triangle and make as many objects as you can that include that shape.
- Expand on the safety items for cars that have already been developed.
- Add decorations to the outside of a house that will increase its beauty.
- Take a character from a famous story and give him/her new qualities.

Curiosity

- Devise an experiment that will cause the cork in a bottle to shoot up and hit the ceiling.
- How do the five senses make us aware of the world around us?
- What would happen if all of a sudden you became blind?
- What do you think the world would be like without trees?
- Did you ever wonder how thermometers work?

Risk Taking

- Predict how the world would look if we did nothing about pollution.
- Given an object in a box, determine how you would go about finding out what it is.
- Explain how you would defend Lee Harvey Oswald if you were his lawyer.
- Make a prediction on the laws governing abortion. Will they change?
- What would happen if you put a thermometer in hot water?

Imagination

- What would happen if you could go to the center of the earth?
- How do you think your street will look ten years from now?
- Draw a picture of the first alien to visit the earth, including his family and space-ship.
- Pretend you are a cloud.
- Suppose Martians landed on the earth and all they found was a penny. How many things can they tell about our society from the penny?

Complexity

- Make a city out of blocks and objects around you.
- Present students with numerous pictures of all types of dogs and ask them to classify them with some new system.
- Ask the students to tell what they would do if they were able to teach.
- What solutions can be developed to stop car hijackers?
- What other ways of evaluation can be used in school besides numerical and letter grades?

Approaches to Educational Programming

Your gifted child may be exposed to two different educational approaches. *Enrichment programs* offer your child a variety of experiences both in and out of the classroom. These enrichment programs attempt to increase your child's exposure by offering him/her all types of new experiences. While enrichment is the most popular alternative used with gifted children, its effectiveness is still unproven. Enrichment strategies include:

- Pullout programs
- Special experiences within a regular classroom
- Tracking
- Special grouping within the regular classroom
- Resource rooms
- Mentor programs
- Guest speakers
- Internships
- Extra-school activities
- Special clubs
- Summer camps and programs
- Special regular classes
- Seminars
- Minicourses
- Team teaching
- Alternative schools
- Field trips
- Cultural programs

To date, *acceleration programs* have received the greatest attention by researchers and as a result studies have indicated that it is a viable alternative for educating gifted children. Some schools may use a variety of acceleration options. One example is *subject matter acceleration*, where the child advances in specific subject areas while remaining in the same grade level. Another approach is called *telescoping*, where children cover more than a full year's work in a given school year. Other viable acceleration options include:

- Honor classes
- Advanced placement classes for college credit
- Early admission to school
- Early admission to college
- Advancing a grade
- Advanced placement tests
- Seminars
- Programmed learning so that the student can accelerate at his/her own pace

- Ungraded classes
- Multi-age classes
- Tutoring
- Correspondence courses
- Classes for extra credit
- Credit by examination
- Independent study
- Continuous progress curriculum
- Year-round school
- Flexible scheduling

Common Characteristics of Program Management

School districts have several educational program options available for dealing with gifted students. The belief by some educators that gifted students just need to be given more of the same is not accepted in today's educational circles. The educational programs provided to gifted children represent an attempt to provide for the unique needs of these students.

Pullout programs offer one viable option. In this program, gifted students are removed from the classroom and placed in an out-of-classroom location for a portion of the school day or week. Grouping in the pullout setting may be by grade or multi-age.

Cluster grouping occurs when identified gifted students from several classes are grouped or clustered into a regular class with other nongifted students. In this type of educational program cluster groups of gifted students within the classroom receive differentiated instruction based on their special needs.

Acceleration is often used by school districts and occurs when gifted students are moved more rapidly through the usual sequence of instruction. In this case, above-grade-level materials are used for instruction. Acceleration may occur in one academic area, for example, mathematics, though in some cases may occur by moving the gifted student into a higher grade.

Homogeneous grouping is used by some school districts and takes all gifted students and places them together in a single class exclusively for them. Many educators tend to shy away from this option because of the feeling of creating an "elite" population which may make other children feel uncomfortable.

Maintaining your gifted student in the *regular classroom* is another option available to schools. In this case, gifted students remain in regular heterogeneous classes and receive individualized instructional approaches. These approaches are used to differentiate the program to meet the needs of gifted students.

A newer attempt to educate the gifted is called the *mentor program*. In this program, gifted students are matched to mentors or guides who work with them in individually selected areas. These programs frequently involve out-of-school experiences for your child. Mentors are frequently community people in business and service areas or the arts. Mentors may assist your gifted child in independent study projects, or acquaint your gifted child with their particular area of expertise.

Terminology for the Gifted

Analysis: Breaking down a concept, problem, or pattern into its component parts.

Associating: Relating objects or thoughts as they come to mind; may be free, controlled, or linked to preceding and following thoughts.

Categorizing: Placing objects, ideas, and phenomena into a given classification system.

Classifying: Establishing an arbitrary system of grouping and subgrouping on the basis of the common characteristics of elements.

Comparing: Determining similarities and differences on the basis of some criteria.

Convergent Thinking: Arriving at one pattern or one solution out of diverse elements, using some criterion.

Creative Thinking: Developing or reorganizing ideas, objects, words, and so on and arriving at a product which is novel, original, unexpected, and imaginative in its new form.

Critical Thinking: A complex process which involves analysis, a weighing of the components (either qualitatively or quantitatively), and making a selection or decision on the basis of the evaluation.

Deduction: Starting with generalizations or universal propositions and arriving at a specific conclusion.

Divergent Thinking: Offering various patterns or solutions to the same problem.

Induction: Using specific situations, objects, and ideas, and arriving at generalizations.

Synthesis: Putting together parts and pieces to form a whole; arranging, rearranging, and combining parts to establish a pattern or product not clearly present before.

Fluent Thinking: The ability to produce different and multiple ideas; thinking of many possibilities; flow of thought.

Flexible Thinking: The ability to produce alternatives; different approaches; variety of ideas; accept variations and modifications.

Original Thinking: The ability to think of novel, unique, or universal possibilities; to be creative, inventive, and innovative.

Elaborate Thinking: The ability to embellish upon an idea to produce a number of detailed steps; to express one-self in greater length or detail; to expand and develop thoroughly.

Curiosity: The willingness to examine things and ideas or the capacity to wonder about things which may lead somewhere; desire to know or learn, especially about something new or strange; inquisitive.

Risk Taking: The courage to try out adventurous tasks or to venture a guess; engages in commitment; judges, disputes, questions; perseveres.

Complexity: The ability to handle challenge and involved details; using intricate ideas.

Imagination: The power to form mental images which have not been experienced; building thought models about situations; ability to deal creatively with reality.

Characteristics of the Gifted and Talented

Many characteristics of the gifted child have been observed over the years. In doing so researchers have found that gifted children tend to share common characteristics with each other. These characteristics are sometimes so unique that they are used by districts to screen children for possible giftedness. These traits are used differently by school districts. Some use these in teacher's observation scales while others use them when questioning parents. It should be kept in mind that your child will probably not exhibit all these characteristics but should exhibit quite a few if he/she is truly gifted. The qualities that have been defined as characteristic of gifted children include:

1. Keen power of observation
2. Sense of the significant
3. Willingness to examine the unusual
4. Power of abstraction
5. High-level conceptualization
6. Interest in inductive learning and problem solving
7. Interest in cause-and-effect relationships
8. Retentiveness
9. Verbal proficiency
10. Large vocabulary
11. Facility in expression
12. Interest in reading
13. Wide range of experiences and information
14. Questioning attitude
15. Intellectual curiosity
16. Inquisitive mind
17. Intrinsic motivation
18. Power of critical thinking

19. Creativeness and inventiveness

20. Power of concentration

21. Intense attention that excludes all else

22. Long attention span

23. Persistent

24. Goal directed

25. High energy levels

26. Alertness

27. Eagerness

28. Independence in work and study

29. Preference for individualized work

30. Self-reliance

31. Need for freedom of movement and action

32. Versatility

33. Diversity of interests and abilities

34. Varied hobbies

Common Disorders Usually First Diagnosed in Infancy, Childhood, or Adolescence

The following chapter contains several sections of common disorders that may first be recognized by you during infancy, childhood, or adolescence. These disorders range from mild to severe and require a variety of educational interventions. This chapter was written for you so that you would have a reference source for the most common disorders that lead to a disability. It is also important for you to understand the educational implications and possible interventions that may be available for each disorder.

Developmental Disorders

Mental Disability

Description: This group of disorders is characterized by severe, delayed development in the acquisition of cognitive, language, motor, or social skills. The general characteristics of this diagnostic category are:

• Consistent and significant subaverage intellectual performance.

• Significant deficits in the development of adaptive functioning.

• Onset prior to the age of 18.

Types: There are several subtypes that are classified by educational or psychological terminology. They are:

Educational Category	DSM–IV Classification	IQ Range	DSM–IV Code
Educable Mentally Disabled	Mild	55–77.5 approx.	317.00
Trainable Mentally Disabled	Moderate	35–55 approx.	318.00
Severely Mentally Disabled	Severe	25–35 approx.	318.10
Profoundly Mentally Disabled	Profound	below 25	318.20

Educational Implications: The more severe the category the greater the possibility of associated features being present like seizures, visual, auditory, or cardiovascular problems. Other educational implications involve poor social skills, severe academic deficits, and possible behavioral manifestations such as impulsivity, low frustration tolerance, aggressiveness, low self-esteem, and in some cases self-injurious behavior.

Possible Least-Restrictive Educational Setting: If your child has this disorder, the least-restrictive educational settings may range anywhere from self-contained in a regular school with mainstreaming options for educable students to institutionalization for profoundly retarded individuals.

Pervasive Developmental Disorders

Autistic Disorder

Description: A very serious developmental disorder characterized by severe impairment in the development of verbal and nonverbal communication skills, marked impairment in reciprocal social interaction (a lack of responsiveness to, or interest in people) and an almost nonexistent imaginative activity. Also known as *Infantile Autism* or *Kanner's Syndrome*.

Educational Implications: If your child has this condition he/she may exhibit poor social skills, and impaired cognitive functioning and language. The onset of puberty may increase oppositional or aggressive behavior. Other complications may include seizures and low intellectual development.

Possible Least-Restrictive Educational Setting: Most children with this condition require the most restrictive educational setting possible. The student teacher ratios are usually 6:1:2 or smaller because of the close supervision required. Those that are not capable of maintaining this type of setting may have to be institutionalized. In rare cases the individual may improve to the point of completing formal education or advanced degrees.

Specific Learning Disorders

Mathematics Disorder

Description: Children with this disorder exhibit a serious marked disability in the development of arithmetic skills. This condition, often called *dyscalculia*, cannot be explained by mental retardation, inadequate teaching, or primary visual or auditory defects, and may be consistent throughout school.

Educational Implications: Your child's seriously impaired mathematical ability which may require modifications like extended time, use of a calculator/flexible setting for tests, and revised test format. Other implications may involve poor self-esteem, social self-consciousness, and avoidance which may increase secondary problems.

Possible Least-Restrictive Educational Setting: Children with this disorder may receive assistance through special educational services like resource room or a consultant teacher, and are usually able to maintain placement within a normal class setting.

Disorder of Written Expression

Description: This disorder is characterized by a serious impairment in the ability to develop expressive writing skills that significantly interfere in the child's academic achievement. This condition is not the result of mental retardation, inadequate educational experiences, visual or hearing defects, or neurological dysfunction.

Symptoms: The symptoms associated with this disorder include an inability to compose appropriate written text, coupled with serious and consistent spelling errors, grammatical or punctuation errors, and very poor organization of thought and text.

Educational Implications: Both you and your child's teacher should be aware that he/she may exhibit a series of symptoms including avoidance, procrastination, denial, and possibly disruptive behaviors when written assignments are involved as a means of covering up the seriousness of the disorder.

Possible Least-Restrictive Educational Setting: Your child may receive assistance through special-educational services like resource room or a consultant teacher, and are usually able to maintain placement within a normal class setting.

Reading Disorder

Description: The more common features of this disorder include a marked impairment in the development of the child's ability to decode or break down words and comprehension skills which significantly interfere in the child's academic performance. As with most developmental disorders, this condition is not the result of mental retardation, inadequate educational experiences, visual or hearing defects, or neurological dysfunction. In the past it was commonly referred to as *dyslexia*.

Symptoms: Typical symptoms of this disorder include a slow, halting reading pace, frequent omissions, loss of place on a page, skipping lines while reading without awareness, distortions, substitutions of words, and a serious inability to recall what has been read.

Educational Implications: You should be aware that early diagnosis of this disorder is crucial to avoid serious secondary symptoms of poor self-esteem, behavior disorders, and educational failure. In school your child's teachers should focus on the possible symptoms exhibited by him/her so that they can assist in early identification of this high-risk problem. Teachers should also be aware of the various reading techniques available to assist your child.

Possible Least-Restrictive Educational Setting: Children with this disorder may receive assistance through special-educational services like resource room or a consultant teacher, and are usually able to maintain placement within a normal class setting.

Expressive Language Disorder

Description: This disorder is characterized by a serious impairment in the child's ability to develop expressive language. This condition is not the result of mental retardation, inadequate educational experiences, visual or hearing defects, or neurological dysfunction.

Educational Implications: Teachers should be aware that from three to ten percent of school-aged children suffer from this disorder, which may greatly hamper a child's social interaction skills as well as academic performance.

Possible Least-Restrictive Educational Setting: Your child may receive assistance through special educational services like resource room, a consultant teacher, or services from a speech therapist. Children are usually able to maintain placement within a normal class setting.

Phonological Disorder

Description: Children with this disorder have consistent problems using developmentally expected speech sounds, including but not limited to misarticulations, substitutions, and omissions often sounding very similar to a more infantile form of speech. This condition is not the result of mental retardation, neurological, intellectual, or hearing disorders, or oral speech mechanism defects.

Educational Implications: If your child has this disorder, the prognosis or outcome for complete recovery is very positive, especially when speech therapy is part of the treatment plan. In some milder cases, the condition may run its course by age 8 without intervention.

Possible Least-Restrictive Educational Setting: Your child may receive assistance through special-educational services like resource room, a consultant teacher, or services from a speech therapist. Children are usually able to maintain placement within a normal class setting.

Receptive Language Disorder

Description: This disorder is characterized by a serious impairment in the child's ability to develop language comprehension. This condition is not the result of mental retardation, inadequate educational experiences, visual or hearing defects, or neurological dysfunction.

Educational Implications: In school your child may have a difficult time communicating with gestures and participating in activities that require imaginary play.

Possible Least-Restrictive Educational Setting: If your child suffers from this condition, he/she may receive assistance through special-educational services like resource room, a consultant teacher, or services from a speech therapist. Children are usually able to maintain placement within a normal class setting.

Common Disruptive Behavior Disorders

Conduct Disorder

Description: This condition is characterized by a persistent pattern of behavior which intrudes and violates the basic rights of others without concern or fear of implications. This pattern is not selective and is exhibited in the home, at school, with peers, and in the child's community. Other behaviors present with this condition may include vandalism, stealing, physical aggression, cruelty to animals, and fire setting.

Categories:

Type	Description	DSM–IV Code
Solitary Aggressive Type	Aggressive behavior towards peers and adults	312.00
Group Type	Conduct problems mainly with peers as a group	312.20
Undifferentiated Type	For those not classified in either above group	312.90

Educational Implications: If your child has this disorder be aware of the possibility that he/she may physically confront teachers and peers, have poor attendance, have high levels of suspension thereby missing a great deal of academic work, and exhibit other forms of antisocial behavior.

Possible Least-Restrictive Educational Setting: Children with this condition may be educated in a special class within a regular school if the condition is mild.

However, the majority of students with this disorder are educated in a more restrictive program housed within special schools, residential schools, or institutions if the antisocial behavior is extreme.

Oppositional Defiant Disorder

Description: This disorder is usually characterized by patterns of negativistic, hostile, and defiant behaviors with peers as well as adults. This disorder is considered less serious than a conduct disorder because of the absence of serious behaviors which violate the basic rights of others. Children with this disorder usually exhibit argumentative behaviors towards adults which may include swearing and frequent episodes of intense anger and annoyance. These symptoms are usually considered to be more serious and intense than those exhibited by other children of the same age.

Educational Implications: Your child may exhibit low frustration tolerance, frequent temper outbursts, low sense of confidence, an unwillingness to take responsibility for his/her actions, consistent blaming of others for his/her own mistakes or problems, and frequent behaviors associated with Attention-Deficit/Hyperactivity Disorder.

Possible Least-Restrictive Educational Setting: If your child has this disorder he/she may be educated in a special class within a regular school if the condition is mild. However, the majority of students with this disorder are educated in a more restrictive program housed within special schools, residential schools, or institutions if the antisocial behavior is extreme.

Common Anxiety Disorders of Childhood

Separation Anxiety Disorder

Description: This disorder is characterized by extreme anxiety associated with separation from someone with whom the child views as a significant other. While this reaction may be common with very young children on their first day of school, continuation of the anxiety for more than two weeks indicates a problem that needs to be addressed. This separation anxiety is frequently exhibited at school and at home. It should be noted that if symptoms of separation anxiety occur in an adolescent, other factors such as social or academic pressure may be the contributing cause.

Educational Implications: In school your child may require a great deal of his/her teacher's attention. Your child may cling, be afraid to try new things, require a great deal of reassurance, and may cry frequently. Panic attacks are common and his/her teacher may find that reasoning does not reduce the anxiety. Physical complaints are common and should never be ignored. However, in cases of separation anxiety these physical symptoms are usually manifestations of the anxiety once medical causes are ruled out.

Possible Least-Restrictive Educational Setting: Your child can usually be maintained in the regular class setting through the help of the school psychologist, who will work with you and your child. If the condition persists and the diagnosis changes, for instance, to major depression, then outside professional help may be required and a more restrictive program, sometimes even homebound instruction if attendance at school is not possible, may have to be instituted.

Avoidant Disorder of Childhood or Adolescence

Description: This disorder results in the child withdrawing from social contact or interaction with an unfamiliar peer or adult to the point of becoming a significant factor in social development.

Educational Implications: Usually, if your child has this disorder, he/she can maintain regular class placement as long as achievement levels do not present problems possibly signifying some other condition. Children with this disorder exhibit social isolation, withdrawal from activity-based assignments, and a complete unwillingness to try new situations involving social interaction with unfamiliar peers. If your child's teacher attempts to force your child into new social interaction situations it may only result in further withdrawal socially as well as verbally. Referring your child to the school psychologist is also highly recommended. Individual outside counseling with a slow lead into small-group counseling should be explored. However, this transition may result in a great deal of resistance on the part of your child.

Possible Least-Restrictive Educational Setting: If your child has this disorder, he/she can usually be maintained in the regular class setting through the help of the school psychologist working with you and your child. However, children with other disabilities may also exhibit this disorder.

Overanxious Disorder

Description: The main feature of this disorder is an excessive level of anxiety or worry extending over a six-month or longer period of time.

Educational Implications: If your child has this disorder be aware of the possibility of poor academic performance because of your child's preoccupation with worry. In school your child's teacher may want to try to reassure and compliment your child as much as possible when he/she is not drawing negative attention to him/herself.

Possible Least-Restrictive Educational Setting: Most children with this disorder can be educated within a regular class placement unless the condition is coupled with more serious disabilities that require a more restrictive setting. Referral to the school psychologist is highly recommended.

Common Eating and Tic Disorders

Anorexia Nervosa

Description: Children with this condition show a marked disturbance and unwillingness to maintain a minimal body weight for their age and height. An extreme, distorted sense of body image exists and intense fears and worries about gaining weight become obsessive. It is not uncommon for Bulimia Nervosa to be an associated feature. In more severe cases, death may occur.

Symptoms: If your child suffers from this disorder he/she may exhibit self-induced vomiting, use of laxatives, increased reduction of food intake, preoccupation with becoming fat, and noticeable increase in the frequency and intensity of exercise. In females, absence of menstrual cycles is common as the child's weight decreases and the body chemistry changes.

Educational Implications: Your child may experience frequent absences because of medical complications. These children are usually high-achieving individuals but because of their medical conditions academic consistency may be difficult.

Possible Least-Restrictive Educational Setting: Children with this type of disorder can be maintained in the regular school setting unless the condition becomes severe enough to warrant hospitalization. In some cases where the child is at home and unable to attend school, homebound instruction is utilized.

Bulimia Nervosa

Description: A condition characterized by recurrent episodes of uncontrolled consumption of large quantities of food (bingeing), followed by self-induced vomiting (purging), and use of laxatives or diuretics over a period of at least two months.

Symptoms: The individual with Bulimia Nervosa exhibits symptoms characterized by bingeing and purging, use of laxatives and diuretics, obsessive preoccupation with body shape and weight, and a feeling of lack of control over food consumption during binge episodes.

Educational Implications: Both you and your child's teachers might not even know that he/she is bulimic. Children hide this "secret" well and may not divulge the problem to anyone, not even to a best friend. This is usually a private disorder until the person feels so out of control that they seek help and support. Consequently, be aware of frequent trips to the bathroom especially in the morning after breakfast or after lunch. Changes in skin color and look may give some indications of problems. However if you suspect anything, let your doctor investigate this further.

Possible Least-Restrictive Educational Setting: Unlike anorexia nervosa, children with bulimia nervosa seldom suffer incapacitating symptoms except in rare cases when the eating and purging episodes run throughout the day. Consequently, in most cases these children can be maintained in the regular school setting unless the condition becomes severe enough to warrant hospitalization.

Tourette's Syndrome

Description: This disorder is characterized by motor and vocal tics which may be exhibited in the form of grunting, coughs, barks, touching, knee jerking, drastic head movements, head banging, squatting, and so on.

Symptoms: The above symptoms may change as the child develops but the course of the disorder is usually lifelong. Associated features include Obsessive Compulsive Disorder (OCD), and Attention-Deficit/Hyperactivity Disorder (ADHD) discussed earlier. The condition is more common in males and family patterns are also common. *Coprolalia* (vocal tic involving the expression of obscenities) is an associated symptom in about thirty-three percent of the cases.

Educational Implications: Students with Tourette's Syndrome encounter social difficulties and confusion when dealing with their peers. Social rejection, isolation, and victimization may be common and the teacher needs to step in to prevent these situations from occurring. In older students with this disorder, the child uses a great deal of energy to control the tics because of social pressure (at the cost of attention) and consistent academic performance. If you have a child with this condition, contact the local Tourette's Syndrome Association in your area for further information and help.

Possible Least-Restrictive Educational Setting: Children with mild forms of this disorder can easily be maintained in a regular educational setting with supportive services. Since the condition does affect performance in many cases, children with this disorder are usually classified as disabled and do receive special-education services, including modifications. More severe cases which do not respond to medication may require a more restrictive setting. Medication, counseling, and special-education services provide a good treatment plan. However, the child may have to try many medications before finding one that relieves the tics. Medications are also taken if Obsessive Compulsive Disorder (OCD) symptoms are associated.

Other Disorders of Childhood and Adolescence

Functional Encopresis

Description: The major symptom of this disorder is repeated involuntary or intentional passage of feces into clothing or other places deemed inappropriate. The condition is not related to any physical condition, must occur for a period of six months on a regular basis, and be present in a child over the age of 4 for diagnosis to take place.

Educational Implications: Your child may experience social ridicule if the occurrences take place in school. The teacher needs to be sensitive to the condition and involve the school psychologist who in turn will contact you. If you suspect this disorder is going on at home, try to intervene as quickly as possible to avoid further embarrassment for your child or secondary complications (such as avoidance).

Possible Least-Restrictive Educational Setting: Your child should have no problem maintaining a regular educational setting unless the condition is associated with other disabilities which require special education placement. However, this condition may create social pressures and isolation for your child.

Functional Enuresis

Description: This disorder is characterized by repeated involuntary intentional elimination of urine during the day or night into bed or clothes at an age which bladder control is expected. A frequency of at least two times per month must be present for the condition to be diagnosed between the ages of five and six and at least once a month for older children.

Educational Implications: This condition may create social pressures and isolation for your child while in school. Social intimidation and ridicule may occur if other children notice the problem. If this occurs, your child may avoid school or begin to suffer physical complaints in the morning, such as stomach pains, in an attempt to ward off impending problems at school.

Possible Least-Restrictive Educational Setting: Children with this condition should have no problem maintaining a regular educational setting unless the condition is associated with other disabilities which require special-education placement.

Elective Mutism

Description: This disorder is characterized by persistent refusal to talk in one or more major social situations, including school, despite the ability to comprehend spoken language and speak. The resistance to speak is not a symptom of any other major disorder.

Educational Implications: If your child has this condition it may create a difficult situation for his/her classroom teacher. The teacher will not be able to measure certain language or social levels, will have to deal with social concerns and comments from classmates, and have a difficult time encouraging your child to participate in necessary class activities or group projects. Individual and family counseling is highly suggested for such a disorder.

Possible Least-Restrictive Educational Setting: Your child can usually be maintained in the regular educational setting as long as he/she maintains sufficient performance levels. However, if your child's academic performance becomes discrepant, and/or social and intellectual factors interfere with performance, then a more restrictive placement may have to be explored.

Anxiety Disorders

Obsessive-Compulsive Disorder

Description: The major characteristics associated with this disorder are persistent obsessions (persistent thoughts) or compulsions (repetitive acts), that significantly interfere with the individual's normal daily social, educational, occupational, or environmental routines.

Educational Implications: Children or adolescents with this disorder will have difficulty concentrating and maintaining consistent academic performance. If your child has this disorder he/she may also experience depression as a result of difficulties and medication may be instituted to relieve the anxiety associated with this disorder.

Possible Least-Restrictive Educational Setting: Your child can usually be maintained in the regular educational setting as long as your child maintains sufficient performance levels. However, if your child's academic performance becomes discrepant, and/or social and intellectual factors interfere in performance, then a more restrictive placement may have to be explored.

Mood Disorders

Dysthymia

Description: The essential feature of this disturbance is a chronic disturbance of the individual's moods involving chronic depression or irritable mood for a period of one year for children and adolescents.

Educational Implications: If your child experiences this disorder, you will experience need to work closely with the teacher, school psychologist, or private therapist if your child is in treatment. You should also alert your child's teacher that medication may be involved and an understanding of the side effects should be discussed.

Possible Least-Restrictive Educational Setting: Your child can usually be maintained in either a regular setting or a more restrictive special-education program, if the symptoms become more intense. The persistence of this disorder rather than the severity usually accounts for a mild or moderate impairment. Consequently, hospitalization is rare unless suicide is attempted.

Specific Personality Disorders

Schizoid Personality Disorder

Description: The child with this disorder exhibits a restrictive range of emotional experiences and expression and indifference to social situations.

Educational Implications: In the classroom your child may be considered unapproachable. He/she will be resistant to group projects or group experiences. If your child is involved, he/she may remain on the outside and not participate in discussions. Other children may eventually ostracize your child. The teacher will also have a very difficult time establishing any meaningful relationship with your child. Therapy and/or medication may be suggested by an outside professional or agency.

Least-Restrictive Educational Setting: Your child may eventually wind up in a special-education setting. However, some remain in the normal mainstream because their academic performance is sufficient but are viewed as "loners" by their classmates.

Antisocial Personality Disorder

Description: This disorder is characterized by a pattern of irresponsible and antisocial behavior. The condition is usually first seen in childhood or early adolescence and continues throughout the child's development. This diagnosis is usually made after the age of 18 and the individual must have had a history of symptoms before the age of 15 indicative of a conduct disorder. If treatment has not been involved up to this point you certainly should try to get your child into either psychotherapy or some type of out-patient program.

Educational Implications: The situation for the classroom teacher can be serious with this type of disorder. Since your child may have little or no regard for the personal rights of others, any antisocial act can occur, even ones that may place the teacher in danger. Medication may help reduce tension while therapy may have limited success.

Possible Least-Restrictive Educational Setting: If your child has this disorder he/she may have aged out and may no longer be part of the educational system. However, if already classified as disabled, he/she would probably be placed in a very restrictive educational setting until the age of 21.

Borderline Personality Disorder

Description: The main features of this disorder include instability of self-image, inconsistent and unfulfilling interpersonal relationships, instability of mood, and persistent identity disturbance (lacking a sense of self, values, goals, and so on).

Educational Implications: In the classroom your child may have a hard time maintaining any consistent academic performance. Frequent outbursts, truancy, hospitalization, legal problems, or school disciplinary actions may provide an inconsistent pattern of attendance and involvement.

Possible Least-Restrictive Educational Setting: Be aware that your child may be placed in a more restrictive special-education setting, hospital program, or institution.

Passive-Aggressive Personality Disorder

Description: Individuals with this disorder exhibit a pervasive pattern of passive resistance to the requests or requirements placed upon them in school, and in their social or occupational venues.

Educational Implications: If your child has this disorder, his/her teachers will find that working with him/her can be very frustrating. He/she may become irritable, sulky, or argumentative, and often blame external causes for his/her lack of production. Assignments may have to be readjusted so that some sense of accomplishment can be obtained. Counseling is strongly suggested.

Possible Least-Restrictive Educational Setting: If your child suffers from this disorder he/she can usually be educated within the normal setting unless he/she exhibits a pattern of constant underachievement. In some cases where the discrepancy becomes significant, a referral for a more restrictive setting may be suggested. A history of severe academic discrepancy resulting from this disorder may result in your child being classified as emotionally disabled.

chapter ten

COMMON MEDICATION INFORMATION

There may be times when a doctor will prescribe or recommend medication. While it is not important to possess a deep knowledge of medications, it is important to understand the nature, reason for its use, and possible side effects which occur. When a child is on medication, it is also helpful to the medical doctor to receive observational reports on the child's reaction to the medication during school and at home. The side effects mentioned do not include all possible conditions to the medication. The more common ones which might be observed in the classroom and at home will be noted. With this in mind this chapter will present information on medications used for special disorders such as Tourette's Syndrome and medications listed by category such as antidepressants.

Medications Used for Specific Disorders

Attention-Deficit/Hyperactivity Disorder

Psychostimulants: These medications have been referred to as paradoxical because they act in the reverse. These are stimulant medications but when used with certain disorders act in the reverse and calm the child down. The main purpose of these medications is to increase attention to task and alertness by either releasing the neurotransmitter *norepinephrine* in the cases of Ritalin®, Cylert®, and Dexedrine®, or brain stimulation as in the case of Pondimin®. These characteristics are usually not present in the behavior of ADHD children who appear to exhibit restlessness, impulsivity, distractibility, and inattention.

Ritalin (methylphenidate)

Ritalin is a mild stimulant that acts upon the central nervous system and is widely prescribed in cases of ADHD. This medication is usually part of a total treatment plan which may also include individual counseling, family counseling, educational intervention, and social behavior modification.

The more common possible side effects may include loss of appetite, nervousness, difficulties sleeping, abdominal pains, and weight loss. Ritalin is usually taken 30–45 minutes before meals and also comes in a sustained or time-release tablet.

Caution is noted in the prescription of this medication when there is a history of Tourette's Syndrome in the family, when the individual is already experiencing a tic disorder, or when there may be a possibility of glaucoma.

Cylert (pemoline)

Cylert is usually taken once a day in the morning and some common side effects may include drowsiness, dizziness, insomnia, headaches, irritability, tics, nausea, yellowing of skin and eyes, and weight loss.

Children who are on Cylert for extended periods of time need to be carefully monitored because it can stunt growth and may affect the kidneys and liver.

Dexedrine (dextroamphetamine)

This medication is available in liquid as well as tablet form and sustained release tablets. It is usually prescribed as part of the treatment plan for children with ADHD, in cases of narcolepsy (unusual number of sleep episodes during the day), and obesity. Possible side effects may include irritability, excessive restlessness, difficulties sleeping, agitation, dry mouth, and may aggravate any tendency that an individual may have towards tics.

This medication is usually taken in the morning because it may cause insomnia. Close monitoring should be done because of the possibility of the medication affecting the child's growth. Unlike Cylert which is rarely prescribed under the age of six, Dexedrine is prescribed for children as young as three years of age.

Other psychostimulants include *Pondimin* and *Prozac*.

Psychosis

Antipsychotic Medication: These medications work by blocking one of the chemical messengers of the central nervous system, *dopamine*. These drugs are sometimes referred to as neuroleptic drugs because they block the dopamine receptors in the brain and correct the imbalance of nerve transmissions associated with psychotic behaviors.

Neuroleptic drugs should be considered very powerful and as a result pose potential risks. Careful monitoring is required and withdrawal symptoms such as headaches, nausea, dizziness, and increased heart rate may occur if abruptly stopped. It should also be noted that alcohol consumption during the time the individual is on these medications may enhance the effects of the drug and increase the risk of depression.

Haldol (haloperidol)

Haldol is frequently prescribed to treat the psychotic behaviors associated with schizophrenia. It is also prescribed for children with oppositional behavior or combative behavior patterns, hyperactivity, and tic disorders.

Some common side effects may include coughing, anxiety, blurred vision, chewing movements, dry mouth, dizziness, drowsiness, lack of muscular coordination, physical rigidity, stupor, and protruding tongue. Withdrawal symptoms may include muscle spasms and twitches.

Mellaril (thioridazine)

Mellaril is commonly used to treat psychotic disorders, depression, and anxiety in adults. It is also used to treat behavior problems in children and panic disorders in the elderly. As with Thorazine, *tardive dyskinesia* (a condition marked by involuntary muscle spasms and twitches in the face and body) may be a side effect.

Some common side effects that may be observed in the classroom include *hypokenesis*, an abnormal lack of movement, muscle rigidity, blurred vision, chewing movements, dry mouth, eye spasms, fixed gaze, and swelling in the throat.

Navane (thiothixene)

Like most neuroleptics, Navane works by lowering levels of dopamine in the brain. Excessive levels of dopamine are associated with a severe sense of distorted reality typical of psychotic disorders.

Some common side effects may include coughing, anxiety, blurred vision, chewing movements, dry mouth, dizziness, drowsiness, lightheadedness, puffing of cheeks, seizures, sensitivity to light, and restlessness.

Navane has been known to mask symptoms of brain tumors and intestinal obstructions. Consequently, close monitoring is important.

Prolixin (fluphenazine)

Prolixin is a neuroleptic medication that is used to reduce the symptoms associated with psychotic disorders such as schizophrenia. Prolixin may also cause tardive dyskinesia and should never be taken with alcohol.

Common side effects may include muscle rigidity, blurred vision, chewing movements, complete loss of movement, dizziness, drowsiness, fixed gaze, muscle spasms, puckering of mouth, twitching, and yellowing of the skin and eyes.

Stelazine (trifluoperazine)

Stelazine is a medication that is used to reduce the symptoms associated with psychotic disorders such as schizophrenia. While not the medication of choice, Stelazine is sometimes used to treat anxiety that does not respond to ordinary tranquilizers. As with most neuroleptics, Stelazine may cause tardive dyskinesia and should not be taken with alcohol.

Some common side effects may include coughing, anxiety, blurred vision, chewing movements, dry mouth, dizziness, drowsiness, lack of muscular coordination, physical rigidity, stupor, and protruding tongue.

Stelazine is usually not prescribed if the individual has liver problems, is already taking central nervous system depressants, or is suffering from blood conditions (consult your physician for specific types of blood conditions).

Thorazine (chlorpromazine)

Thorazine is a medication that is used to reduce the symptoms associated with psychotic disorders such as schizophrenia. During treatment with Thorazine, individuals may experience a condition marked by involuntary muscle spasms and twitches in the face and body called tardive dyskinesia. This may be a chronic condition.

Some possible side effects of Thorazine may include chewing movements, difficulty breathing, drooling, difficulty swallowing, eye problems observed as a fixed gaze, and twitching in the body.

Trilafon (perphenazine)

Trilafon is used to reduce severe anxiety associated with psychotic disorders and to reduce the symptoms of hallucinations and delusions. Common side effects include drowsiness, tardive dyskinesia, and dry mouth.

Other antipsychotic medications may include: *Serentil, Moban, Loxitane, Compazine, Orap,* and *Clozaril.*

Tourette's Syndrome

Tourette's syndrome is a disorder characterized by motor and vocal tics which may be exhibited in the form of grunting, coughs, barks, touching, knee jerking, drastic head movements, head banging, squatting, and so on. A variety of medications are used to reduce the symptoms which can be so severe at times that they may be mistaken for seizures. With many patients, one medication may be given for the tics, and one for the symptoms of OCD or obsessive compulsive disorder, while still other medications may be given to reduce the side effects of those already administered. The more common medications used to treat this disorder include the following.

Orap (pimozide)

Orap is an oral medication that is usually prescribed with Haldol, a primary choice medication. Orap reduces the intensity of physical and verbal tics, jerking motions, twitches, and verbally bizarre outbursts. This medication should only be used when the tics are so severe that it hampers the individual's ability to function.

Some side effects may include increase in appetite, blurred vision, trembling of hands, drooling, dizziness, changes in handwriting, loss of movement, swelling around the eyes, and excessive thirst.

Catapres (clonidine)

Catapres is usually prescribed for high blood pressure but has been used with Tourette's Syndrome as well. The more common side effects include dry mouth, skin reactions, dizziness, and drowsiness.

Haldol (haloperidol)

Haldol is a widely used medication to suppress the symptoms associated with Tourette's Syndrome.

Depression

Antidepressants: These drugs affect the symptoms associated with depression by adjusting the levels of neurotransmiters in the brain such as *dopamine, serotonin,* and *epinephrine.* These medications are usually prescribed when the treatment of the condition is considered long term. Doctors do not usually like to use such powerful tricyclic antidepressants for short-term or transitory depression.

These medications tend to elevate the individual's mood, improve sleep patterns, increase energy levels and physical activity, and restore perception to a more positive level.

In the case of some antidepressants, once the doctor feels comfortable with the levels of medication attained, he/she may prescribe a single dose at night, a practice called *night-loading.*

Elavil or Endep (amitriptyline hydrochloride)

Elavil (other brand name, Endep) is usually prescribed for the relief of severe mental depression. Some possible side effects may include abnormal movements, speech difficulties, dry mouth, lightheadedness, fatigue, fainting, hallucinations, insomnia, loss of coordination, tingling, and pins and needles.

Tofranil or Janimine (imipramine)

Tofranil (other brand name, Janimine) is a commonly used tricyclic antidepressant. It is also used to treat *enuresis,* bedwetting, on a short-term basis. It is a powerful medication that needs to be monitored closely. It is usually not prescribed for individuals who are already on MAO inhibitors (*monoamineoxidase*) or antidepressants such as Nardil or Parnate.

Some common side effects may include sensitivity to light, abdominal cramps, frequent urination, agitation, sore throat, fatigue, loss of appetite, nausea, insomnia, and inflammation of the mouth. It is not usually administered to children under the age of 6.

Norpramin (desipramine)

Norpramin is prescribed for the relief of symptoms associated with severe mental depression such as the inability to fall asleep, inability to concentrate, loss of appetite, feelings of despondency, low energy levels, and feelings of helplessness.

Some common side effects may include black tongue, red, black, or blue spots on the tongue, sensitivity to light, abdominal cramps, frequent urination, agitation, sore throat, fatigue, loss of appetite, nausea, insomnia, and inflammation of the mouth.

Pamelor (nortriptyline)

Pamelor seems to be more successful with *endogenous depression*, depression resulting from physical causes within the body.

This medication is never prescribed if the individual is already taking a MAO inhibitor such as Nardil, Parnate, or Marplan because high fevers, convulsions, and death have occurred with this combination of medications.

Some common side effects may include black tongue, red, black, or blue spots on the tongue, sensitivity to light, abdominal cramps, frequent urination, agitation, sore throat, fatigue, loss of appetite, perspiration, ringing in the ears, nausea, insomnia, and inflammation of the mouth.

Prozac (fluoxetine)

Prozac is a very popular medication that is prescribed for the treatment of long-term depression that has impaired the individual's ability to function on a daily basis. Prozac should never be taken with any MAO inhibitor because of serious complications.

Some possible side effects may include convulsions, dilation of pupils, dimness of vision, ear pain, eye pain, hostility, irrational ideas, and vague feelings of body discomfort.

Other tricyclic antidepressants include: *Sinequan, Adapin, Desyrel, Wellbutrin, Parnate, Vivactil, Surmontil, Asendin, Ludiomil, Marplan, Eutonyl, Elderyl,* and *Limbitrol.*

Anxiety or Panic Disorders

ANTIANXIETY AGENTS: These medications work by diminishing the activity parts of the brain, called the *limbic system*. The symptoms associated with anxiety may include tension, agitation, irritability, panic attacks, feelings of dying or going crazy. Physical symptoms include excessive sweating, heart palpitations, chills, fainting, racing pulse and flushes. Anxiety may be a disorder by itself or a component of other psychiatric disorders.

Valium (diazepam)

Perhaps one of the more widely used antianxiety medications, Valium is used in the short-term treatment of the symptoms associated with anxiety. This medication is also prescribed in the treatment of acute alcohol withdrawal, as a muscle relaxant, and to treat along with other medications certain convulsive disorders. Valium belongs to a class of agents known as *benzodiazepines*.

Concerns about possible dependence need to be considered and close monitoring is suggested. Serious withdrawal symptoms may occur if the medication is stopped abruptly.

Side effects may include loss of muscle coordination, lightheadedness, and nausea.

Librium or Libretabs (chlordiazepoxide)

Librium (other brand name, Libretabs) is used in the short-term treatment of the symptoms associated with anxiety. This medication is also prescribed in the treatment of acute alcohol withdrawal and anxiety or apprehension before surgery.

As with Valium, concerns about possible dependence need to be considered and close monitoring is suggested. Serious withdrawal symptoms may occur if the medication is stopped abruptly.

Side effects may include confusion, drowsiness, and unsteadiness. Symptoms due to abrupt withdrawal may include convulsions, tremors, vomiting, muscle cramps, and sweating.

Xanax (alprazolam)

Xanax is a tranquilizer prescribed for the short-term treatment of symptoms associated with anxiety as well as panic disorders. This medication is also used to treat anxiety associated with depression. Xanax is considered a short-acting drug in that it acts quickly and unlike Valium leaves the body relatively quickly. Regardless of the nature and course of action, Xanax has a high dependency factor and should be closely monitored.

Some side effects may include dizziness, fainting, poor coordination, abnormal involuntary movement, agitation, confusion, dry mouth, and tremors.

Ativan (lozazepam)

Like Xanax, Ativan belongs to a group of drugs called benzodiazepines, is considered short-acting and enters and leaves the body rapidly. It is usually prescribed for short-term treatment, about four months, and produces the fewest cumulative effects of all the medications in this group. It is commonly prescribed with other antidepressive or antipsychotic medications in the treatment of other psychiatric disorders.

Use should taper off slowly since rapid stoppage may result in irritability, insomnia, convulsions, depressed mood, and tremors. Other antianxiety agents include Buspar, Catapres, Inderal, Tranxene, Centrax, Paxipam, and Serax.

In conclusion, while medication can be a positive influence for your child in terms of reducing negative and stressful symptoms, monitoring by a trained professional is crucial. You should never administer an extra dosage or reduce the amount given to your child without consultation. If you have a child who is on medication you will need to inform the school nurse so that he/she will have the information on file in case of an emergency or bad reaction to the medication.

Medications by Category

Psychostimulants

Psychostimulants have been around for a long time. These drugs tend to stimulate the nervous system and increase certain chemical levels of the brain thereby affecting mood and state of mind. Since many psychostimulants may have dependent liabilities, they may be used as a secondary medication to antidepressants. However some (such as *methylphenidate* and *pemoline*) still play a role in the treatment of childhood/adolescent behavior problems. Usually, psychostimulants may not be used in children under the age of twelve, except under medical supervision. Some of these drugs may lose their effectiveness within a few weeks and when this occurs, you should stop using these drugs and consult your physician. Do not increase the dosage. Examples include:

Medication	Generic Name
1. Amphedroxyn	methamphetamine
2. Benzedrine	amphetamine
3. Biphetamine	amphetamine+dextroamphetamine
4. Cylert	pemoline
5. Deaner	deanol
6. Desoxyn	methamphetamine
7. Dexedrine	dextroamphetamine
8. Pondimin	fenfluramine
9. Ritalin	methylphenidate

Sedatives/Hypnotics

These drugs are used to reduce pain and are not drugs used to hypnotize people. Sedatives should always be used carefully with children. Some children may experience side effects including irritability, excitability, tearfulness, or aggression. One of the major concerns associated with these drugs is related to their continued use since, over time, your body may develop a tolerance. When this occurs the drug becomes less effective and some people tend to increase the dosage, a practice that can lead to dependency. Examples of these drugs include:

Medication	Generic Name
1. Alurate	aprobarbital
2. Amytal	amobarbital
3. Dalmane	flurazepam
4. Doral	quazepam
5. Doriden	gluthimide
6. Halcion	triazolam
7. Mebaral	mephobarbital
8. Nembutal	pentobarbital
9. Noludar	methyprylon
10. Nortec	chloralhydrate
11. Paral	paraldehyde
12. Placidyl	ethchlorvynol
13. ProSom	estazolam
14. Quaalude	methaqualone
15. Restoril	temazepam
16. Seconal	secobarbital
17. Solfoton	phenobarbital
18. Tuinal	secobarbital+amobarbital

Antipsychotic Medications

These medications work by blocking one of the chemical messengers of the central nervous system: dopamine. These drugs are sometimes referred to as neuroleptic drugs because they block the dopamine receptors in the brain and restore the imbalance of nerve transmissions associated with psychotic behaviors.

Neuroleptic drugs should be considered very powerful and as a result pose potential risks. Careful monitoring is required and withdrawal symptoms such as headaches, nausea, dizziness, and increased heart rate may occur if abruptly stopped. It should also be noted that alcohol consumption during the time the individual is on these medications may enhance the effects of the drug and increase the risk of depression.

Medication	Generic Name
1. Clozaril	clozapine
2. Compazine	prochlorperazine
3. Daxoline	loxapine
4. Etrafon	perphenazine+amitriptyline
5. Haldol	haloperidol
6. Inapsine	droperidol
7. Loxitane	loxapine
8. Mellaril	thioridazine
9. Moban	molindone
10. Navane	thiothixene
11. Orap	pimozide
12. Orazine	chlorpromazine
13. Permitil	fluphenazine
14. Prolixin	fluphenazine
15. Serentil	mesoridazine
16. Serpasil	reserpine
17. Sparine	promazine
18. Stelazine	trifluoperazine
19. Thorazine	chlorpromazine
20. Tindal	acetophenazine
21. Triavil	perphenazine+amitriptyline
22. Trilafon	perphenazine
23. Vesprin	triflupromazine

Antidepressant Medications

Sometimes referred to as tricyclic drugs, these drugs affect the symptoms associated with depression by adjusting the levels of neurotransmiters in the brain such as dopamine, serotonin, and epinephrine. These medications are usually prescribed when the treatment of the condition is considered long term. Doctors do not usually like to use such powerful tricyclic antidepressants for short-term or transitory depression.

These medications tend to elevate the individual's mood, improve sleep patterns, increase energy levels and physical activity, and restore perception to a more positive level.

In the case of some antidepressants, once the doctor feels comfortable with the levels of medication attained, he/she may prescribe a single dose at night, a practice called *night-loading*.

Medication	**Generic Name**
1. Adapin	doxepin
2. Anafranil	clomipramine
3. Asendin	amoxapine
4. Aventyl	nortriptyline
5. Desyrel	trazadone
6. Elavil	amitriptyline hydrochloride
7. Endep	amitriptyline
8. Etrafon	perphenazine+amitriptyline
9. Janimine	imipramine
10. Limbitrol	chlordiazepoxide+amitriptyline
11. Ludiomil	maprotiline
12. Marplan	isocarboxazid
13. Nardil	phenelzine
14. Norpramin	desipramine
15. Pamelor	nortriptyline
16. Pertofrane	desipramine
17. Parnate	tranylcypromine
18. Prozac	fluoxetine
19. Sinequan	doxepin
20. Surmontil	trimipramine
21. Tofranil	imipramine
22. Vivactil	protriptyline
23. Wellbutrin	buproprion
24. Zoloft	sertraline

Antianxiety Medications

These medications work by diminishing the activity of certain parts of the brain, called the limbic system. The symptoms associated with anxiety may include tension, agitation, irritability, panic attacks, feelings of dying or going crazy. Physical symptoms include excessive sweating, heart palpitations, chills, fainting, racing pulse, and flushes. Anxiety may be a disorder by itself or a component of other psychiatric disorders.

Medication	Generic Name
1. Atarax	hydroxyzine
2. Ativan	lozazepam
3. BuSpar	buspirone
4. Catapres	clonidine
5. Centrax	prazepam
6. Corgard	nadolol
7. Dalmane	flurazepam
8. Deprol	meprobamate+benactyzine
9. Doral	quezepam
10. Equanil	meprobamate
11. Halcion	triazolam
12. Klonopin	clonazepam
13. Inderal	propranolol
14. Librium	chlordiazepoxide
15. Libritabs	chlordiazepoxide
16. Lopressor	metoprolol
17. Miltown	meprobamate
18. Paxipam	halazepam
19. Restoril	temazepam
20. Serax	oxazepam
21. Tenormin	atenolol
22. Tranxene	chlorazepate
23. Transcopal	chlormezanone
24. Valium	diazepam
25. Valrelease	diazepam
26. Vistaril	hydroxyzine
27. Xanax	alprazolam

Anticonvulsive Medications

Medication	Generic Name
1. Amytal	amobarbitol
2. Anxanil	amobarbitol
3. Celontin	methsuximide
4. Depakene	valproic acid
5. Depakote	divalproex
6. Diamox	acetazolamide
7. Dilantin	phenytoin
8. Gemonil	methobarbital
9. Klonopin	clonazepam
10. Mebaral	mephobarbital
11. Mesantoin	mephenytoin
12. Milontin	phensuximide
13. Myidol	primidone
14. Mysoline	primidone
15. Nebutal	pentobarbital
16. Peganone	ethosuximide
17. Phenurone	phenacemide
18. Seconal	secobarbital
19. Tegretol	carbamazepine
20. Tridione	trimethadione
21. Tranxene	chlorazepate
22. Valium	diazepam
23. Zarontin	ethosuximide

chapter eleven

PRACTICAL PARENTING SUGGESTIONS

How You Can Help Your Children With Homework

Every night in millions of homes across the country you can imagine the scenario being played out. It depicts the age-old problem of homework. The scene may have different characters, but the script is usually the same. Parents have always attempted to work with their children on homework. This help ranges from a short occasional explanation to total completion of the task by the parent. Whatever the case, numerous problems exist. In an attempt to cope, you may use trial-and-error methods, bribery, threats, reasoning, and anything else that may appear to work.

There seems to be little doubt that your motives are genuine. Who could find fault with the motive of concern? However, it is not the motive that creates the anxiety and tension for both you and your child, but the techniques employed.

For some children, school can be a rather stressful place. When one takes into account work demands, social pressures, concern over parental approval, fear of failure, and so much more, children may need the home as a haven to unwind. If they encounter stress in the form of parental agitation during homework, then where can one "hang one's hat?" For those of us who work, it might be comparable to working all day at a job that has its share of stresses and coming home to a tense environment. Think of how long you might be able to handle such a situation. Also keep in mind the alternatives that we have as adults if the pressure gets to be too great. Children do not have the same options.

The following techniques are provided to facilitate the process of homework and prevent frustration, anger, and disappointment.

1. **Try to set up a homework schedule**. Many children would benefit from a set homework schedule. For some children, the responsibility of deciding when to sit down and do homework is too difficult. Children may decide to do their homework after school or after dinner. This is a personal choice and has to do with *learning style*. However, once the time is determined, the schedule should be adhered to as realistically as possible. This will also relieve the problem of having to "hunt down" or "corral" children in order to get them to do their homework. After a while, this will become a natural part of their schedule. It should be noted that during this time no interruptions should be allowed. Phone calls, TV, and everything else can wait until the time is up.

2. **Prioritize assignments**. For some children, the decision about what to do first becomes a major chore. They may dwell over this choice for a long period of time. Some children use *horizontal perspective*. This occurs when everything takes on the same level of importance and no priority is seen.

   Suggest which assignment to do first. Many children tend to use a *quantity orientation* (number of assignments left) rather than a *qualitative orientation* (difficulty of assignment). This means that if they have five things to do, have them finish the four easy ones first. In their eyes, they have only one assignment left even though it may be a more difficult task.

3. **Avoid sitting next to your child while he/she does homework**. This is usually a very big problem for some parents. Parents employing this technique are not only setting themselves up for tremendous frustration and anger, but are also creating *learned helplessness*.

   Many parents will say that their children cannot work unless they are sitting next to them. It is not that many children are unable to work, they choose not to work. The work stoppage on the part of children occurs when a parent attempts to break away and no longer affords them undivided attention. This "dependency" is very unhealthy because it is not imitated in the classroom. Consequently, such children may procrastinate in doing classwork, bringing the unfinished work home. In this way they may gain mommy or daddy's full attention. After a hard day's work, parents are tired and the thought of sitting down with children for up to three hours doing homework can only lead to problems.

   If you are already locked into this type of situation, you should not break away all at once. You should *desensitize* children a little at a time. Sit at the end of the table for a few days. Then slowly increase the distance between yourself and the child's work until he/she is working alone.

4. **Check correct problems first**. Parents sometimes have a habit of zeroing in on the incorrect problems first. Next time your child brings you a paper to check, mention to him/her how well he/she did on the correct problems, spelling words, and so on. For the ones that are incorrect say, "I bet if you go back and

check these over you may get a different answer." Now the child will go back and redo the problems without any animosity or feelings of inadequacy. If you were to zero in on the incorrect problems and become angry, there is a good chance that when the child returns to the work area he/she will be more involved in dealing with the loss of parental approval rather than finishing the task.

5. **Set reasonable homework periods**. Sometime you may allow your child to work on homework for several hours or until he or she finishes. This is fine if the performance of your child is consistent or the assignment realistically calls for such a commitment of time. However, in the event that your child is no further along in his performance after one or two hours than he/she was ten minutes into the assignment, the homework should be stopped. The only thing accomplished by allowing your child to linger on hour after hour with very little performance is increased feelings of inadequacy. You may choose to end the work period after a reasonable amount of time, and write the teacher a note explaining the circumstances. Such concerns can be worked out at a meeting with the teacher as well.

There may be several reasons for such a behavior pattern. First, your child may not have understood the concept in class and therefore will not be able to finish the assignment at home. Second, your child may already have feelings of helplessness, and may wait for you to complete the assignment. Third, your child may have serious learning difficulties, especially if this is a pattern, and may be overwhelmed by a series of assignments.

6. **Discuss homework questions before your child reads the chapter**. Most textbooks, except for the newer ones, have the chapter questions at the end. When this procedure occurs, your child may not be aware of what he/she should be looking for while reading. Discuss and talk about the questions before your child begins reading. By using this strategy, he/she will know what important information to look for in the chapter.

Some children have a tendency of trying to remember everything. You may want to give your child a pencil and suggest that he/she lightly note a passage or word that sounds like something in one of the questions. This will help children when they have to skim back over the many pages in the chapter.

7. **Check small groups of problems at a time**. Many children benefit from immediate gratification. Have your child do five problems and then come back to you for checking. Zero in on the correct ones and after they are checked send the child back to do the next group. In this way the child gets immediate feedback and approval and the necessary motivation for the next assignment. Also, if your child is doing the assignment incorrectly, the error can be detected and explained, preventing the child from having to redo the entire assignment.

8. **Place textbook chapters on tape**. Research indicates that the more sensory input children receive, the greater the chance the information will be retained. Therefore, tape record some science or social studies chapters so that children

can listen while they read along. This will allow both *auditory and visual input* of information. From time to time you may want to add a joke, a song, or a message to keep the interest of the child.

9. **Darken page lines for children learning how to write**. Sometimes, when children are first learning how to write, they will experience problems with control. While this can be a normal developmental problem, it is suggested that you darken top and bottom lines so that the children have a reinforced boundary. This boundary can help maintain control and help them focus on letter formation. This technique can also be used for older children who have visual motor problems which are manifested in their handwriting.

10. **Check homework assignments at the end of the night**. Anxiety is exhibited by some children over the thought of possibly bringing incorrect homework to school. Therefore, it is very important for you to take time each night to check homework. This offers children a feeling of accomplishment, a source of positive attention, and a sense of security that the work is correct. This sense of academic security may carry over to the classroom and offer your child a greater sense of confidence with classwork. However, if it is clear that your child does not understand a particular concept, the teacher should be made aware of it.

11. **Be aware of negative nonverbal messages**. Nonverbal communication is a large part of overall communication. Since this is possible, many messages, especially negative ones, can be communicated easily without your awareness. Grimaces, body stiffness, sighs, raised eyebrows, and other types of body language are all nonverbal responses. If children are sensitive, they will pick up these messages which can only add to the tension of the homework relationship. This is extremely important with younger children who cannot distinguish between loss of parental approval and loss of love. Such a state can only add stress to their ability to perform.

12. **Avoid finishing assignments for your child**. Some parents will complete an entire assignment for their children. While the motivation may be to help finish a difficult assignment, the end result may be very destructive. Children tend to feel inadequate when a parent finishes homework. First, they feel a sense of failure. Second, they feel a sense of inadequacy since they can never hope to do the assignment as well. This can only foster increased dependency and feelings of helplessness on the part of children.

     If children cannot complete an assignment, and they have honestly tried, write the teacher a note explaining the circumstances. Most teachers will understand the situation.

To recap, before you sit down to work with your children, please make sure that they are not exhibiting symptoms which may reflect more serious concerns. When parents attempt to work with children who have severe learning problems or a high tension level they may be faced with tremendous frustration, anger, and disappointment. Following basic guidelines when helping with homework can result in a more rewarding situation for both parents and children.

How You Can Use Effective Discipline

Many parents find the use of discipline and reward very difficult. What makes it difficult is your confusion over what is either too strict or too lenient. The added pressure of confrontation with its built-in unpopularity further adds to this discomfort. Certain techniques and attitudes are basic when it comes to this area of child rearing. It is very important that you develop a healthy mental set about this area so you can be realistic, consistent, and supportive. The following techniques are offered as "tools." Not all these techniques may work for all people, and some may take several tries before results are observed. However, the following tools may represent conservation of energy and reduce the possibility of "parent burnout."

1. **Necessary limits and guidelines for a child's emotional development**. For children, limits and guidelines represent a "safety net" within which they can behave. Children will know that any act of poor judgment will be brought to their attention if limits are well defined. Consequently, they will be led back to the safety net. If children are not bound by well-defined limits, then there is no buffer between them and the outside world. The result may be a high level of tension and frequent inappropriate behavior.

2. **All behavior must have a consequence**. This means appropriate behavior is rewarded and negative behavior punished. However, the consistency of such rewards and punishments from day to day is also crucial. Consistency of consequence, whether reward or punishment, will aid the child in developing a frame of reference.

3. **Rewards need not be monetary**. Although this is one possibility, rewards can also be verbal praise, written notes of thanks, extended playtime or bedtime, and so on. They should be natural and not mechanical. Variety is also nice in dealing with rewards.

4. **Punishment only will not be effective in changing negative behavior**. Punishment tells your child what not to do, but rewards tell him/her what behavior is acceptable. If long-term changes in behavior are desired, then reward must be included. You may tend to shy away from rewards because you feel that doing what is expected should not be rewarded. However, all human beings need positive stroking regardless of whether or not the behavior is expected. Rewarding your child for cleaning a room without having been told to do so, reinforces the continuation of that behavior. This type of reward may come in the form of a positive comment of appreciation. This is not to say that every behavior should be verbally rewarded. The key to any system is discrimination.

5. **Limit punishments to something that you can control**. Quantity is not always important. For very young children with no concept of time, 5 minutes in a "time out" chair (controllable) rather than 50 minutes (uncontrollable) is just as good. On the other hand, delaying a teenager's departure for two hours on a Friday or Saturday night can be just as effective and more easily controlled than being grounded for a week. The most important thing to remember with disci-

pline is that the parent begin it and end it. Maintaining both boundaries is crucial. Consequently, parents should avoid very harsh (you are grounded till you get married) punishments. This will only confuse children and distort their frame of reference. Even worse, you will most likely be the one punished if long unrealistic consequences are chosen.

6. **Never trade a punishment for a reward**. If children do something inappropriate and then something appropriate, the two incidents should be treated separately. You may want to say that while you appreciate their appropriate behavior and feel good about their choice, the poor judgment they have shown with the other incident cannot be overlooked. If you begin to trade off, your child will learn to avoid punishment merely by doing something appropriate.

7. **Try to project a united front when using discipline.** If one parent should disagree with the other's tactics or reasoning, discuss it at a private moment. Open disagreement concerning a disciplinary action can sometimes confuse children and place them in the uncomfortable position of having to choose between parents.

8. **Focus on the inappropriate behavior, not the personality**. Remember, your child is not stupid, his/her inappropriate behavior is unacceptable. You may want to use phrases such as "poor judgment, inappropriate behavior" when confronting the act. Focusing on the act allows children to save face. It may also allow them to better understand and accept more appropriate options for the next time. Children who grow up in a home where personalities are attacked tend to model that behavior in their social relationships. They tend to be less tolerant and more critical of their peers.

9. **Choose your battlegrounds wisely.** Try to view energy like money. In this way you will be deciding whether an issue is worth a $2 or $200 investment. Overinvesting can only lead to parent burnout.

   Sit down with each other and discuss what you feel are the more important issues. As long as your child is not verbally abusive or destructive, statements of frustration or healthy anger should be tolerated. However, if these statements become loudly vocalized to the point of screaming at the "top of their lungs," then limits must be set and he/she should be taught more appropriate ways of venting feelings. It is very destructive to allow your child to use verbal abuse in any form because you may feel that they must be allowed to vent feelings. For the purposes of this particular section, verbal abuse should be defined as any verbal act directed at the parent using cursing, vulgar comments or attacks (jerk, idiot, and so on). There are healthy ways to communicate anger rather than verbal abuse.

10. **Never allow temper tantrums an audience**. Children will sometimes choose the most inopportune place to throw a tantrum, such as a supermarket, visiting a relative's house, and so on. Regardless of the location, you should not allow them control of the situation. Removal from the audience is crucial.

    Further, the more you try to reason with your child when he/she is in this state, the more control you are relinquishing. Tell your child that you will be more than happy to discuss his/her concerns when the tantrum is over. But remember, no audience. Removal to a room, a car, or some isolated area may be necessary.

When your child is in a more rational state, teach him/her other ways to discuss concerns. Further inform him/her that if a tantrum is chosen rather than communication, there will be a consequence. Remember to reward any behavior that approaches verbal communication.

11. **Try not to conceal problems with children from the other parent**. Some parents will choose this direction to "protect" children. You may actually increase your child's anxiety level if this approach is used. Children tend to lose a frame of reference in regard to the other parent when it comes to anger. The message is that the other parents should be feared. If many incidents are held back, children begin to ponder the other parent's reaction if he/she should find out. This fantasy fear may increase internal tension and preoccupy their minds with unbiased fears.

In most cases, it is better for your child to gain a sense of reality rather than fantasize what might happen. The only exception occurs when one parent is prone to violence and abuse. In this case, such protection is a form of survival.

12. **Try not to relinquish power to your spouse**. Relinquishing power—"Wait until Daddy gets home"—gives off a very negative message to children. It implies that you cannot control the situation. What may be the real issue is that you have run out of techniques and are feeling frustrated. If this is the case delay dealing with your children. Send them to their rooms and tell them that you will deal with this later. Regroup your own control rather than pass it off to the other parent. Further, relinquishing power tends to reduce your feelings of self-esteem.

13. **Try to use a forced choice technique whenever possible**. Choose two options that are both acceptable to you. Then, say to children, "You may do . . . or . . . Which do you prefer?" This technique is more realistic than an open-ended "What would you like to do?" In this case you may either get no response or one that is not acceptable to you. Using a forced-choice technique allows children to feel that they are making the decision. Either choice will be acceptable. If children reply, "Neither" remind them that "Neither" is not an option and they may only choose either of the two presented. Usually after a few minutes of testing most children will make a choice.

14. **Don't be afraid to delay a consequence when you are very angry**. The use of delay allows for a different perspective than that viewed at the height of anger. There is nothing wrong with saying, "I am so angry right now that I don't want to deal with this situation. Go to your room and I'll deal with you in 15 minutes." The use of delay will also reduce impractical consequences.

In conclusion, be aware that parenting is not a popularity contest but a responsibility. The opportunity to select from a variety of tools when confronted with a positive or negative situation can only enhance the difficult but rewarding job of child rearing.

How to Communicate Better with Your Children

Communication is one of the major factors behind any good relationship, whether between boyfriend and girlfriend, husband and wife, or parents and children. However, many parents are at a loss when it comes to communicating with their children. What may start out as communication may wind up as a lecture, argument, or worse.

Communication comes in many forms and knowledge of certain techniques can greatly enhance a relationship. The following guidelines should be kept in mind to allow positive interaction with children.

1. **Communication is a two-way street**. The technique of "I'll talk and you listen and then you talk and I'll listen" is a first step and should be taught to children as soon as possible. Many people think they are communicating but in a sense they never listen. The technique of active listening is a first step in the development of communication skills.

2. **Try not to attack when communicating**. Communication will tend to deteriorate if either party feels they are being attacked. This feeling can come in many forms but the most usual way is through the use of the word "you." This word more than any other creates a defensive structure and interrupts the flow of communication. When communicating feelings, try using the words "I," "We," or "Me" as often as possible. Even if someone has done something to hurt you, focus on your feelings rather than the behavior. Inform the individual as to how the behavior affected you.

3. **Teach children to label feelings properly**. There are many times when the only difference between communication and an argument is the choice of words. Many arguments could be avoided if either party used more appropriate labels. The ability to label one's feelings is an important factor in communication. Nowhere is that more evident than in the case of children. Children may have a very hard time communicating because they lack experience in labeling their feelings. When children are unable to correctly label an internal feeling, it becomes trapped and the frustration may be become manifested in behavior problems, physical symptoms, and so on. When such feelings are manifested in these forms, they are usually misunderstood or misinterpreted. Therefore, it is crucial that you assist your children in correctly labeling a feeling or emotion. You may want to say for example, "While the feeling you are expressing sounds like anger, it is really frustration and frustration is. . . ." It is also helpful to have children develop an emotional vocabulary so that feelings and communication can flow more easily.

4. **Use connective discussion whenever possible**. Parents will often use direct communication such as, "Tell me what is wrong," "Tell me what you feel," or "Tell me why you did that." It is this line of questioning that has the least chance of obtaining a response from the child, since most children do not possess the labels or experiences in communication necessary for such an answer. What parents may want to use instead is *connective discussion*. This technique assumes

something and offers children reasonable labels for what they may be experiencing. For example, parents may say "It seems to me that you are feeling upset over your new baby brother. I think you may be feeling somewhat jealous because you feel he gets more attention than you." Another example may be to say, "I get the feeling from your behavior that you are trying to say something. I think what you may be trying to say is . . . ." If you are close you may observe some nonverbal reaction, an intense denial, crying, or some other similar response. At this point children should have an easier time expressing themselves since they have a foundation from which to work.

5. **Remember that all behavior has a trigger**. Sometimes this trigger may be unconscious and not available for identification. However, in many cases the trigger is conscious and the knowledge that an intense response will always follow some incident or feeling can be helpful. If parents can trace children's responses back to the source or trigger, they will have a very good chance of identifying the real problem. In fact, it may be good practice to have children do just that if they become upset or show inappropriate behavior. Ask them to think about what took place immediately prior to the behavior. If they cannot and you are aware of the problem, use connective discussion to make the bridge.

6. **Be aware of nonverbal misinterpretations**. Children are very prone to nonverbal misinterpretations. They may, for instance, misread the look on a parent's face and personalize it into something negative. This is very typical of younger children.

If parents are upset, angry, or frustrated with something other than their children, they should let them know that fact in a verbal way. You do not have to go into detail but merely say, "I am very upset right now with something. But I wanted to tell you that it has nothing to do with you and after I think for awhile we will get together."

This small piece of communication may prevent some very anxious moments for children.

7. **Use written communication whenever possible**. Another useful form of communication is writing. The use of writing to communicate feelings is an excellent tool in that it allows parents and children to phrase thoughts as desired for the best results. Notes thanking a child for some positive behavior are great. Notes telling children to have a nice day, that you love them very much, or you appreciate their cooperation are all examples of written communication.

Notes can also be used to register a complaint without nose-to-nose confrontation. This is nice to use when the issue at hand is not a major one.

Spontaneity with written communication is also a very nice message. Notes in a lunchbox, notebook, or slipped into a textbook are excellent. Discrimination with any technique is suggested.

8. **Try to use direct love as often as possible**. Many clients in therapy will often talk about the way their parents expressed love to them. The need to feel loved and cared for is a primary need for any individual at any age. Many of these clients as well as other adults with whom I have spoken, express the indirectness on the part of their parents when it came to communicating feelings of love and caring.

For instance, when asked the question, "How did you know your father or mother loved you?", some will respond by saying, "Because they used to take care of me when I was sick." Other responses included "bringing home things when I was good; being kept neat and clean, helping with homework." All these messages are fine except they all represent *indirect love*.

If indirect love is the only "game in town," then the individuals receiving it from parents must utilize interpretation and assumption. These individuals have all assumed the fact that because of "A," "B" must be true. Such a need for assumption when dealing with indirect messages of love can be dangerous. The same assumption can be made and is often made that such love is conditional. The individual assumes that illness, injury, and other situations are the conditions for love and caring.

Be aware of this factor and utilize as many direct messages of love as you can. Direct messages of love require no interpretation or assumption by children. Even teenagers, who on some verbal level will reject such expressions of love, need to hear it anyway. Direct messages include verbal statements like, "I am a very lucky parent to have a son/daughter like you." "You mean a great deal to me," or " There may be times when I am angry with you, but I want you to know I always love you." Don't assume your children know that you feel this way. Communicate to them directly.

Examples of Alternate Responses

Avoid	**Try**
Use of the word "you."	Use the words:
	"I," "Me," or "We"
"Tell me what you feel."	"I get the feeling that . . ."
	"It seems to me that . . ."
	"I get the feeling from your behavior that you are trying to say . . ."
"You listen to me."	"I'll talk and you listen and then you can talk and I'll listen."
"What would you like?"	"You can choose between ____ and ____. Which do you prefer?"
"Speak with me later."	"Let's get together in 10 minutes."
"Clean your room."	"Please clean your room and by clean I mean the following . . ."
"Be home early."	"Please be home between ____ and ____."
"I don't trust you . . ."	"Trust is not the issue. It's your sense of judgment that concerns me."
"You are grounded forever."	"I am so angry. I'll deal with you later."

Another very necessary and important example of *direct love* is through the use of physical demonstration of feelings. When dealing with children, demonstrating love by hugging, kissing, cuddling, holding, allowing them to sit on your lap, and other expressions should be an everyday part of communication. While not every adult has "learned ability" to use such direct messages, the absence of this form of communication in a parent-child relationship may have adverse effects for the child in later life.

The higher your *approachability factor*, the easier it is for children to express and show direct love to you. In later life, your child may have an easier time using direct forms of love in relationships. The lower the approachability factor, the more difficult it is for children to communicate love to their parents. In later life, they may have unproductive relationships.

In conclusion, the ability to communicate using proper labels will relieve both your emotional turmoil and benefit the relationship in the long run.

How to Improve Your Child's Self Esteem

Self-esteem is feeling good about yourself. Because it is a feeling, self-esteem is expressed in the way that people behave. However, success is important for the growth of positive feelings about oneself. High self-esteem will allow your child to keep failure situations in proper perspective. Whether or not a failure situation is perceived as a learning experience, or as a self-punishment, depends on one's level of self-esteem.

Children as well as adults will vary in the type of self-esteem exhibited. We all feel more confident on some days than others. Feeling low self-esteem from time to time is not a problem. However, a pattern of low self-esteem should be observed in order for there to be a concern. You can easily observe your child's self-esteem by seeing what he/she does and how he/she accomplishes it.

A Child With High Self-Esteem Will:

- feel capable of influencing another's opinions or behaviors in a positive way
- be able to communicate feelings and emotions in a variety of situations
- behave independently
- approach new situations in a positive manner
- exhibit a high level of frustration tolerance
- take on and assume responsibility
- keep situations in proper perspective
- communicate positive feelings about him/herself
- be willing to try a new situation without major resistance

Such children will possess an internal locus of control. Consequently, they feel whatever happens to them is a direct result of their own behavior or actions. These children will therefore feel a sense of power over their environment.

Children With Low Self-Esteem Will:

- communicate self-derogatory statements
- exhibit a low frustration tolerance
- become easily defensive
- listen to other's judgment rather than his/her own
- be resistant to new situations and experiences
- constantly blame others for their failures and problems
- have very little feeling of power and control
- lose perspective easily (blow things out of proportion)
- avoid any situation that creates tension
- be unwilling to reason

Such children will possess an external locus of control. Consequently, these children feel that whatever happens to them is the result of fate, luck, or chance.

In order to fully understand self-esteem, one must consider the factors involved. self-esteem occurs when children experience the positive feelings of satisfaction associated with feeling:

Connected. A child feels good relating to people, places, and things that are important to her and these relationships are approved and respected by others.

Unique. A child acknowledges and respects the personal characteristics that make him special and different, and receives approval and respect from others for those characteristics.

Powerful. A child uses the skills, resources, and opportunities that he/she has in order to influence the circumstances of his/her own life in important ways.

The following suggestions are offered to enhance your child's positive feelings about him/herself. These recommendations require consistency, genuineness and discrimination on your part. No one suggestion by itself will have long-lasting effects. A combination of techniques will have greater impact. However, you should always keep in mind that many other factors, not within your child's control such as peer group, school success or failure, perception and so on, will also contribute to his/her self-esteem. However, your role as a parent is a crucial one and can offset difficulties in other areas.

1. **Be solution-oriented**. An important step in building children's self-esteem is to teach solutions rather than blame. Some families are very "blame-oriented."

When something goes wrong, everyone is quick to "point the finger" at each other. Children who grow up in this type of environment not only become easily frustrated, but never learn how to handle obstacles. Teaching children solutions begins with simple statements like "Who's at fault is not important. The more important question is what can we do so that it doesn't happen again." Being solution-oriented allows children a sense of control and resiliency when confronted with situations that could be ego-deflating.

2. **Allow children the right to make decisions**. While the statement "No one promised them a democracy" may hold true in some parental situations, allowing children the right to make decisions that affect their daily life can only enhance their self-esteem. Decisions about clothing, room arrangement, friends to invite at a party, menu for dinner, and so on can make children feel some sense of control in what happens to them. Coupled with solution orientation, mistakes can be used as a positive learning experience.

3. **Offer alternative ways when handling a situation**. Some people know only one or two alternatives in handling situations. After these fail, frustration occurs. Conditioning children to see many alternative ways of handling a situation or obstacle can also enhance their self-esteem. Asking children what they have tried and offering them options to other possible solutions, increases their "tool box." The more "tools" we have at our disposal, the easier life becomes. Individuals with limited "tools" tend to use avoidance and flight.

4. **Teach children the proper labels when communicating feelings**. The ability to correctly label one's feelings is a factor in self-esteem. Children tend to have a very difficult time communicating because they lack the proper labels for their feelings. When your child is unable to label an internal feeling, it becomes trapped and the frustration may become manifested in behavior problems, physical symptoms, and so on. When such feelings are manifested in other forms, they are usually misunderstood or misinterpreted. You can offer your child the correct labels. For example, you may want to say, "While the feeling you are expressing sounds like anger, it is really frustration and frustration is ____. Now that you know this, is there anything that is causing you frustration?"

   Building an emotional vocabulary allows communication to flow more easily and reduces a child's unwillingness to deal with situations.

5. **Allow children the opportunity to repeat successful experiences**. Whenever possible, allow children the chance to handle any job or responsibility in which they have proven success. A foundation of positive experiences is necessary for self-esteem. Since the child has mastered skills required for the job, any opportunity to repeat success can only be ego-inflating. Jobs such as cooking dinner, cutting the lawn, fixing something around the house, and making the shopping list are examples of repetitive experiences.

6. **Allow avenues for disagreement**. Children with higher self-esteem will always feel they have an avenue to communicate their concerns. Even though the result

may not go in their favor, the knowledge that a situation or disagreement can be discussed allows the child to feel some involvement in his/her destiny. This factor becomes important when one sees that many children with low self-esteem feel a loss of power in affecting change.

7. **Help your child set realistic goals**. This is a very crucial issue in helping children improve their self-esteem. Some children will set unrealistic goals, fall short and feel like a failure. Repeated over a period of time, the child begins to feel a sense of urgency leading to more unrealistic goals. This circular behavior sometimes results with children becoming unwilling to venture out or take chances. The more limited children become in their experiences, the less chance for success. Avoidance, passivity, rejection of an idea or experience will only reinforce feelings of inadequacy.

   Help your child by defining his/her objective. You may want to ask your child what he/she wants to accomplish. After this, try to help him/her define the steps necessary to accomplish the task. Each step becomes a goal in itself. Your child should be taught not see one final goal, but a series of smaller goals leading to a final point. In this way he/she will feel accomplishment at every step.

8. **Use a reward system to shape positive behavior**. Punishment tells your child what not to do, while rewards inform them of what to do. Rewarding positive behavior increases self-esteem. Children enjoy winning your approval, especially when it comes to a job or task. You may want to use rewards such as notes indicating how proud you feel about what the child has accomplished. Rewards can also be special trips, special dinners with one parent, extra time before bed, a hug and a kiss. The use of monetary rewards can also be utilized every so often.

9. **Don't pave all your child's roads**. Some parents make the mistake of reducing frustration for children to the point where the child receives a distorted view of the world. Children with high self-esteem get frustrated. However, they tend to be more resilient because they have previously handled frustrating situations and worked out the solutions themselves. When you rush to the aide of your child, or change the environment to prevent him/her from becoming frustrated, you are unwittingly reinforcing children's low self-esteem. After awhile, your child may become so dependent upon you to "bail them out" when he/she is confronted with frustration. The need to master the environment and find solutions to challenges is crucial to positive self-esteem. The old saying, "Catch me a fish and I'll eat today, teach me to fish and I'll eat forever," seems to apply.

In conclusion, evaluate your own feelings of self-esteem. If you are experiencing feelings of inadequacy, changing your child's feelings about him/herself will be difficult. Improving your child's self-esteem is a process that needs to be viewed in a positive way. Altering feelings of low self-esteem offers your child a more positive future.

How You Can Recognize Possible Learning Disabilities in Your Children

As parents you should be aware of the possible signals that may indicate your child is experiencing a learning disability. Many diagnostic characteristics are exhibited by children with this disorder. Some of these are diagnosed by school officials through observation and evaluation. However, other important information is derived from your observation and records. If you suspect that your child may have a learning disability (refer to Chapter 4, *How Parents Can Observe Their Children for Suspected Disabilities*) then contact a school official immediately. This may be the school psychologist, the special-education coordinator, or the resource-room special-education teacher in your child's school.

Information that would come from the school would include:

Intellectual Requirements: Children with learning disabilities usually exhibit intellectual potential within the average range and above. This usually translates into a score of 90 or better. Such potential should only be measured by an individual intelligence test like the Wechsler Intelligence Scale for Children—Revised.

Academic Requirements: Children with learning disabilities usually exhibit mild academic deficits (6 months to 1 year below grade level), moderate academic deficits (1 to 2 years below grade level) or severe academic deficits (more than 2 years below grade level). These deficits may exhibit themselves in any one of the following areas:

- Decoding (word attack skills)
- Reading Comprehension
- Mathematical Computation
- Mathematical Reasoning
- Written Expression
- Oral Expression
- Listening Comprehension

Exclusion Requirements: Children with learning disabilities are not mentally disabled, primarily emotionally disturbed, hearing impaired, visually impaired, slow learners, or the result of inadequate instructional practices, or cultural or economic disadvantages.

Processing Requirements: Children with learning disabilities usually exhibit deficits in the learning process. The strengths or weaknesses in this process are usually measured by process (perceptual) tests such as the Slingerland, Woodcock Johnson, Detroit Tests of Learning Aptitudes, or the ITPA. However, the following list indicates some difficulties exhibited by children with processing problems in the following areas:

Visual Motor Disability

- Poor motor coordination

- Poor perception of time and space
- Gets lost easily

- Poor handwriting, artwork, drawing
- Restless, short attention span

- Awkward, frequent tripping, trouble skipping

Auditory-Vocal Disability

- Appears not to listen or comprehend
- Responds with one-word answers
- May emphasize wrong syllables in words
- Offers little in group discussions
- Follows directions better after he is shown
- Trouble with rote memory (such as math facts)

Auditory Association Disability

- Fails to enjoy being read to
- Has difficulty comprehending questions
- Slow to respond, takes a long time to answer
- Relies heavily on picture clues

Visual Association Disability

- Unable to tell a story from pictures
- Unable to understand what he/she reads
- Fails to handle primary-level workbook
- Needs auditory cues and clues

Manual Expressive Disability

- Handwriting and drawing are poor
- Poor at game playing, can't imitate others
- Clumsy, uncoordinated
- Poor at acting out ideas or feelings

Verbal Expression Disability

- Mispronounces common words
- Uses incorrect word endings

- Difficulty in sound blending
- Omits correct verbal endings

Auditory Memory Disabilities

- Fails to remember instructions
- Can't memorize nursery rhymes, poems
- Doesn't know alphabet

- Unable to count

Visual Memory Disabilities

- Misspells own name frequently
- Inconsistent word identification

- Frequent misspellings, even after practice
- Can't write alphabet, numbers

Information that would involve your observation and input includes:

Background Requirements: Children with learning disabilities usually exhibit a history of learning, social, and developmental difficulties dating back to early grades. Children with learning disabilities may have other relatives or family members who exhibited the same types of problems.

Behavioral Requirements: Children with learning disabilities usually exhibit several of the following both at home and at school:

- Variability in performance across subject areas
- Attention problems (distractibility, poor concentration)
- Organizational problems with information, space, or time
- Poor motivation and attitude due to repeated academic failure
- Memory problems
- Language deficits in listening, speaking, or writing
- Poor motor abilities in fine motor (small muscle) or gross motor (large muscle)
- Inappropriate social behavior (inability to make friends, poor reactions to social situations)

Frequently Asked Questions Concerning Learning Disabilities

1. Q—What is a learning disability?

A—In general, a learning disability is a problem in acquiring and using skills required for listening, speaking, reading, writing, reasoning, and mathematical ability. Such problems in the acquisition of skills cannot be traced to inadequate intelligence, school environment, emotional problems, visual or hearing defects, cultural deprivation, or lack of motivation.

2. Q—How many children have learning disabilities?

A—This is somewhat difficult depending upon the definition used. The U.S. Department of Education reports approximately 5% of a school's population may be learning disabled. According to statistics taken in 1984, this represented 1,811,451 students throughout the country.

3. Q—What causes learning disabilities?

A—Several theories have been proposed concerning the cause of learning disabilities. Some of the more widely-held theories center around heredity, complications of pregnancy, or some subtle neurological impairment, sort of like crossed wires in a telephone line.

4. Q—Can a true learning disability show up in later grades with no earlier indications?

A—This is a widely held misconception. In most cases a true learning disability has a historical pattern with symptoms appearing as early as a child's first school experience or sooner. A fifth-grade child who is referred by a teacher for suspected learning disabilities and has *no* prior educational difficulties should be considered a low-risk LD youngster.

5. Q—Are dyslexia and learning disabilities the same?

A—No. Dyslexia is a specific and severe form of a learning disability. Dyslexia refers to a severe problem in learning how to read. All learning-disabled children are not dyslexic. However, all dyslexic children are learning disabled.

6. Q—Are reversals an indication of a learning disability?

A—This symptom has been greatly inflated by the media. Parents should keep in mind that reversals of letters and numbers may be very common in children up to grade three and may not by themselves indicate any learning disability. However, if a child frequently reverses letters and numbers along with other symptoms, or continues after age 8, you should discuss this with a professional as soon as possible.

7. Q—Can a child be learning-disabled in only one area?

A—Yes. Some children may have a learning disability in the area of short-term memory, mathematical computations, or spelling or reading comprehension. Of course, the more areas affected, the more serious the disability.

8. Q—What kinds of symptoms signal a possible learning disability?

A—There are a variety of symptoms that may signal the presence of such a problem. Some of the more common include: disorganization, poor muscle coordination, impulsivity, distractibility, short attention span, trouble in completing assignments, poor spelling, poor handwriting, poor social skills, low reading level, difficulty in following directions, discrepancy between ability, and performance and language difficulties.

9. Q—What is the first thing to do if I suspect that my child may have a learning disability?

A—Hopefully the school would have identified this possibility before you. However, if this is not the case, immediately contact the school psychologist, or head of the school's child study team and make him/her aware of your concerns. If you do not wish to go through the school, then contact a qualified professional in the field, or a clinic that specializes in learning disabilities. They will be happy to evaluate your child. However, keep in mind that such an evaluation can be very expensive while it is free through the school.

10. Q—Must my child be referred to the committee on special education if he/she has a learning disability?

A—The answer in most cases will be yes. It is the legal and moral responsibility of every school district to refer such a child for a review before the CSE (Committee on Special Education). A review does not mean immediate classification. It just means that enough evidence exists to warrant a "look" by the district. If the child has a learning disability and is encountering frustration in school, then the services he/she will receive should greatly reduce such problems.

What You Need to Know About Retention

Retention of a student's grade placement is a very difficult decision for both parents and educators. In some cases the decision is based on a single factor such as classroom performance. In other cases several factors are considered. Whatever the input, it is a decision that should not be taken lightly. The implications for your child and your family can have long-lasting effects.

When you are first presented with this suggestion by the school, you may become very overwhelmed and confused. Instead of looking into the possible reasons, you may get angry and exert more pressure on your child. You may see this action as a social stigma, rather than an educational recommendation. In other cases, you may agree to the school's recommendation without question. If you are presented with this option, then great care should be taken in examining all the variables that will affect the outcome.

We have all heard stories from friends, neighbors, teachers, and family on the results of grade retention. Some adults will say that the decision was a positive step and gave them the opportunity to "catch up." However, others express negative feelings surrounding the ridicule, family pressure, loss of self-esteem, social problems, and continued difficulties in school even after retention.

Present research seems somewhat divided about the use of such an educational alternative. Some studies have shown that the greatest success for such an action occurs in kindergarten and first grade. The chances for success dramatically decrease as children become older. Other studies seem to indicate that if retention is exercised as an option in kindergarten and first grade, boys seem to benefit most. This result seems to support the developmental pattern of a more advanced social and academic maturity in girls. Some parents have even chosen to wait an extra year before enrolling their sons in school. Since most referrals to psychologists, resource rooms, and special-education class in elementary school are boys, this "waiting period" should be explored further. However, the emphasis with today's education is to begin earlier, around age 4, not later. Consequently, further research is needed.

Since you should be involved in the decision of retention, it is important that you become educated in this area. The following factors should be taken into consideration prior to the final action.

Present Grade Placement: As previously mentioned, the greatest chance for retention to work is in kindergarten and first grade. By the time children are in fourth or fifth grade, the chances for success decrease dramatically.

Immature Behavior Patterns: The level of interpersonal relations exhibited by children is also a factor to consider. If they tend to play with children much younger than themselves, retention will have fewer consequences. However, if children choose peers that are equal or older in age, retention may have more negative results.

Age of the Child: Children who are younger than their classmates will experience fewer problems with retention. However, children who are one or two years above their classmates may have more serious adjustments to this action.

Brothers and Sisters: Children without siblings seem to make a better adjustment when repeating a grade. Others with brothers or sisters in the same grade or one year below find retention much more difficult. Children in this category find the experience ego-deflating and feel a loss of familial status.

Attendance: The more time a child is out from school, the greater the reason for retention. Children who are ill and miss over 25 days of school are prime candidates. This is especially important in the early grades where the foundations of reading and basic skills are taught. Some children with excellent attendance are less suitable candidates.

Intellectual Ability: Children with average intelligence have the better chance of success with retention. However those with below average (lower two to ten percent) or superior ability (upper two to ten percent) tend to have more difficulty. Children who fall into these categories may be having difficulties in school for other reasons which would not be addressed by retention (emotional problems, retardation).

Physical Size: Children who are smaller in stature make better candidates. Those who are physically larger than their present classmates will have more problems when retained.

Student's Gender: Boys in kindergarten and first grade make the best candidates. After fourth grade both boys and girls will have little chance of success when it comes to retention.

Present Classroom Performance: Students who are performing one year behind in most academic subjects may find retention a help. Those who are more than two years behind may need an alternate type of program such as special-education class or resource room. There are times when some schools might recommend retention because of maturation or behavior problems. Children who are functioning on grade level or above should be reviewed carefully.

Present Emotional State: Children who do not exhibit any signs of serious emotional difficulties, such as impulsivity, nervous habits, distractibility, unwillingness to reason, and tantrums, have a better chance when retained. Children who exhibit serious emotional concerns should not be considered for retention. However, other educational options should be explored.

Your Attitude About Retention: This factor is crucial. Children will have the best chance of adjusting to retention when their parents see it as a positive step. Frustrated, angry, and disappointed parents will negate any chance of success.

Number of Schools Attended: Children who have attended several schools within their first two years of school will have less success with retention because of added social stress and lack of consistency.

Student's Attitude: Children who see retention as an opportunity to "catch up" will have a better chance of success. Children who become very upset, exhibit denial about poor performance, or show indifference may have greater difficulty.

Evidence of Learning Disabilities: Children with intact learning skills and processes have a greater chance for success when it comes to retention. Children who have been diagnosed as having learning disabilities should receive alternate educational support. In such cases, retention should not be considered an option.

The above factors are offered as a general guide for you to follow. There may be other factors that should be considered as well. Regardless, your input into this decision is crucial.

chapter twelve
THE TRANSITION OF SPECIAL-EDUCATION STUDENTS TO ADULT LIFE

Congratulations! You have come this far. Your next goal and your child's next goal will be to graduate from secondary school and move on to his/her next level of transition. The transition process begins at the junior-high-school or middle-school level. This process culminates with a high school diploma, IEP diploma or certificate of attendance. New Federal regulations require your school district to assist you in this process. This chapter was developed to help you address and meet the needs of your children in their transition to adult life. It will also help you understand the requirements for Transitional IEPs under the new Individuals with Disabilities Education Act (IDEA).

In October, 1990, Congress passed and President Bush signed into law the *Education of the Handicapped Amendments of 1990, P.L. 101–476* or *IDEA*. This chapter is to acquaint you with each of the sections within the law and the new proposed Rules and Regulations that directly relate to transition. This provides you with insight on how transition is an integral part of your child's Transitional IEP.

The purpose of this chapter is to summarize the key components of transition services and to assist you with planning and implementing your child's transitional services.

Transitional Services

Transition into the adult world can present challenges for your child. The process of transition is difficult for children with disabilities and requires specific strategies to enable them to achieve the maximum possible independence. Your child needs to plan for the future in an adult world where there will be few services available. Under IDEA (Individuals with Disabilities Education Act), Transitional services are a coordinated set of activities designed to prepare your child for positive experiences in adult life. These activities may include employment, vocational training, adult education, adult services, independent living, and community participation. The set of activities for your child will need to be based on his/her individual needs. The activities should include community experiences, instruction, and development of employment or other postschool adult-living objectives.

As part of your child's Transitional IEP, secondary-education students with disabilities, ages 15 through 21, are eligible to receive transition services. This transitional process could be initiated earlier for students younger than age 15, who are considered to be at risk for dropping out of school. Cultural and linguistic backgrounds of disabled children must be taken into consideration when delivering transitional services.

Federal requirements defining transition services for students with disabilities are consistent. The key difference is that some states require that Transition services be provided by age 15 rather than 16, as Federal law provides.

Districts are required to develop a strategic plan for incorporating transition services within the Individualized Education Program (IEP) process. They will need to implement transition planning and services. The CSE will need to identify postschool outcomes for your child and will need to include activities in the transitional IEP that prepares your participation in adult community.

The intent of transition process provided by your district is to enable your disabled child to live, work, and continue to learn in the community with supports if necessary as adults. The process of developing transition plans involves the following:

- Active student participation
- Cooperative family member's participation
- Community service agency's participation
- Supportive participation by school-district personnel

A documented, sequential transitional process should include services that are provided for students from linguistically and culturally diverse backgrounds, a focused plan that is measured in terms of your child's ability to successfully achieve in the transition to adult life, and timely support and services that are agreed upon in the ITEP by you and your child.

Vocational Assessments

A vocational assessment is the responsibility of your district's special-education program. They begin by assessing referrals for special-education services and continue throughout subsequent annual reviews. The planning of transitional services includes the CSE's development of transitional employment goals and objectives based on your child's needs, preferences, and interests. These will be identified through the child-centered vocational-assessment process.

A good vocational assessment should include the collection and analysis of information about your child's vocational aptitudes, skills, expressed interests, and occupational exploration history (volunteer experiences, part-time or summer employment, club activities). The collection of this information should also take into account your child's language, culture, and family.

A *Level I Vocational Assessment* is administered at the beginning of your child's transitional process and is based on your child's abilities, expressed interests, and needs. This Level I assessment may include a review of existing school information and the conducting of informal interviews. A *Level II Vocational Assessment* usually includes the administration of one or more formal vocational evaluations. A *Level III Vocational Assessment* usually involves the analyses of your child's success in a real or simulated work setting. This is usually reported by a job coach, employer, or vocational evaluator. The transitional process should not be used to limit the student's educational or career aspirations. Ideally, it allows districts to provide opportunities at an earlier age.

Level I takes a look at your child from a vocational perspective. A trained vocational evaluator or knowledgeable special-education teacher should be designated to collect the Level I assessment data. The information gathered for analyses should include existing information from:

- Cumulative records
- Student interviews
- Parent/guardian, and teacher interviews
- Special-education eligibility data
- A review of your child's aptitudes, achievements, interests, behaviors
- Occupational exploration activities

The informal student interview involved in a Level I assessment should consider your child's vocational interest, interpersonal relationship skills, and adaptive behavior.

Level II assessment follows and is based upon the analyses obtained from the Level I assessment. This may be recommended by the CSE at any time to determine the level of a student's vocational skills, aptitudes, and interests but not before the age of 12. The same knowledgeable staff members involved in prior assessments should be used. Collected data should include:

- Writing
- Learning styles
- Interest inventory
- Motor skills (dexterity, speed, tool use, strength, coordination)
- Spatial discrimination

- Verbal
- Reading
- Perception (visual/auditory/tactile)
- Speaking
- Numerical skills (measurement, money skills)
- Comprehension (task learning, problem solving)
- Attention (staying on task)

Level III vocational assessment is a comprehensive vocational evaluation that focuses on real or simulated work experiences. This assessment is the basis for vocational counseling. Unlike a Level I and Level II assessment, a trained vocational evaluator should administer or supervise this level of assessment. Level III assessment options include:

- *Vocational evaluations* including aptitudes and interests which are compared to job performance to predict vocational success in specific areas. Work samples must be valid and reliable.
- *Situational vocational assessments* which occur in real work settings. This on-the-job assessment considers what has been learned and how.
- *Work study assessments* are progress reports from supervisors or mentors who provide information on your child's job performance. A standard observational checklist may be utilized.

If your child plans a postsecondary educational program, he/she may benefit from two types of assessments:

1. *General assessments of postsecondary education skills* are necessary to determine your child's academic skills, critical thinking skills, requirements for reasonable accommodations, social behaviors, interpersonal skills, self-advocacy and self-determination skills, learning strategies, time management, and organizational skills. This information is usually obtained through consultation with peers or teachers, or through self-evaluation.
2. *Assessments specific to field of study or setting* are necessary to assess your child's needs in relation to daily-living skills that may be experienced in a classroom setting or college campus. You need to identify additional skills that your child must plan for to be an effective member of a postsecondary educational setting including:
   - Dormitory living vs. commuting
   - Lab work
   - Large lecture vs. seminar courses

You may wish to visit campuses that provide supportive services for children with disabilities. Sources of information regarding colleges that provide these services can be obtained in your local library or bookstore.

In order to involve the expertise of community-based nonschool personnel in the transitional planning process the matter of confidentiality must be addressed. Under the *Family Education Rights and Privacy Act (FERPA)* aka, *Buckley Amendment*, your rights to confidentiality must be maintained. You may need to sign releases to get written consent during the transition process to benefit from the resources available to you in the community. This does not commit you or your child to a specific service if you later feel you do not want or need it. Ask your district about the rules of confidentiality regarding the release of information, the use of information by community agencies, and the storage of information once it is released by the district.

Individualized Transitional Education Program (ITEP)

The ITEP should include long-term adult outcomes from which annual goals and objectives are defined. Transition services should prepare your child to pursue his/her desired long-term adult goals through a variety of activities including:

- Instruction
- Community experiences
- Development of employment
- Postschool adult-living objectives
- Activities of daily living
- Functional vocational evaluation

The following should be addressed in the ITEP:

1. A statement of transition services should be responsive to your child's preferences, interests, and needs. The beginning date for the service should be provided.
2. Annual goals and objectives should include the following 10 areas:
   - Education (college)
   - Legal/advocacy (guardianship)
   - Independence/residential (private residence vs. group home)
   - Recreation/leisure (joining sports activities)
   - Financial/income (banking and checking accounts)
   - Medical/health (health insurance, physician selection)
   - Employment (sheltered workshop vs. competitive employment)
   - Transportation (public vs. private)
   - Postsecondary/continuing education (college vs. vocational training)
   - Other support needs (clergy, fraternal organizations)

3. Long-term adult outcomes in the IEP should include statements on your child regarding his/her performance in employment, postsecondary education, and community living.

4. A coordinated set of activities must be included on the ITEP. It must demonstrate the use of various strategies, including community experiences, adult-living objectives, instruction. If one of these activities is not included in the IEP in a particular year, then the IEP must explain why that activity is not reflected in any part of the student's program. Activities of daily living and functional vocational evaluation activities should also be included.

5. A list of participants involved in the planning and development of the Individualized Transitional Educational Program.

Under existing regulations, the Committee on Special Education must notify you when an initial evaluation, review, or reevaluation is being conducted.

Student and Family Participation

What is your role as a family in the transition process? Listed are steps that your family can take to assist in the transitional process:

- Explore your community for useful community resources.
- Discuss transition options with other families.
- Provide peer support to other parents.
- Seek out information about occupational, educational, and living options.
- Work along with the school, finding ways to increase your child's academic, career, and personal independence skills.
- Set achievable goals for your child.
- Help your child develop the ability to communicate his/her needs, preferences, and interests to school staff, and other professionals.
- Observe the kinds of things your child can do independently and the areas in which he/she may need assistance.
- Participate actively in meetings with the school and other professionals.
- Make sure you plan and prepare well in advance for your child's future financial, medical, and housing resource needs, as appropriate by: (a) assisting with application for Social Security Disability or Supplemental Security Income (SSI) benefits; (b) developing a will; (c) determining guardianship; (d) applying for financial aid for postsecondary education or training.
- Help your child obtain key identification documents, such as a social security card, driver's license or nondriver identification card.
- Help your child develop independent decision-making and communication skills.
- Help your child explore options, set realistic goals for the future.

- Enhance your child's positive self-esteem and assist him/her to develop independence, including self-reliance, self-advocacy, and self-management skills.
- Use actual home-life opportunities to teach your child daily-living skills: banking, shopping, cooking, cleaning, laundry.
- Promote good money management, budgeting, and savings.
- Encourage your child to become aware of the world of work, such as by talking with neighbors.
- Help your child to locate and obtain a part-time job.
- Reinforce work-related behaviors at home (grooming, etiquette, following directions, completing chores).
- Provide opportunities for leisure time activities (sports, daily exercise, or hobbies).
- Encourage your child to participate in social activities with peers.
- Teach your child how to utilize community-based resources (library, recreation, transportation, stores).
- Work actively with your CSE to make sure the plan is successful.
- Stay in close contact with your child's teachers.

TRANSITION PLANNING TIMELINE

The following is a series of events that you may need to consider during your child's transition process. All items will not be applicable to all students or to all State regulations. The list is provided to serve as an optional planning tool.

Age Range   **Action**

12–15   _____ Initial vocational assessment.
                      _____ Develop and implement strategies to increase responsibilities and independence at home.
                      _____ Discuss the following curriculum area at CSE meetings:
                          Academic
                          Social
                          Language/communication
                          Occupational
                          Self-help skills
                          Self-advocacy skills

14–16   _____ Introduce and discuss transition services.
                      _____ Notify parents that transition services will be incorporated into the IEP beginning at age 15.
                      _____ Assure that copies of work-related documents are available:
                          Social security card

> Birth certificate
> Obtain working papers (if appropriate)

_____ Obtain parental consent so that the appropriate adult/ agency representative can be involved.

_____ Develop transition component of IEP and annually thereafter.

_____ Complete periodic vocational evaluations.

15–21 _____ Discuss adult transition with CSE.

_____ Consider summer employment/volunteer experience.

_____ Explore community leisure activities.

_____ Consider the need for residential opportunities, including completing applications, as appropriate.

_____ Complete periodic vocational evaluations.

16–21 _____ Obtain personal ID card.

_____ Obtain driver's training and license.

_____ Develop transportation/mobility strategies such as:
> Independent travel skills training
> Public or paratransit transportation
> Needs for travel attendant

_____ Investigate SSDI/SSI/Medicaid programs.

_____ Consider guardianship or emancipation.

_____ Develop and update employment plans.

_____ Involve state vocational rehabilitation agencies, as appropriate within two years of school exit.

_____ Research possible adult-living situations.

_____ Investigate postschool opportunities
> (further educational vocational training, college, military).

_____ Complete periodic vocational evaluations.

18–21 _____ Seek legal guardianship.

_____ Apply for postschool college and other training programs.

_____ Male students register for the draft (no exceptions).

_____ Register to vote.

_____ Review health insurance coverage: inform insurance company of son/daughter disability and investigate rider of continued eligibility.

_____ Complete transition to employment, further education or training, and community living, affirming arrangements are in place for the following:
1. Postsecondary/continuing Education
2. Employment
3. Legal/advocacy
4. Personal independence/residential
5. Recreation/leisure

6. Medical/health
7. Counseling
8. Financial/income
9. Transportation/independent travel skills
10. Other

Sample Transitional IEP

STUDENT TRANSITION ACTION PLAN—PAGE 1

Descriptive Information   **Date Plan Initiated**:

Student Name: **Age**:   **DOB**:   **Case Coordinator**:

Social Security #:   **Disability**:   **Phone**:

Parent Guardian Name: **Parent Home Phone #**:

Home Address: **Parent Work #**:

Grade: Teacher: County of Residence:

Class Location: School Phone: Social Worker:

Vocational Education Placement: Home School District:

Contact Person (Name and Phone):   Contact Person (CSE):

Additional Vocational/Technical Placements/Program:

Participants in Transition Planning

Name: Role/Agency   Name: Role/Agency

Additional Services Needed:

STUDENT TRANSITION ACTION PLAN—PAGE 2

Employment Responsibilities	Date	Activities Accomplished

Employment Responsibilities

_____ Competitive Employment
          (no need for services)
_____ Competitive Employment
          (time-limited support)
_____ Supported Employment
          (infrequent support)
_____ Supportive Employment
          (daily support)
_____ Sheltered Workshop
_____ Day Treatment
_____ Volunteer Work
_____ Summer Employment
_____ Other
_____ Not Applicable

Postsecondary Education and Training

_____ Community College or University
          (no support needed)
_____ Community College or University
          (support needed)
_____ Technical/Trade School
          (no support needed)
_____ Technical/Trade School
          (support needed)
_____ Adult Education Classes
_____ Other
_____ Not Applicable

Residential

_____ Parents or Relatives
_____ Intermediate Care Facility
_____ Community Residence
_____ Supervised Apartment
_____ Supported Apartment
_____ Independent Living
_____ Foster Care/Family Care
_____ Respite
_____ Section 8 Housing
_____ Other

STUDENT TRANSITION ACTION PLAN—PAGE 3

	Date	Activities Completed
Transportation Responsibilities		

Transportation Responsibilities

_____ Independent
_____ Family Transportation
_____ Car Pool
_____ Public Transportation
_____ Specialized Transportation
_____ Agency Transportation
_____ Other
_____ Not Applicable

Recreation/Leisure

_____ Independent Recreation
_____ Family-Supported Recreation
_____ Church Groups
_____ Local Clubs
_____ Community Parks and Recreation
_____ Specialized Recreation for
      Individuals with Disabilities
_____ Other
_____ Not Applicable

Personal/Home/Money Management

_____ Independent (no support needed)
_____ Citizenship Skills
_____ Insurance Coverage
_____ Money Management
_____ Use of Community Resources
_____ Meal Preparation
_____ Housekeeping Skills
_____ Self-Care
_____ Other

Advocacy/Legal

_____ Guardianship
_____ Wills/Trusts
_____ Self-Advocacy
_____ Client Assistance Program (CAP)
_____ Other

STUDENT TRANSITION ACTION PLAN—PAGE 4

Medical   **Date**   **Activities Completed**
Responsibilities
_____ Medical Care, Daily Care
_____ Intermediate Care
_____ Medical Services—General Check-Ups,
            Specialists, Medical Supervision
_____ Dental Care
_____ Use of Free Clinics
_____ Therapy (OT/PT. Sp./Lan.)
_____ Family Insurance
_____ Individual Insurance
_____ Medicaid
_____ Visiting Nurse/Home Health
_____ Aide
_____ Medication
_____ Other

Social/Sexual
_____ Individual Counseling
_____ Group Counseling/Support
_____ Family-Planning Services
_____ Other

Financial/Income
_____ Earned Wages
_____ Unearned Income (family support, gifts)
_____ SSI/SSDI
_____ Food Stamps, Housing Subsidy
_____ Other

Communication
_____ Braille
_____ Assistive Technology
_____ Computer Applications
_____ Interpreter Services
_____ Other

Transition From School to Work

Your child will be facing transition from school to work in the near future with increasingly difficult barriers. Two specific problems currently facing your children and those who serve them are the lack of effective, community-based transition programs from school-to-work and inability of a tested coordinated service. There is no process that enables education, rehabilitation, and business professionals in local communities to have effective services to meet the needs of these youths and employers who will help them coordinate the process of transition.

Ten years ago there were over 150 million people in the United States between the ages of 15 and 64. Eighteen percent (27 million) of those people had some type of disability that interfered with their functioning in major life roles, such as work. According to the U.S. Bureau of the Census 1985, at least three million of these people were students. Since the Education for All Handicapped Children Act of 1975, there have been significant changes and improvements in the availability for children with disabilities. The law provides a free and appropriate education for youth with disabilities, but appropriate vocational training and opportunities are not guaranteed. What does this mean for your child? It means your child will be at risk for training and acquiring quality employment.

There are significant differences in education and employment statuses between children with and without disabilities. Statistically these quarters of graduates without disabilities compared to just over half of the disabled population, graduate and find employment. What is worse, income is also lower for disabled adults. Recent studies indicate that there are about 4.5 million students with disabilities being educated today. Better than a third of these students attend special programs or are attendance problems in school. Almost two-thirds have problems in and out of school activities who are disabled where less than 5% of the more handicapped population have similar problems out of school. Teachers feel that disabled youths have many more problems compared to their counterparts. They also score lower on tests, have lower grade averages, and are less likely to attend college.

In the workplace they also have more problems. Beyond high school, they have problems learning new skills, adapt less to change. They exhibit difficulties with interpersonal relationships in the workplace. Effective work habits, initiative, and reliability are also deficient skills. Employers today need self-sufficient people who can think for themselves, and show initiative. Is your child a self-starter who can fend for himself or is he/she dependent on others to complete a task?

Today employers are looking for people who take responsibility, are creative, and have good social skills. The research shows that inappropriate behavior is one of the major problems with our disabled youth. They need to learn that social skills are important in today's communication economy. Your child's social skills will either be an asset or a liability. Social skills need to be an intregal part of your child's education. Successful transition from school to work was a priority of the National Council on Disabilities ten years ago.

Most school districts currently do not have a comprehensive program that assists children in the transition process from school to work. They just don't teach disabled students the necessary skills to be successful in the workplace. There are vocational programs and academic programs, but transitions from these programs to positions in the workplace, business, or industry usually do not occur. Students are given very little career counseling and are generally naive about securing meaningful employment.

Studies show that early intervention programs work well for students with disabilities. Coordinated efforts are successful, but as secondary and postsecondary considerations arise, families find fewer and fewer coordinated programs that they or their children can access. The Association of Retarded Citizens (ARC) point out that three-fourths of mentally retarded youths could be self-sufficient, employed adults if they had appropriate coordinated community support.

Much work needs to be done to change the transition process and make it workable and productive for our disabled youth today. You can see that it's a big step in your child's educational career. You need to be on top of what is available to your child and you need to be aware that the training needs to consider the total child, not just academic or vocational components.

Features you should consider when selecting transition programs are: active parent group, area-wide transportation system for graduates, job club, follow-up services, on-the-job training, curriculum that focuses on the development of employment preparation, career skills, daily-living skills, an awareness of health and safety measures, job development, and placement activities.

Transition to Posthigh-School Programs

Up until now we have talked about mandated programs that provide services and regulations to assist your disabled child. At graduation or at age 21 many of the supports disappear for most disabled young adults. It is now up to the individuals to transition themselves into the adult world. Hopefully what you learned has helped you and your child to be a self-sufficient, well-rounded graduate ready for the world of higher education.

When your child attends college he/she must be aware that the Law 94–102 that provided special education to them does not apply anymore. Responsibilities now shift from the system to the individual. Many students are not ready for the rude awakening. Is your child? It is the responsibility of your guidance office to explain the differences your child will be experiencing. They will now learn a new law, Section 504 of the Rehabilitation Act of 1977. Students with disabilities have the right to auxiliary aids and compensating services under Section 504. The statute, however, is not specific about support services. A postsecondary educational facility must be provided if they receive federal funding.

Postsecondary Schooling

Section 504 states that postsecondary schools need to be free from discrimination, and quotas are prohibited. It also states that reasonable academic programs should ensure maximum participation for students with disabilities in such programs. Program access requires that postsecondary schools make course information available to disabled students in a format that they can understand. They should have items like:

- Taped textbooks
- Readers
- Tape recorders
- Calculators
- Dictionaries

They should also have extended time to complete a program, and if they can't do full-time study, they can take courses for part-time study.

To compare secondary and postsecondary settings is to compare night to day. The school-aged youngster has many rights under 94–142 compared to limited access under Section 504. For example, school-aid services are prescribed and mandated from postsecondary programs. Call for reasonable accommodations.

As stated before, Section 504 is applicable in all secondary education programs that receive Federal funds. Under the provisions of Section 504, a college or university may not limit the number of students with disabilities admitted; nor may they make preadmission inquiries as to whether an applicant is disabled. They may not use admission tests or criteria that inadequately measure the academic level of visually impaired, hearing impaired, or otherwise disabled applicants because special provisions were not made for them. You must make sure that the college of your choice follows the rules for your child. You must be in constant support of your child.

Things to Consider When Looking Into Postsecondary Education

1. What are admission requirements?
2. What is the grade point average? ACT? SAT?
3. Are there special accommodations for your child to take entrance exams?
4. Do they have special incentive programs?
5. Is there a disabled student service office on campus?
   Does it have a full-time person there or is it part time?
6. What kind of documentation is required to verify disabilities?
7. Is there a disabled student organization on campus? How can one contact them?
8. How are the faculty informed of the necessary accommodations if needed?
9. Is tutoring available? Is it individualized or group? Is there a cost involved?
10. Are notetakers and readers available? Is there a cost involved? How are they trained?

11. Is it possible to arrange for tape-recorder classes, computers, untimed testing, test readers?

12. Is it possible to relocate classes to more accessible sites?

13. What is the college's policy regarding course substitutes or waiver of curriculum requirements?

14. Are there developmental courses available? In what areas?

You as a parent need to work closely with your child to prepare him/her for post-secondary education. It is important that you investigate several college programs to find a good fit for your child.

Parents, counselors, teachers, and LD students may use the following as a reminder of helpful skills and necessary steps to take as a high-school student with a learning disability, to begin to make the transition to college. Ensure that the psychological testing is up-to-date. Many students with disabilities will look towards vocational and second-year colleges close to home. You, your child, your school pupil, and personnel staff may wish to use the following helpful hints as your begin the transition to college.

Vocational assessment is a way to amplify present and future goals. Each state should have agencies that are responsible for vocational assessment and training. These agencies can be of assistance as can your guidance counselor. The junior-high level is not too early to consider vocations. Contact local Vocational and Educational Services for Individuals with Disabilities office before graduation. These agencies offer a variety of services to eligible students with learning disabilities such as vocational assessments, job placements, and so on. (Increase their independent accounts, do their own laundry, cleaning, some cooking, improve socialization skills.) Have a good understanding of their particular learning disability. They should know and articulate their strengths and weaknesses. Know what compensation techniques and accommodations work best for them. Know Section 504 of the Rehabilitation Act. Help students understand how their disability is connected to social experiences with peers, families, and employers. A visual discrimination deficit, and/or an attention-deficit/hyperactivity disorder frequently leads to missed cues and inappropriate timing in conversation. Know the symptoms of learning disabilities.

When your child is accepted into a postsecondary school, responsibilities that he/she needs to take in order to become successful is to learn skills to communicate their needs to their friends, to their instructors, to the clerical and clinical staff in their school.

Some basic clues to relationships with instructors are:

- They are a key part of your education.
- They are paid to teach you.
- Like you they will expect to be treated with respect.
- Instructors expect you to be an adult.
- Ask for help when you need it.
- Accept responsibility for mistakes you make.

Practical Advice for Students Considering Postsecondary Education

Make up your own mind about a teacher. Some instructors are good for you but not for others. Get to know your instructors firsthand. Talk to them. They are also human. Sometimes they may look intimidating, but don't judge a book by its cover. The vast majority of instructors want to help you succeed.

Arriving early for class is a good habit. You can relax and speak to your instructor or classmates or just sit and review notes. Always be ready with paper, pencils, and any reading materials needed for a particular class. Being prepared makes you feel confident and shows commitment on your part. It would be a good idea to sit in the front of the class, close to the professor and to the blackboard. If you are a distance from the front of the room, you may have a tendency not to focus. This will only get you into trouble. Remain focused. It can be hard, but if you keep doing it things will come easier. In the long run everyone will be happy and you will be learning the materials and skills to help you succeed in life. Always ask questions, participate in class, but don't interrupt the lesson—wait for the professor to stop and then raise your hand. Also, if you do not understand something, ask your professor to repeat himself/herself. If you do not understand the lesson, speak to the professor after class so he/she gets to know you and feel your interest in the class. Don't be adverse to criticism—it is another way of learning and not meant as a personal insult. It is the teacher's job to set you on a correct path.

Submit your work as you would to an employer. Be proud of your work. Do not be discouraged if your work needs revision; your teacher will know you are trying. If you are having problems with a particular subject or need answers and want some privacy with your teacher, the best rule is to set up a meeting. Keep the appointment. Be there early or at least on time. It is common courtesy. If you must cancel, do it as early as you possibly can and only if you have no choice. The best way is to leave a phone message or note taped on the mailbox or door. Give your teacher an idea of what the meeting is about. If you do this, he/she will probably have the answer to most of your questions. Remember instructors are real people who are there to help you.

Here are the most common questions students ask themselves about postsecondary education:

1. Why do you want college?
2. How do your parents feel about you going to college?
3. What would you like to major in?
4. What is your learning disability? Know how it affects you.
5. What are your weaknesses?
6. What things are easy for you to learn?
7. What things are difficult for you to learn?
8. What helped you learn in the past?

9. What help do you need from our program to make it in college?
10. Will you spend extra exam time and effort to be successful in college?

The following are certain pointers to keep in mind while you are in school:

The Buckley Amendment: Gives you the right to inspect your educational records. There are only two exceptions: confidential letters of recommendation received, and financial records of your parents that may be on file at the school. You may waive this right to confidential recommendations. Usually this waiver is printed directly on recommendation forms available through the college. You must give your written consent before any personally identifiable information from your educational records are released. You have the right to seek correction in your educational records as appropriate.

Using the Phone: Make sure you have your number listed somewhere in your room. The phone is a magic machine that will help you save time and energy.

Laundry: If you live at home, anything goes. It's up to you and your parent. If you're going away to school, plan on taking over all or most of the job. Some colleges provide laundry services that deliver clean sheets and towels to you each week for a fee. Most dorms have pay laundry facilities, but you have to do it all yourself. If you have money some laundromats do everything for you. Most of the time, you have to take on the responsibility of washing your own clothes.

Nutrition and Your General Health: What you eat is up to you and nobody else. If you go away to school or even stay at home, you have to take care of your own nutrition. At school there are nutrition experts who plan the menus, and at home, it's your responsibility. If you do not have a clue how to go about it on campus, buy a meal card. It tells you how many meals you are entitled to. If you live at home, you can still purchase a meal card because most of the time you are on campus. Remember, eating healthy keeps you healthy. Starving yourself is not the answer. Food is for the brain. Eat right. Eat a variety of healthy foods every day.

You are the expert on your body. You live with it every day. If you are sick, get help. Even if it may not be serious, check it out with a doctor, not your friends. Untreated illness or injury often causes more serious problems than would occur had you received prompt attention. Be aware of serious weight loss, sores, scabs that do not heal, a mole that bleeds, itches, changes in shapes and color, persistent or severe headaches, and sudden vomiting. Any time your body isn't working as you know it to work, check it out with a physician. College health centers provide free or inexpensive treatment for minor problems. They may also treat emergencies and provide health-related counseling. They also make referrals for services they cannot provide. Some campuses have on-campus child-care facilities for students who are parents. They may be provided through an education department or through separate services. Inquire within the department for the fees.

Plagiarism: You should also be aware of plagiarism. Most colleges have dismissal policies if you copy others' work. Whether it's someone else's test paper or something published, it could result in your being asked to leave.

Parental Contact: Your parents may never be contacted except in specific situations. They may be invited to parent day or they may be called in case of a medical emergency. Some schools will call you to give them permission to release information and authorize them to mail data to your home, such as grades and other related assessment materials. Many schools prefer to keep parents fully aware of the educational programs. In some cases they do not have the right to withhold information from your parents, especially grades. In many cases, the school will contact your parents about possession of illegal substances, alcohol abuse, having an accident on campus, and other serious situations.

Tutoring: Many colleges provide tutoring programs to mainstreamed as well as disabled students. Before you decide on a college, find out if tutoring is available. You should check to see if there is a special-education center, an office for disabled students, and an advisor department. Some tutoring is staffed by professors or sometimes by students in a particular area of study. If there are services, use them as necessary. Sometimes there is an extra cost involved.

Testing Modifications: Modifying your test is a function that can only be provided by your professor. He/she is the first person you will need to discuss your disability with. If you had test modifications in high school, there are *no guarantees* that you will have them in college. Remember *you* are your best advocate. You have to express your needs, explaining your disability and how you were successful in situations in high school by modifying your exams. You may need extended time and special locations to take the exams. Remember, speak up. Try to make it happen if you need help on exams.

Legal Advice: Some colleges do have a lawyer or one who is employed part time for student advisement. If not a lawyer, perhaps a legal assistance office can help you. Keep in mind that some community advocacy agencies may be helpful for your problem. Refer to the listing of student-service offices.

Syllabus: You need to read your syllabus every day until it is gospel. You need to check to see whether the syllabus contains course objectives. If so, it represents what the professor wants you to be able to do as a result of the course. Study this carefully because it will help you to know what is considered most important in projects, assignments, and exams.

Organization for success in college occurs when work is steady over the semester; class attendance is regular; good notes are reviewed before class; papers are started early; a daily routine is good policy; a quiet study place is a must; emotional problems are under control; and time spent on school work is closely self-monitored.

Time Management: Time management is an important part of success in school. Include long-range scheduling of important events and responsibilities. Include weekly and daily lists of things to do. Your personal schedule should include time for preparing papers, projects, and assignments separate from regular study time. Personal schedules should also be realistic, including adequate time for chores, recreation, nonacademic responsibilities, and leisure activity. Academic work time should be paced throughout the day rather than scheduled in one block of time. Areas of most importance or difficulty should be scheduled for the times when your individual concentration is best. For many people, that means early in the morning.

Examinations: When it comes time to take examinations in your courses, consider the following:

- The format the test will take. Ask the professor ahead of time what types of questions will be included. Most professors will tell you the information.

- The time allowed for the test. Many learning-disabled students are allowed to take more time on the test. If this is the case, always check with the professor during the class before the test is to take place to make sure there are no problems. Learning-disabled students are sometimes permitted to take their tests in a quiet location away from others. Arrangements should be made for this ahead of time. If you are permitted to use a computer to take tests, you should know exactly where to go and which computers are available to you.

- What choices do you have in answering the exam questions? Must you answer all questions, or may you skip some? Is there a choice of essay topics? What form should your answer take? Should you check, circle, or underline a word, darken a space on an answer sheet, fill in words, letters, sentences, or phrases? How do you indicate true or false? The instructor who grades the test will be expecting a certain kind of answer. Give precisely what is expected of you. Make sure you know if testing aids are allowed while you are taking the test—the use of scratch paper, calculators, dictionaries, a thesaurus, or other reference books. Know this before you take the test. Make sure to follow all directions. If you do not understand the directions, raise your hand and ask for help.

chapter thirteen
APPENDICES

Appendix A—Terminology

Educational Terminology Associated With Special Education

1. **Ability Grouping**: The grouping of children based on their achievement in an area of study.

2. **Accelerated Learning**: An educational process that allows students to progress through the curriculum at an increased pace.

3. **Achievement**: The level of a child's accomplishment on a test of knowledge or skill.

4. **Adaptive Behavior**: Refers to an individual's social competence and ability to cope with the demands of the environment.

5. **Adaptive Physical Education**: A modified program of instruction implemented to meet the needs of special students.

6. **Advocate**: An individual, either a parent or professional, who attempts to establish or improve services for exceptional children.

7. **Age Norms**: Standards based on the average performance of individuals in different age groups.

8. **Agnosia**: Inability to recognize objects and their meaning usually resulting from damage to the brain.

9. **Amplification Device**: Any device that increases the volume of sound.

10. **Anecdotal Record**: A procedure for recording and analyzing observations of a child's behavior; an objective, narrative description.

11. **Annual Goals**: Yearly activities or achievements to be completed or attained by the disabled child that are documented on the Individual Educational Plan.

12. **Aphasia**: The inability to acquire meaningful spoken language by the age of three usually resulting from damage or disease to the brain.

13. **Articulation**: The production of distinct language sounds by the vocal chords.

14. **At Risk**: Usually refers to infants or children with a high potential for experiencing future medical or learning problems.

15. **Attention-Deficit/Hyperactivity Disorder (ADHD)**: A psychiatric classification used to describe individuals who exhibit poor attention, distractibility, impulsivity, and hyperactivity.

16. **Baseline Measure**: The level or frequency of behavior prior to the implementation of an instructional procedure that will later be evaluated.

17. **Behavior Modification**: The techniques used to change behavior by applying principals of reinforcement learning.

18. **Bilingual**: Having the ability to speak two languages.

19. **Career Education**: Instruction that focuses on the application of skills and content area information necessary to cope with the problems of daily life, independent living, and vocational areas of interest.

20. **Categorical Resource Room**: An auxiliary pullout program which offers supportive services to exceptional children with the same disability.

21. **Cognition**: The understanding of information.

22. **Consultant Teacher**: a supportive service for disabled children in which the services are provided by a specialist in the classroom.

23. **Criterion-Referenced Tests**: Tests in which the child is evaluated on his/her own performance to a set of criterion (not in comparison to others).

24. **Declassification**: The process in which a disabled child is no longer considered in need of special-education services. This requires a meeting of the CSE and can be requested by the parent, school, or child if over the age of 18.

25. **Deficit**: A level of performance that is less than expected for a child.

26. **Desensitization**: A technique used in reinforcement theory in which there is a weakening of a response, usually an emotional response.

27. **Diagnosis**: Refers to the specific disorder(s) identified as a result of some evaluation.

28. **Distractibility**: Refers to difficulty in maintaining attention.

29. **Due Process**: Refers to the legal steps and processes outlined in educational law that protects the rights of disabled children.

30. **Dysfluency**: Difficulty in the production of fluent speech as in the example of stuttering.

31. **Dyscalculia**: A serious learning disability in which the child has an inability to calculate, apply, solve, or identify mathematical functions.

32. **Dysorthographia**: A serious learning disability that affects a child's ability to spell.

33. **Dyslexia**: A severe type of learning disability in which a child's ability to read is greatly impaired.

34. **Dysgraphia**: A serious learning disability in which the child has an inability or loss of ability to write.

35. **Enrichment**: Providing a child with extra and more sophisticated learning experiences than those normally presented in the curriculum.

36. **Exceptional Children**: Children whose school performance shows significant discrepancy between ability and achievement, and as a result require special instruction, assistance, and/or equipment.

37. **Etiology**: The cause of a problem.

38. **Free Appropriate Public Education (FAPE)**: Used in PL94–142 to mean special education and related services that are provided at public expense and conform to the state requirements and the individual's IEP.

39. **Group Homes**: A residential living arrangement for handicapped adults, especially the mentally retarded, along with several nonhandicapped supervisors.

40. **Habilitation**: An educational approach used with exceptional children which is directed toward the development of the necessary skills required for successful adulthood.

41. **Homebound Instruction**: A special-education service in which teaching is provided by a specially trained instructor to students unable to attend school. A parent or guardian must always be present at the time of instruction. In some cases, the instruction may take place on a neutral sight and not in the home or school.

42. **Hyperactivity**: Behavior which is characterized by excessive motor activity or restlessness.

43. **Impulsivity**: Nongoal-oriented activity that is exhibited by individuals who lack careful thought and reflection prior to a behavior.

44. **Individualized Educational Plan**: A written educational program that outlines a disabled child's current levels of performance, related services, educational goals, and modifications. This plan is developed by a team including the child's parent(s), teacher(s), and support staff.

45. **Inclusion**: The education of disabled children in their home school so that they may be educated with nonhandicapped children in the same classroom.

46. **Interdisciplinary Team**: The collective efforts of individuals from a variety of disciplines in assessing the needs of a child.

47. **Intervention**: Preventive, remedial, compensatory, or survival services made on behalf of a disabled individual.

48. **Itinerant Teacher**: A teacher hired by a school district to help in the education of a disabled child. The teacher is employed by an outside agency and may be responsible for several children in several districts. An itinerant teacher meets the needs and roles outlined by the hiring district. This may include a resource room model, consultant-teacher model, and so on.

49. **Learning Disability**: Refers to children with average or above average potential intelligence who are experiencing a severe discrepancy between their ability and achievement.

50. **Least-Restrictive Environment**: The least-restrictive setting in which the disabled child can function without difficulty. This placement is determined by the CSE and can change if the child requires more or less restriction.

51. **Mainstreaming**: The practice of educating exceptional children in the regular classroom.

52. **Mental Age**: The level of intellectual functioning based on the average for children of the same chronological age. When dealing with severely disabled children, the mental age may be more reflective of levels of ability than chronological age.

53. **Mental Retardation**: A disability in which the individual's intellectual level is measured within the subaverage range and there are marked impairments in social competence.

54. **Native Language**: The primary language used by an individual.

55. **Noncategorical Resource Room**: A resource room in regular school that provides services to children with all types of classified disabilities. The children with these disabilities are able to be maintained in a regular classroom.

56. **Norm-Referenced Tests**: Tests used to compare a child's performance to the performance of others on the same measure. For example, a child's reading skills are compared to the scores by all other children his age.

57. **Occupational Therapist**: A professional who programs and/or delivers instructional activities and materials to assist disabled children and adults to participate in useful daily activities. Occupational therapists focus on the skills that would be necessary for a disabled child to function in school (such as fine motor skills).

58. **Paraprofessionals**: A trained assistant or parent who works with a classroom teacher in the education process.

59. **Physical Therapist**: A professional trained to assist and help disabled individuals maintain and develop muscular and orthopedic capability and to make correct and useful movements.

60. **Positive Reinforcement**: Any stimulus or event which occurs after a behavior has been exhibited that affects the possibility of that behavior occurring in the future.

61. **Pupil Personnel Team**: A group of professionals from the same school who meet on a regular basis to discuss children's problems and offer suggestions or a direction for resolution.

62. **Pupils With Special Educational Needs (PSEN)**: Students defined as having math and reading achievement lower than the 23rd percentile and requiring remediation. These students are not considered disabled but are entitled to assistance to elevate their academic levels.

63. **Pupils With Handicapping Conditions (PHC)**: Refers to any child classified as disabled by the Committee on special-education.

64. **Related Services**: Services provided to disabled children to assist in their ability to learn and function in the least-restrictive environment. Such services may include in-school counseling, speech and language services, and so on.

65. **Remediation**: An educational program designed to teach children to overcome some deficit or disability through education and training.

66. **Resource Room**: An auxiliary service provided to disabled children for part of the school day. It is intended to service children's special needs so that they can be maintained within the least-restrictive educational setting. This service may be rendered in either a categorical or noncategorical model.

67. **Screening**: The process of examining groups of children in hopes of identifying potential high-risk children.

68. **Section 504**: Refers to Section 504 of the Rehabilitation Act of 1973 in which guarantees are provided for the civil rights of disabled children and adults. It also applies to the provision of services for children whose disability is not severe

enough to warrant classification, but could benefit from supportive services and classroom modifications.

69. **Self-Contained Class**: A special classroom for exceptional children usually located within a regular school building.

70. **Sheltered Workshops**: A transitional or long-term work environment for disabled individuals who cannot or who are preparing for work in a regular setting. Within this setting the individual can learn to perform meaningful, productive tasks and receive payment.

71. **Surrogate Parent**: A person other than the child's natural parent who has legal responsibility for the child's care and welfare.

72. **Token Economy**: A system of reinforcing various behaviors through the delivery of tokens. These tokens can be in the form of stars, points, candy, chips, and so on.

73. **Total Communication**: The approach to the education of deaf students which combines oral speech, sign language, and finger spelling.

74. **Underachiever**: A term generally used in reference to a child's discrepancy between his/her ability and academic achievement in school. However, it is important that the school identify the underlying causes of such underachievement since it may be a symptom of a more serious problem.

75. **Vocational Rehabilitation**: A program designed to help disabled adults obtain and hold a job.

Medical Terminology

1. **Albinism**: A congenital condition marked by severe deficiency in or total lack of pigmentation.

2. **Amblyopia**: A dimness of sight without any indication of change in the eye's structure.

3. **Amniocentesis**: A medical procedure done during the early stages of pregnancy for the purpose of identifying certain genetic disorders in the fetus.

4. **Anomaly**: Some irregularity in development or a deviation from the standard.

5. **Anoxia**: A lack of oxygen.

6. **Aphasia**: The inability to acquire meaningful spoken language by the age of 3 as a result of brain damage.

7. **Apraxia**: Pertains to problems with voluntary, or purposeful muscular movement with no evidence of motor impairment.

8. **Aqueous Humor**: The jelly-like fluid which fills most of the interior of the eyeball.

9. **Astigmatism**: A visual defect resulting in blurred vision caused by uneven curvature of the cornea or lens. The condition is usually corrected by lenses.

10. **Ataxia**: A form of cerebral palsy in which the individual suffers from a loss of muscle coordination, especially those movements relating to balance and position.

11. **Athetosis**: A form of cerebral palsy characterized by involuntary, jerky, purposeless, and repetitive movements of the extremities, head, and tongue.

12. **Atrophy**: The degeneration of tissue.

13. **Audiogram**: A graphic representation of the results of a hearing test.

14. **Audiologist**: A specialist trained in the evaluation and remediation of auditory disorders.

15. **Binocular Vision**: Vision using both eyes working together to perceive a single image.

16. **Blind, Legally**: Visual acuity measured at 20/200 in the better eye with best correction of glasses or contact lenses. Vision measured at 20/200 means the individual must be 20 feet from something to be able to see what the normal eye can see at 200 feet.

17. **Cataract**: A condition of the eye in which the crystalline lens becomes cloudy or opaque. As a result, a reduction or loss of vision occurs.

18. **Catheter**: A tube inserted into the body to allow for injections or withdrawal of fluids or to maintain an opening in a passageway.

19. **Cerebral Palsy**: Refers to an abnormal amount of human movement or motor functioning resulting from a defect, insult, or disease of the central nervous system.

20. **Cochlea**: Referred to as the organ of hearing, this part of the ear is responsible for sending impulses to the brain.

21. **Conductive Hearing Loss**: A hearing loss resulting from obstructions in the outer or middle ear or some malformations that interfere in the conduction of sound waves to the inner ear. This condition may be corrected medically or surgically.

22. **Congenital**: Present at birth.

23. **Cretinism**: A congenital condition associated with a thyroid deficiency that can result in stunted physical growth and mental retardation.

24. **Cyanosis**: A lack of oxygen in the blood characterized by a blue discoloration of the skin.

25. **Cystic Fibrosis**: An inherited disorder affecting the pancreas, salivary, mucous, and sweat glands that causes severe, long-term respiratory difficulties.

26. **Diplegia**: Paralysis that affects either both arms or both legs.

27. **Down's yndrome**: A medical abnormality caused by a chromosomal anomaly which often results in moderate to severe mental retardation. The child with Down's Syndrome will exhibit certain physical characteristics such as a large tongue, heart problems, poor muscle tone, and broad, flat bridge of the nose.

28. **Electroencephalogram (EEG)**: A graphic representation of the electrical output of the brain.

29. **Encopresis**: A lack of bowel control that may also have psychological causes.

30. **Endogenous**: Originating from within.

31. **Enureusis**: A lack of bladder control that may also have psychological causes.

32. **Exogenous**: Originating from external causes.

33. **Fetal Alcohol Syndrome**: A condition usually found in the infants of alcoholic mothers. As a result, low birth weight, severe retardation, and cardiac, limb, and other physical defects may be present.

34. **Field of Vision**: The area of space visible with both eyes while looking straight ahead; measured in degrees.

35. **Glaucoma**: An eye disease characterized by excessively high pressure inside the eyeball. If untreated, the condition can result in total blindness.

36. **Grand Mal Seizure**: The most serious and severe form of an epileptic seizure in which the individual exhibits violent convulsions, loses consciousness, and becomes rigid.

37. **Hemiplegia**: Paralysis involving the extremities on the same side of the body.

38. **Hemophilia**: An inherited deficiency in the blood-clotting factor which can result in serious internal bleeding.

39. **Hertz**: A unit of sound frequency used to measure pitch.

40. **Hydrocephalus**: A condition present at birth or developing soon afterwards from excess cerebrospinal fluid in the brain and resulting in an enlargement of the head and mental retardation. This condition is sometimes prevented by the surgical placement of a shunt which allows for the proper drainage of the built-up fluids.

41. **Hyperactivity**: Excessive physical and muscular activity characterized by extreme inattention, excessive restlessness, and mobility. The condition is usually associated with Attention-Deficit Disorder or learning disabilities.

42. **Hyperopia**: Farsightedness; a condition causing difficulty with seeing near objects.

43. **Hypertonicity**: Refers to heightened state of excessive muscle tension.

44. **Hypotonicity**: Refers to an inability in maintaining muscle tone or an inability in maintaining muscle tension or resistance to stretch.

45. **Insulin**: A protein hormone produced by the pancreas that regulates carbohydrate metabolism.

46. **Iris**: The opaque, colored portion of the eye.

47. **Juvenile Diabetes**: A children's disease characterized by an inadequate secretion or use of insulin resulting in excessive sugar in the blood and urine. This condition is usually controlled by diet and/or medication. However in certain cases, control may be difficult and if untreated, serious complications may arise such as visual impairments, limb amputation, coma, and death.

48. **Meningitis**: An inflammation of the membranes covering the brain and spinal cord. If untreated can result in serious complications.

49. **Meningocele**: A type of spina bifida in which there is protrusion of the covering of the spinal cord through an opening in the vertebrae.

50. **Microcephaly**: A disorder involving the cranial cavity characterized by the development of a small head. Retardation usually occurs from the lack of space for brain development.

51. **Monoplegia**: Paralysis of a single limb.

52. **Multiple Sclerosis**: A progressive deterioration of the protective sheath surrounding the nerves leading to a degeneration and failure of the body's central nervous system.

53. **Muscular Dystrophy**: A group of diseases that eventually weakens and destroys muscle tissue leading to a progressive deterioration of the body.

54. **Myopia**: Nearsightedness; a condition which results in blurred vision for distance objects.

55. **Neonatal**: The time usually associated with the period between the onset of labor and 6 weeks following birth.

56. **Neurologically Impaired**: Exhibiting problems associated with the functioning of the central nervous system.

57. **Nystagmus**: A rapid, rhythmic, and involuntary movement of the eyes. This condition may result in difficulty reading or fixating upon objects.

58. **Ocular Mobility**: Refers to the eye's ability to move.

59. **Optometrist**: A professional trained to examine eyes for defects and prescribe corrective lenses.

60. **Ophthalmologist**: A medical doctor trained to deal with diseases and conditions of the eye.

61. **Optic Nerve**: The nerve in the eye which carries impulses to the brain.

62. **Optician**: A specialist trained to grind lenses according to a prescription.

63. **Ossicles**: The three small bones of the ear that transmit sound waves to the eardrum. They consist of the *malleus, incus,* and *stapes.*

64. **Osteogenesis Imperfecta**: Also known as "brittle bone disease," this hereditary condition affects the growth of bones and causes them to break easily.

65. **Otitis Media**: Middle-ear infection.

66. **Otolaryngologist**: A medical doctor specializing in diseases of the ear and throat.

67. **Otologist**: A medical doctor specializing in the diseases of the ear.

68. **Otosclerosis**: A bony growth in the middle ear which develops around the base of the stapes, impeding its movement and causing hearing loss.

69. **Organic**: Factors usually associated with the central nervous system that cause a handicapping condition.

70. **Paralysis**: An impairment to or a loss of voluntary movement or sensation.

71. **Paraplegia**: A paralysis usually involving the lower half of the body, including both legs as a result of injury or disease of the spinal cord.

72. **Perinatal**: Occurring at or immediately following birth.

73. **Petite Mal Seizures**: A mild form of epilepsy characterized by dizziness and momentary lapse of consciousness.

74. **Phenylketonuria**: Referred to as PKU, this inherited metabolic disease usually results in severe retardation. However, if detected at birth, a special diet can reduce the serious complications associated with the condition.

75. **Photophobia**: An extreme sensitivity of the eyes to light. This condition is common in albino children.

76. **Postnatal**: Occurring after birth.

77. **Prenatal**: Occurring before birth.

78. **Prosthesis**: An artificial device used to replace a missing body part.

79. **Psychomotor Seizure**: Epileptic seizures in which the individual exhibits many automatic seizure activities of which he/she is not aware.

80. **Pupil**: The opening in the middle of the iris which expands and contracts to let in light.

81. **Quadriplegia**: Paralysis involving all four limbs.

82. **Retina**: The back portion of the eye, containing nerve fibers which connect to the optic nerve on which the image is focused.

83. **Retinitis Pigmentosa**: A degenerative eye disease in which the retina gradually atrophies, causing a narrowing of the field of vision.

84. **Retrolental Fibroplasia**: An eye disorder resulting from excessive oxygen in incubators of premature babies.

85. **Rh Incompatibility**: A blood condition in which the fetus has Rh-positive blood and the mother has Rh-negative blood leading to a build-up of antibodies that attack the fetus. If untreated, can result in birth defects.

86. **Rheumatic Fever**: A disease characterized by acute inflammation of the joints, fever, skin rash, nosebleeds, and abdominal pain. This disease often damages the heart by scarring its tissues and valves.

87. **Rigidity Cerebral Palsy**: A type of cerebral palsy characterized by minimal muscle elasticity, and little or no stretch reflex which creates stiffness.

88. **Rubella**: Referred to as German Measles, this communicable disease is usually only of concern when developed by women during the early stages of pregnancy. If contracted at that time, there is a high probability of severe handicaps of the offspring.

89. **Sclera**: The tough white outer layer of the eyeball which protects as well as holds contents in place.

90. **Scoliosis**: A weakness of the muscles which result in a serious abnormal curvature of the spine. This condition may be corrected with surgery or a brace.

91. **Semicircular Canals**: The three canals within the middle ear that are responsible for maintaining balance.

92. **Sensorineural Hearing Loss**: A hearing disorder resulting from damage or dysfunction of the cochlea.

93. **Shunt**: A tube that is inserted into the body to drain fluid from one part to another. This procedure is common in cases of hydrocephalus to remove excessive cerebrospinal fluid from the head and redirect it to the heart or intestines.

94. **Spasticity**: A type of cerebral palsy characterized by tense, contracted muscles, resulting in muscular incoordination.

95. **Spina Bifida Occulta**: A type of spina bifida characterized by a protrusion of the spinal cord and membranes. This form of the condition does not always cause serious disability.

96. **Strabismus**: Crossed eyes.

97. **Tremor**: A type of cerebral palsy characterized by consistent, strong, uncontrolled movements.

98. **Triplegia**: Paralysis of three of the body's limbs.

99. **Usher's Syndrome**: A genetic disorder that may result in a combination of visual and hearing impairments.

100. **Visual Acuity**: Sharpness or clearness of vision.

Psychological Terminology

1. **Affective Reactions**: Psychotic reactions marked by extreme mood swings.

2. **Anxiety**: A general uneasiness of the mind characterized by irrational fears, panic, tension, and physical symptoms including palpitations, excessive sweating, and increased pulse rate.

3. **Assessment**: The process of gathering information about children in order to make educational decisions.

4. **Baseline Data**: An objective measure used to compare and evaluate the results obtained during some implementation of an instructional procedure, (such as the amount of time a child spends sitting in his/her seat).

5. **Compulsion**: A persistent, repetitive act which the individual cannot consciously control.

6. **Confabulation**: The act of replacing memory loss by fantasy or by some reality that is not true for the occasion.

7. **Defense Mechanisms**: The unconscious means by which an individual protects him- or herself against impulses or emotions that are too uncomfortable or threatening. Examples of these mechanisms include the following:

   • **Denial**: A defense mechanism in which the individual refuses to admit the reality of some unpleasant event, situation, or emotion.

- **Displacement**: The disguising of the goal or intention of a motive by substituting another in it's place.
- **Intellectualization**: A defense mechanism in which the individual exhibits anxious or moody deliberation, usually about abstract matters.
- **Projection**: The disguising of a source of conflict by displacing one's own motives to someone else.
- **Rationalization**: The interpretation of one's own behavior so as to conceal the motive it expresses by assigning the behavior to another motive.
- **Reaction Formation**: A complete disguise of a motive, expressed in a form that is directly opposite to its original intent. For instance, a child jealous and angry over a new baby may overly "love" the child through some play to the point of hurting the child.
- **Repression**: Refers to the psychological process involved in not permitting memories and motives to enter consciousness but are operating at an unconscious level.
- **Suppression**: The act of consciously inhibiting an impulse, affect, or idea, as in the deliberate act of forgetting something so as not to have to think about it.

8. **Delusion**: A groundless, irrational belief or thought, usually of grandeur or of persecution. It is usually a characteristic of paranoia.

9. **Depersonalization**: A nonspecific syndrome in which the individual senses that he/she has lost personal identity, that he/she is different, strange, or not real.

10. **Echolalia**: Refers to the repetition of what other people say as if echoing them.

11. **Etiology**: Refers to the cause(s) of something.

12. **Hallucination**: An imaginary visual image that is regarded as a real sensory experience by the person.

13. **Magical Thinking**: Refers to primitive and prelogical thinking in which the child creates an outcome to meet fantasy rather than the reality.

14. **Neologisms**: Made up words that only have meaning to the child.

15. **Obsessions**: A repetitive and persistent idea that intrudes into a person's thoughts.

16. **Panic Attack**: A serious episode of anxiety in which the individual experiences a variety of symptoms including palpitations, dizziness, nausea, chest pains, trembling, fear of dying, and fear of losing control. These symptoms are not the result of any medical cause.

17. **Paranoia**: A personality disorder in which the individual exhibits extreme suspiciousness of the motives of others.

18. **Phobia**: An intense irrational fear, usually acquired through conditioning to an unpleasant object or event.

19. **Projective Tests**: Evaluative methods used by psychologists and psychiatrists to study personality dynamics. These tests require the child or adult to make up

answers when presented with a series of inkblots, pictures, or sentences. In this way, the professional will be able to see how the individual feels about certain things in his/her life that he/she may not be aware of on a conscious level.

20. **Psychosis**: A serious mental disorder in which the individual has difficulty differentiating between fantasy and reality.

21. **Rorschach Test**: An unstructured psychological test in which the individual is asked to project responses to a series of ten inkblots.

22. **School Phobia**: A form of separation anxiety in which the child's concerns and anxieties are centered around school issues and as a result he/she has an extreme fear about coming to school.

23. **Symptom**: Refers to any sign, physical or mental, that stands for something else. Symptoms are usually generated from the tension of conflicts. The more serious the problem or conflict, the more frequent and intense the symptom.

24. **Syndrome**: A group of symptoms.

25. **Thematic Apperception Test**: A structured psychological test in which the individual is asked to project his/her feelings onto a series of drawings or photos.

26. **Wechsler Scales of Intelligence**: A series of individual intelligence tests measuring global intelligence through a variety of subtests.

Occupational and Physical Therapy Terminology

1. **Abduction**: Movement of limb outwards away from body.

2. **Active Movements**: Movements a child does without help.

3. **Adaptive Equipment**: Devices used to position or to teach special skills.

4. **Asymmetrical**: One side of the body different from the other—unequal or dissimilar.

5. **Associated Reactions**: Increase of stiffness in spastic arms and legs resulting from effort.

6. **Ataxic**: No balance, jerky.

7. **Athetoid**: Uncontrolled and continuously unwanted movements.

8. **Atrophy**: Wasting of the muscles.

9. **Automatic Movements**: Necessary movements done without thought or effort.

10. **Balance**: Not falling over, ability to keep a steady position.

11. **Bilateral Motor**: Skill and performance in purposeful movement that requires interaction between both sides of the body in a smooth manner.

12. **Clonus**: Shaky movements of spastic muscle.

13. **Compensatory Movement**: A form of movement that is atypical in relation to normal patterns of movement.

14. **Congenital**: From birth.

15. **Coordination**: Combination of muscle in movement.

16. **Contracture**: Permanently tight muscle or joint.
17. **Crossing the Midline**: Refers to skill and performance in crossing the vertical midline of the body.
18. **Deformity**: Body or limb fixed in abnormal position.
19. **Diplegia**: Legs mostly affected.
20. **Distractable**: Not able to concentrate.
21. **Equilibrium**: Balance.
22. **Equilibrium Reactions**: Automatic patterns of body movements that enable restoration and maintenance of balance against gravity.
23. **Equinus**: Toe walks.
24. **Extension**: Straightening of the trunk and limbs.
25. **Eye-Hand Coordination**: Eye is used as a tool for directing the hand to perform efficiently.
26. **Facilitation**: Making it possible for the child to move.
27. **Figure-Ground Perception**: To be able to see foreground against background.
28. **Fine Motor**: Small muscle movements, use of hands and fingers.
29. **Flexion**: Bending of elbows, hips, knees, and so on.
30. **Fluctuating Tone**: Changing from one degree of tension to another, for example, from low to high tone.
31. **Form Constancy**: Ability to perceive an object as possessing invariant properties such as shape, size, color, and brightness.
32. **Gait Pattern**: Description of walking pattern.
33. **Gait Swing**: Walking with crutches or walker by moving crutches forward and swinging body up to crutches and beyond them.
34. **Genu Valgus**: Knocked knee.
35. **Genu Varum**: Bowlegged.
36. **Gross Motor**: Coordinated movements of all parts of the body for performance.
37. **Guarding Techniques**: When a student requires hands-on contact to maintain balance.
38. **Guarded Supervision**: When an individual is close to the student to provide physical support if balance is lost while sitting, standing, or walking.
39. **Head Control**: Ability to control the position of the head.
40. **Hemiplegia**: One side of the body affected.
41. **Hypertonicity**: Increased muscle tone.
42. **Hypotonicity**: Decreased muscle tone.
43. **Inhibition**: Positions and movements which stop muscle tightness.
44. **Involuntary Movements**: Unintended movements.
45. **Kyphosis**: Increased rounding of the upper back.
46. **Lordosis**: Sway back or increased curve in the back.

47. **Manual Muscle Test**: Test of isolated muscle strength.

48. *Normal—100%*

49. *Good—80%*

50. *Fair—50%*

51. *Poor—20%*

52. *Zero—0*

53. **Mobility**: Movement of a body muscle, body part, or movement of the whole body from one place to another.

54. **Motivation**: Making the student want to move or perform.

55. **Motor Patterns**: Ways in which the body and limbs work together to make movement, also known as *praxis*.

56. **Nystagmus**: Series of automatic back-and-forth eye movements.

57. **Organization**: A student's ability to organize himself/herself in approach to and performance of activities.

58. **Orthosis**: Brace.

59. **Paraplegia**: Paralysis of the lower half of the body with involvement of both legs.

60. **Passive**: Anything that is done to the student without his/her help or cooperation.

61. **Pathological**: Due to or involving abnormality.

62. **Perseveration**: Unnecessary repetition of speech or movement.

63. **Positioning**: Ways of placing an individual that will help normalize postural tone and facilitate normal patterns of movement and that may involve the use of adaptive equipment.

64. **Position in Space**: Child's ability to understand the relationship of an object to himself/herself.

65. **Postural Balance**: Refers to skill and performance in developing and maintaining body posture while sitting, standing, or engaging in an activity.

66. **Praxis**: Ability to think through a new task which requires movement, also known as *motor planning*.

67. **Pronation**: Turning of the hand with palm down.

68. **Prone**: Lying on the stomach.

69. **Quadriplegic**: Whole body affected.

70. **Range of Motion**: The extent to which an individual is able to move joints and limbs.

71. **Reflex**: Stereotypic posture and movement that occurs in relation to specific eliciting stimuli outside of conscious control.

72. **Righting Reactions**: Ability to put head and body right when positions are abnormal or uncomfortable.

73. **Right/Left Discrimination**: Skill and performance in differentiating right from left and vice versa.

74. **Rigidity**: Very stiff movements and postures.

75. **Rotation**: Movement of the trunk, the shoulders move opposite to the hips.

76. **Sensation**: Feeling.

77. **Sensory-Motor Experience**: The feeling of one's own movements.

78. **Scoliosis**: C or S curvature of the spine.

79. **Spasm**: Sudden tightness of muscles.

80. **Stair Climbing**: Methods of climbing including mark stepping, stairs (ascending or descending), one step at a time, or alternating steps (step over step).

81. **Stereognosis**: The identification of forms and nature of object through the sense of touch.

82. **Subluxation**: A partial dislocation where joint surfaces remain in contact with one another.

83. **Supniation**: Turning of hand with palm up.

84. **Symmetrical**: Both sides equal.

85. **Tactile**: Pertaining to the sense of touch of the skin.

86. **Tandem Walking**: Walks in a forward progression placing heel to toe.

87. **Tone**: firmness of muscles.

88. **Visual Memory**: Ability to recall visual stimuli, in terms of form, detail, position, and other significant features on both short- and long-term basis.

89. **Visual-Motor Integration**: The ability to combine visual input with purposeful voluntary movement of body parts involved in the activity.

90. **Voluntary Movements**: Movements done with attention and with concentration.

Commonly Used Terms in the Employment of Disabled Individuals

1. **Accessible**: easy to approach, enter, operate, participate in, and/or use safely and with dignity by a person with a disability (site, facility, work environment, service, or program).

2. **Affirmative Action**: Positive action to increase the employment opportunities of certain groups, which may involve goals, timetables, or specifically outlined steps to be undertaken to assure that objectives are reached.

3. **Americans With Disabilities Act (ADA)**: A comprehensive Civil Rights law which makes it unlawful to discriminate in private-sector employment against a qualified individual with a disability. The ADA also outlaws discrimination against individuals with disabilities in state and local government services and employment, public accommodations, transportation, and telecommunication. The law was enacted in July of 1990. The private sector employment provisions (Title I) became effective for employers with 25 or more employees on July 26, 1992, and on July 26, 1994, for employers of 15 or more employees.

4. **ADA Affirmative Action**: The ADA does not mandate affirmative action for persons with disabilities, but does require that covered entities ensure nondiscrimination. Title V, Section 503 of the Rehabilitation Act does require that affirmative action be taken in employment considerations of persons with disabilities by Federal contractors (see Title V definition in this section).

5. **Auxiliary Aids and Services**: Devices or services that accommodate a functional limitation of a person with a communication disability. The term includes qualified interpreters and communication for persons who are deaf or persons who are hard of hearing; qualified readers, taped texts, Braille, or other devices for persons with visual impairments; adaptive equipment or similar services and actions for persons with other communication disabilities.

6. **Equal Employment Opportunity**: Nondiscrimination in hiring, firing, compensation, promotion, recruitment, training, and other terms and conditions of employment regardless of race, color, sex, age, religion, national origin, or disability.

7. **Essential Job Functions**: The fundamental job duties of the employment position that the individual with a disability holds or desires. The term "essential functions" does not include marginal functions of the position.

8. **Individual With a Disability**: A person who has a physical or mental impairment that substantially limits one or more of that person's major life activities, has a record of such impairment, or who is regarded as having such an impairment.

9. **Major Life Activity**: Basic activities that the average person in the general population can perform with little or no difficulty, including caring for oneself, performing manual tasks, walking, seeing, hearing, speaking, breathing, learning, and working.

10. **Qualified Individual With a Disability**: An individual with a disability who satisfies the requisite skill, experience, education, and other job-related requirements of the employment position such individual holds or desires, and who, with or without reasonable accommodation, can perform the essential functions of such position.

11. **Readily Achievable**: Easily accomplished and able to be carried out without much difficulty or expense. In determining whether an action is readily achievable, factors to be considered include nature and cost of the action, overall financial resources, and the effect on expenses and resources, legitimate safety requirements, impact on the operation of a site, and, if applicable, overall financial resources, size, and type of operation of any parent corporation or entity.

12. **Reasonable Accommodation**: Modification or adjustment to a job-application process that enables a qualified applicant with a disability to be considered for the position desired; or modifications or adjustments to the work environment, or to the manner or circumstances under which the position held or desired is customarily performed, that enables qualified individuals with disabilities to perform the essential functions of that position; or modifications or adjustments that enable a covered entity's employee with a disability to enjoy equal benefits and

privileges of employment as are enjoyed by its other similarly situated employees without disabilities.

13. **Title V Of The Rehabilitation Act of 1973**: Title of the law which prohibits discrimination on the basis of a disability by the Federal government, Federal contractors, by recipients of Federal financial assistance, and in Federal programs and activities.

14. **Undue Hardship**: With respect to the provision of an accommodation, significant difficulty, or expense incurred by a covered entity, when considered in light of certain factors. These factors include the nature and cost of the accommodation in relationship to the size, resources, nature, and structure of the employer's operation. Where the facility making the accommodation is part of a larger entity, the structure and overall resources of the larger organization would be considered, as well as the financial and administrative relationship of the facility to the larger organization.

15. **Vocational Rehabilitation**: Programs designed to assist individuals with disabilities to enter or reenter gainful employment.

Source: Adapted from "Glossary of Commonly Used Terms," President's Committee on Employment of People with Disabilities, 10/94, Original sources for definitions include the *Americans With Disabilities Act* and its implementing regulations and *Title V of the Rehabilitation Act of 1973*.

Abbreviations Associated With Special Education

ACLC—Assessment of Children's Language Comprehension

ADHD—Attention-Deficit Hyperactivity Disorder

AE—Age Equivalent

AUD.DIS—Auditory Discrimination

BINET—Stanford Binet Intelligence Test

BVMGT—Bender Visual Motor Gestalt Test

CA—Chronological Age

C.A.T.—Children's Apperception Test

CEC—Council for Exceptional Children

C.P.—Cerebral Palsy

CSE—Committee on Special Education

DAP—Draw a Person Test

Db—Decibel-Hearing Measurement

DDST—Denver Developmental Screening Test

DQ—Developmental Quotient

DTLA–3—Detroit Tests of Learning Aptitude–3

ED—Emotionally Disturbed

EMR—Educable Mentally Retarded

FAPE—Free Appropriate Public Education

fq—Frequency Range-Hearing Measurement

GE—Grade Equivalent

GFW—Goldman-Fristoe-Woodcock Test of Auditory Discrimination

HH—Hard of Hearing

HTP—House-Tree-Person Test

Hz—Hertz-Hearing Measurement

IEU—Intermediate Educational Unit

IHE—Institutions of Higher Education

IQ—Intelligence Quotient

ITPA—Illinois Tests of Psycholinguistic Abilities

LA—Learning Aptitude

L.D—Learning Disabled

LEA—Local Education Agency

LPR—Local Percentile Rank

MA—Mental Age

MBD—Minimal Brain Dysfunction

MH—Multiply Handicapped

MMPI—Minnesota Multiphasic Personality Inventory

MR—Mentally Retarded

MVPT—Motor-Free Visual Perception Test

NPR—National Percentile Rank

PHC—Pupils With Handicapping Conditions

PIAT—Peabody Individual Achievement Test

PINS—Person in Need of Supervision

PLA—Psycholinguistic Age

PQ—Perceptual Quotient

PPVT—Peabody Picture Vocabulary Test

PR—Percentile Rank

PS—Partially Sighted

PSEN—Pupils With Special Educational Needs

PTA—Pure Tone Average-Hearing Measurement

SAI—School Abilities Index

SCSIT—Southern California Sensory Integration Tests

SEA—State Education Agency

SIT—Slosson Intelligence Test

SRT—Speech Reception Threshhold—Hearing Measurement

SSDI—Social Security Disability Insurance

SSI—Social Security Insurance

TACL—Test for Auditory Comprehension of Language

TAT—Thematic Apperception Test

TMR—Trainable Mentally Retarded

TOWL—Test of Written Language

TWS—Larsen-Hammill Test of Written Spelling

VAKT—Visual/Auditory/Kinesthetic/Tactile

VIS.DIS—Visual Discrimination

VMI—Beery-Buktenica Developmental Test of Visual Motor Integration

WAIS–R—Wechsler Adult Intelligence Scale–Revised

WISC–R—Wechsler Intelligence Scale for Children–Revised

WISC–III—Wechsler Intelligence Scale for Children–III

WPPSI–R—Wechsler Preschool and Primary Scale of Intelligence–Revised

WRAT–R—Wide Range Achievement Test–Revised

Appendix B—Special-Education Forms

Suggested Materials for CSE Presentations

A school may be required to gather materials for the CSE for several reasons:

1. An initial review of a new student who may have a suspected disability.
2. An annual review meeting where the child's present disability and placement are reviewed.
3. A triennial evaluation.
4. A request for a special CSE meeting (for example, a change in an existing IEP).

Once the review is requested, the school should prepare a packet of information for a presentation at your child's meeting. While state requirements may differ, a complete and well-organized packet should be sufficient for any situation.

In order to accomplish this task, one person from the school may be designated as the coordinator of the case and it would be his/her responsibility to ensure that all required material is placed in the packet. Once this is accomplished, the packet is then sent to the chairperson of the CSE prior to the meeting. Be aware that you should see the completed packet before the meeting and are entitled to a copy of the packet for your records.

A well-organized presentation packet could include the following information:

DATA PROCESSING SHEET

This form gives the CSE office all the necessary identifying data on a child with a potential disability. It can also serve as a worksheet for the CSE chairperson during the meeting. The following is an example of how this form may look.

Goals submitted and attached to packet?_____Yes _____No   Student ID No.:_____

Goals Changed (Review)_____Yes _____No   Student Date of Birth:_____

CSE DATE _____ **(FOR CSE USE ONLY)**

COMMITTEE _____

Also Present (for CSE use only) _____

Case Presented by _____

Student Name _____

Parent Name(s) _____

Status: Married_____Single_____Divorced_____Widowed_____

Address _____

All correspondence and information should be sent to:
Mother_____ Father _____ Both _____ Legal Guardian _____

Current School _____

Current Teacher (Elem. Level Only) _____

Current Grade _____

Current Contact Teacher if Previously Classified
(Mid. Sch. and H.S. Only) _____

Guidance Counselor _____

Dominant Language—Student _____

Dominant Language—Home _____

Ethnicity _____

Reason for the Meeting:

(Check One) Initial Review _____ Review of Present Classification _____
 Declassification _____ Review of Placement _____

Pendency _____ Annual Review _____ Triennial Review _____

Date Entered Program (For a review case only) _____

Diploma Type _____

Other _____

Evaluation Information (Test names and score type)
IQ Test Information

Test _____ VIQ _____ % Rank _____ PIQ _____%
Rank _____ FSIQ _____% Rank _____

Psychoeducational Test Information
Area Measured

Test Name _____ Percentile _____ Test Date _____

Test Name _____ Percentile _____ Test Date _____

Test Name _____ Percentile _____ Test Date _____

Examiner: Psychological _____ Educational _____ Speech/Language _____

STUDENT NAME _____ CSE DATE _____

STUDENT ID _____ STUDENT DOB _____ SCHOOL _____

FOR CSE USE ONLY
Recommended:

1. **Classification** _____ **Sec.Con.** _____

2. **Placement** _____ **Staff Ratio** _____

3. **Related Service** _____ **Times/wk** _____

   Related Service _____ **Times/wk** _____

   Related Service _____ **Times/wk.** _____

4. **Adaptive Devices** _____

5. **Mainstreamed Classes** _____

   _____

6. **Test Modifications** _____

   _____

   _____

7. **Transportation Y** _____ **N** _____ **Triennial Date** _____

8. **Special Trans. Needs**: _____

   _____

9. **Foreign Language Exempt** **Yes** _____ **No** _____ **NA** _____

10. **Service Start Date for Placement** _____ **For Related Service** _____

11. **Related Service Provider(s)** _____

12. **Recommended Teacher or Contact Teacher** _____

13. **Least-Restrictive Statement** _____

CSE Packet Checklist

This checklist is a good tool to ensure that the school or task coordinator has included all the necessary materials required by the CSE for a particular type of review. An example of this form follows.

Name of Student _____ School _____ Grade _____

Type of Meeting: Initial _____ Special _____ Annual Review _____

INITIAL REFERRAL:

REQUIRED FORMS:
- ____ A-Initial Referral to CSE From School Staff
- ____ B-Initial Referral to CSE From Parent/Guardian
- ____ C-Parent Consent for Evaluation

EVALUATION:
- ____ Social History
- ____ Medical Report
- ____ Classroom Observation
- ____ Psychological
- ____ Educational
- ____ Speech/Language
- ____ Vocational (Secondary Level Only)
- ____ Other (Occupational Therapist, Physical Therapist, ESL, Reading)

Specify _____, _____, _____

GUIDANCE MATERIALS:
- ____ Child's Schedule
- ____ Transcript of Past Grades
- ____ Latest Report Card
- ____ Teacher Reports

OTHER:
- ____ Discipline Information
- ____ PPT-Related Documents (minutes)
- ____ Standardized Achievement Test Scores
- ____ Report Cards
- ____ Needs (Levels of Development: Social, Physical, Academic, Management)
- ____ Recommended Goals and Objectives (Draft)
- ____ Attendance Records
- ____ Other

SPECIAL MEETING:

Name of Current/Contact Teacher____
Special Meeting Referral Form____
Current Teacher Report____
Recom. Goals and Objectives____
New Evaluations if Completed____
Other Documents—Specify:_____

ANNUAL REVIEW:
- ____ Prep Sheet_____
- ____ Current IEP_____
- ____ Evaluations Completed _____
  —Specify: _____
- ____ Needs (Social, Physical)_____
- ____ Recommended Goals/Obj._____
- ____ Other Documents
  —Specify: _____

TRIENNIAL
EVALUATION DOCUMENTS:
- ____ Parent Notice of Triennial Evaluation Form
- ____ Psychological
- ____ Educational
- ____ Speech/Language
- ____ Medical Report
- ____ Social History Update
- ____ Transcript of Grades
- ____ Child's Schedule
- ____ Recent Report Cards
- ____ Teacher Reports
- ____ Other
  —Specify:_____

Recommended CSE Participants:
Case Manager: **Date:**

There are several forms that may have to be used when referring a case for a CSE review. These forms are used for initial reviews, special meetings, and triennial evaluations.

INITIAL REFERRAL TO CSE FROM PARENT/GUARDIAN

This initial referral may be initiated by any school staff member (teacher, counselor, administrator, psychologist) or by a parent. However, if a parent requests an initial review by the CSE, a different form may be used.

Date: _____

To: _____
　　　　　Principal or CSE Chairperson

I am writing to refer my child _____, aged _____, to the Committee on Special Education. I am asking you to conduct an individual evaluation to determine whether a handicapping condition exists that would make my child eligible for Special-Education Services.

I am concerned about my child's educational difficulties in the following areas:

Please contact me as soon as possible to discuss my referral.

Sincerely,

Parent/Guardian _____ Phone _____

Address _____

State _____ Zip _____

Child's Birthdate _____ School _____ Grade _____

Date received by CSE _____

PARENT CONSENT FOR EVALUATION

State laws and/or district policies usually mandate that parent(s) must sign a consent form allowing the school to administer an evaluation of their child. As previously mentioned, the school usually obtains this form at the initial meeting with the parent to discuss the reasons for the referral or through the mail. Either way, this consent is required before any evaluation can take place. An example of such a form may look like the following:

To the Parent/Guardian of: _____ **Birth Date**: _____

School: _____ **Grade**: _____

We would like to inform you that your child _____ has been referred for individual testing because of the suspicion of a disability. Testing results will help us in determining your child's educational needs and in planning the most appropriate program. The evaluation procedures and/or tests may include the following:

Intelligence: _____

Communication/Language/Speech: _____

Physical: _____

Behavior/Emotional: _____

Academic:_____

Vocational: _____

Other: _____

Before we can begin testing, it is necessary that the School District CSE have your written permission to evaluate your child. You have had the opportunity to discuss the need for this testing and the possibilities for special-education services with the school principal/designee.

The evaluation(s) will be conducted by the multidisciplinary team who will share the results of said evaluation with you at a building-level meeting. Both this meeting and a CSE meeting will be held within 30 school days of receipt of this notice.

I grant permission for the evaluation(s) mentioned above: _____

I do not grant permission for the evaluation(s) mentioned above: _____

Date:_____ **Parent Signature**: _____

Date:_____ **Administrator/Designee**: _____

Explanation of Evaluations

1. **Psychological Evaluation**: A full psychological evaluation including all identifying data, reason for referral, background and developmental history, prior testing results, observations, tests administered, test results (including a breakdown of scaled scores), conclusions and recommendations is required. This evaluation must be conducted within one year of the CSE meeting. It may also be helpful to include any prior evaluations done over the years.

2. **Educational Evaluation**: A psychoeducational evaluation including identifying data, reason for referral, academic history, prior testing results, observations, tests administered, test results, conclusions, and recommendations is required. This report should identify achievement strengths and weaknesses and perceptual strengths and weaknesses.

3. **Speech/Language Evaluation**: A speech/language evaluation including identifying data, reason for referral, observations, tests administered, test results, conclusions and recommendations should be included if applicable. A description of the severity of the language deficit should also be included, and if possible, the prognosis.

4. **Reading Teacher's Report**: If indicated, a full reading evaluation including identifying data, reason for referral, observations, prior standardized reading test percentiles, tests administered, test results, conclusions, and recommendations should be included. A description of the severity of the deficit should also be included which outline the specific areas in need of remediation.

5. **Vocational Evaluation-Aptitude Test Results—Middle School and High School Only (e.g. DAT)**: A copy of the child's Differential Aptitude Test results or other measures of vocational aptitude should be included if applicable.

6. **Outside Reports**: From time to time, parents will have a variety of reports from outside agencies (medical, neurological, psychological, audiological, visual training). These reports should be included only when they are relevant to the possible disability. If outside reports are to be used in lieu of the district's own evaluations, they should be fairly recent (within the past 6 months to 1 year).

7. **Assessments Related to the Suspected Disability as Required**: These measures may include the following areas: communication skills, motor abilities, hearing, vision, gross motor abilities, fine motor abilities, physical therapist's evaluation, occupational therapist's evaluation, adaptive physical-education evaluation.

Required Academic Data

1. **Standardized Achievement Test Data From All Grades**: This information should reflect standardized test score results including percentiles as far back as possible. This is included to allow the members to see patterns, strengths, and weaknesses in the child's group scores.

2. **Report Cards**: *Elementary Level*: Copies of all report cards including teacher comments (Grades K–6). *Secondary Level*: These copies should reflect quarter grades, final grades, and absences beginning from grade 7.

3. **Classroom Teacher's Reports**: This report should include a behavioral description of the child's academic, social, intellectual, behavioral, and physical status. Observations should be worded in behavioral terms and any informal testing results should be included.

4. **Attendance and Disciplinary Reports**: *Elementary Level–Secondary Level*: A listing of all disciplinary reports, including reason for referral and disposition should be included. An accurate attendance record should also be included.

5. **Student Class Schedule**: A copy of the child's present class schedule should be included which clearly outlines the level of classes he/she is enrolled in (modified, regents) and teacher's names.

6. **Classroom Observation Sheet**: This form must be completed by either the Special-Education Teacher, Psychologist, Administrator, Social Worker or Guidance Counselor. This form must be included in the CSE packet for an initial referral. An example of this type of form can be found in the section on *Observations*.

SOCIAL AND DEVELOPMENTAL HISTORY FORM

This form should be filled out in full with the parent present if possible. It is important that it include answers to all the information requested so that the committee members have a thorough understanding of the child's history.

Date _____

Name _____ Sex _____

School _____Grade _____ DOB _____

Address _____

Telephone _____

Natural Parents _____ **Child Resides with** _____ (check one)

Father's Name _____ Age _____ Education _____

Occupation _____ Business Phone _____

Mother's Name _____ Age _____ Education _____

Occupation _____ Business Phone _____

Guardians or Other Individual's
Name With Whom Child Resides _____ Name _____

Relationship _____ Relationship _____

Employment _____ Employment _____

Business Phone _____ Business Phone _____

Siblings _____

Names _____ Ages _____ School _____

Others in Home

Names _____

Relationships _____

Ages _____

Name _____ **School** _____ **(Page 2)**

Presenting Problem (As perceived by respondent)

_____

_____

_____

Developmental History: Birth and Infancy Periods—Prenatal, birth, and postnatal facts. Include any unusual aspects in attainment of developmental milestones, such as critical stages, traumatic experiences, falls or injuries, hospital stays, previous testing, medical conditions, or medications used. Include any medical facts which might have an implication in the outcome of this case.

_____

_____

_____

Family History _____

_____

_____

Social History: Include indications of child's conduct in social skills, involvement in groups or organizations, relationship to peers, hobbies or interests.

_____

_____

_____

School Adjustment: Age and grade entrance to school, attendance, retention, change of schools, previous psychological evaluations or prior reviews by CSE in another district.

_____

_____

_____

Behavioral Patterns: (eating, sleeping, relationship with adults)

_____

_____

_____

Name _____ **School** _____ **(Page 3)**

Other Residences: (Hospitals, schools, relatives, foster homes)

_____

_____

_____

Recommendations

_____

_____

Individual Filling Out Form _____ **Title** _____

MEDICAL REPORT FOR THE CSE

This form is usually filled out by the nurse/teacher, forwarded to the psychologist, and attached to the CSE Packet. It contains all the child's pertinent medical history and should include results from a medical examination within the past year.

To be completed by the nurse/teacher and included in the CSE Packet.

Date _____

Student's Name _____ **Grade** _____

Address _____

State _____ Zip _____

Date of last medical examination _____

Name and address of physician _____

_____

_____

Medical findings (attach copy if pertinent) _____

_____

Last vision exam _____ Results _____

Last hearing exam _____ Results _____

Speech _____

Additional information which might have implications in determining the outcome of this case:

Other Required Information and Procedures

Written Consent for Evaluation: A copy of this signed form should be included in the packet so that the Committee has a record of this consent and has an indication of the 30-day time limit requirement.

Draft of Recommended Objectives and Goals: Appropriate members of the PPT should develop a draft of initial goals and objectives. These goals and objectives will be used in the development of the Individual Educational Plan (IEP) at the time of the CSE meeting. These goals and objectives may be modified at the time of the meeting. The form, specific goals, and objectives from which to choose and other factors may differ from district to district.

Statement of Least-Restrictive Environment: If a Pupil Personnel Team is recommending additional services under a classifying condition, please state the reasons why additional services or less-restrictive environment would be necessary. This statement is also very important if the PPT feels that the child's needs may be better served in an out-of-district placement. While the final decision for placement is up to the CSE, the school still needs to substantiate its recommendation.

Parent Given Rights Booklet Prior to CSE Meeting: A parent must be given a copy of the State booklet on parent rights prior to the CSE meeting. This will give the parent an opportunity to become familiar with the procedure and allow him/her time to develop any questions that he/she might have.

Agreement to Withdraw CSE Referral

There may be times when the parent and school agree that the evaluation and findings do not seem to substantiate the suspected disability that was originally considered. When this occurs the school and parent must meet and discuss other methods that will be used to remedy the problem(s). At the time of the meeting, an *Agreement to Withdraw the CSE Referral* form must be filled out and forwarded to the principal and then to the CSE chairperson. This will officially withdraw the original referral and stop the CSE process.

There are usually time requirements and constraints on the professional involved with this procedure so check with the district and state policies. For instance, in some states the professionals must secure this release no later than ten days from the date the testing release was initially signed or the case must go to the CSE.

AGREEMENT TO WITHDRAW CSE REFERRAL

INITIAL CONFERENCE

Student Name _____ **Date of Agreement** _____

Date of Birth _____ Date of Referral _____

Current Program _____ Name of Referring Party _____

Position of Referring Party _____

Persons Present at Conference _____

The following method(s) will be used to attempt to resolve _____ identified learning difficulties: (Attach additional sheets, as needed)

_____

_____

If necessary, a follow-up conference to review the student's progress will be held on:

_____

_____

We agree to the above conditions. The referral is hereby withdrawn.

Referring Party Signature _____ **Date** _____

Parent/Guardian Signature _____ **Date** _____

cc: Student's Cumulative Educational Record
Parent/Guardian
Referring Party

LEARNING PROFILE

Name: _____ **Grade**: _____

School _____ **DOB** _____

Address _____

State _____ **Zip** _____

Phone _____ **Date** _____

  1. Self-Concept: _____

_____

  2. Peer Relationships: _____

_____

  3. Adult Relationships: _____

_____

  4. Intellectual Characteristics: _____

 5. **Academic Characteristics**: _____

 6. **Modality Strengths and Weaknesses**: _____

 7. **Environmental Factors**: _____

 8. **Classroom Structure**: _____

 9. **Prior Evaluations**: _____

10. **Attention to Task:** _____

11. **Motivation**: _____

12. **Response to Pressure**: _____

13. **Response to Difficulty**: _____

14. **Organizational Ability**: _____

15. **Special Skills, Talents, Interests**: _____

16. **Home Environment**: _____

17. **Medical or Physical Problems**: _____

Early Childhood Screening Program Checklist

School _____ No. of Children _____

Dates _____ Person responsible _____

Testing Materials   **Student Materials**

_____ Obstacle course   _____ Name tags
_____ Fine-motor activities   _____ Pencils
_____ School entrance checklist   _____ Crayons
_____ Screening summary sheets   _____ Paper (drawing and writing)
_____ Parent handbooks   _____ Puzzles
_____ Assessment profiles   _____ Books
_____ Screening instruments   _____ Blocks
_____ Checklist of tests   _____ Misc. toys (puppets,
_____ Student folders   clay, riding toys)

Elementary Screening Program

Name of Child _____ Mother's name _____

Date of Birth _____ Father's name _____

Name of Nursery School _____ Address _____

_____

Any special problems? _____ Telephone Number _____

Native language spoken in the home _____

Is your child presently taking any medication? Yes_____ No_____

Please list _____

_____

_____

1. (a) Have you ever suspected that your child may have defective eyesight?

   _____

   (b) If so, has he or she ever been seen by an optometrist or an eye specialist?

   _____

   (c) What was the result of the examination and recommendations, if any?

   _____

2. (a) Have you ever suspected that he or she may have defective hearing?

   _____

   (b) If so, has he or she ever had his or her hearing tested?

      Yes _____ No _____ Date_____

(c) What was the result of the examination and recommendation, if any?

_____

3. (a) Has your child had any other screening or evaluations?

Yes _____ No _____ Date_____

(b) If yes, what were the results?

_____

_____

4. (a) Has your child been hospitalized at all since birth?

Yes _____ No _____ Date_____

(b) If so, what was the reason?

_____

_____

(c) Any other serious illness or injuries?

5. (a) Has your child ever seen a dentist?

Yes _____ No _____ Date_____

(b) If so, for what reason?

_____

6. Does your child have any allergies?

Yes _____ No _____

Please list_____

_____

_____

7. By the age of 3 1/2 did he or she tend to omit words?

(for example "I going to school.")

Yes _____ No _____

8. Can he/she remember a short message or a telephone number?

Yes _____ No _____

9. Additional Comment: _____

_____

_____

_____

10. I understand that all reports and testing results will be tested confidentially.

Date _____ Parent/Guardian Signature _____

Appendix C—Organizations and Publications

Selected Organizations for Exceptional Children

- Alexander Graham Bell Association for the Deaf, Inc., 3417 Volta Place, NW Washington, DC 20007
- American Academy for Cerebral Palsy, University Hospital School, Iowa City, IA 52240
- American Association for Rehabilitation Therapy, PO Box 93, North Little Rock, AR 72116
- American Association for the Advancement of Behavior Therapy, 420 Lexington Avenue, New York, NY 10017
- American Association for the Education of Severely and Profoundly Handicapped, 1600 West Armory Way, Garden View Suite, Seattle, WA 98119
- American Association on Mental Deficiency, 5201 Connecticut Avenue, NW, Washington, D.C. 20015
- American Diabetes Association, 18 E. 48th Street, New York, NY 10017
- American Foundation for the Blind, 15 West 16th Street, New York, NY 10011
- American Heart Association, 44 E. 23rd Street, New York, NY 10016
- American Lung Association, 1790 Broadway, New York, NY 10019
- American Mensa, 1701 W. 3rd Street, Suite 1–R Brooklyn, NY 11223
- American Occupational Therapy Association, 6000 Executive Blvd., Rockville, MD 20852
- American Physical Therapy Association, 1156 15th Street NW, Washington, DC 20005
- American Printing House for the Blind, 1839 Frankfort Avenue, Louisville, KY 40206
- American Psychological Association, 1200 17th Street NW, Washington, DC 20036
- American Speech-Language Hearing Association, 10801 Rockville Pike, Rockville, MD 20852
- Association for Children and Adults with Learning Disabilities, 4900 Gerard Rd., Pittsburgh, PA 15236
- Association for Children with Retarded Mental Development, 902 Broadway, New York, NY 10010
- Association for Education of the Visually Handicapped, 206 N. Washington Street, Alexandria, VA 22314
- Association for Retarded Citizens, 2709 Avenue E. East, Arlington, TX 76011
- Association for the Gifted, The Council for Exceptional Children, 1920 Association Drive, Reston, VA 22091

- Association for the Severely Handicapped. 7010 Roosevelt Way, N.E., Seattle, WA 98115
- Association on Handicapped Student Service Programs in Postsecondary Education, PO Box 21192, Columbus, OH 43221
- Box 118, Teachers College, Columbia University, New York, NY 10027
- Canadian National Institute for the Blind, 1921 Bayview Avenue, Toronto, Ontario MG43E8
- Center on Human Policy, 216 Ostrom Ave., Syracuse, NY 13210
- CHADD—Children and Adults with Attention Deficit Disorder, 499 Northwest 70th Avenue, Suite 308, Plantation, Florida 33317
- Chicago Institute for Learning Disabilities (social adjustment, language) University of Illinois at Chicago Circle, Box 4348, Chicago Il 60680
- Children's Defense Fund, 1520 New Hampshire Ave., Washington, DC 20036
- Clearinghouse on the Handicapped, Rm 3106, Switzer Bldg, Washington, DC 20202
- Closer Look, 1201 16th Street NW, Washington, D.C. 20036
- Conference of Executives of American Schools for the Deaf, 5043 Wisconsin Avenue, NW Washington, DC 20016
- Coordinating Council for Handicapped Children, 407 S. Dearborn St. Rm 680, Chicago, Il 60605
- Council for Children with Behavior Disorders, The Council for Exceptional Children, 1920 Association Drive, Reston, VA 22091
- Council for Exceptional Children, 1920 Association Drive, Reston, VA 22091
- Council for Learning Disabilities, Department of Special Education, University of Louisville, KY 40292
- Creative Education Foundation, State University College at Buffalo, 1300 Elmwood Avenue, Buffalo, NY 14222
- Division for Children with Communication Disorders, Council for Exceptional Children, 1920 Association Drive, Reston, VA 22091
- Division for Children with Learning Disabilities, 850 Hungerford Drive, Rockville MD 20850
- Division for Early Childhood, The Council for Exceptional Children, 1920 Association Drive, Reston VA 22091
- Division for the Visually Handicapped, Council for Exceptional Children, 1920 Association Drive, Reston, VA 22091
- Division of Mental Retardation, The Council for Exceptional Children, 1920
- Division on Career Development, The Council for Exceptional Children, 1920 Association Drive, Reston, VA 22091
- Education Development Center, 55 Chapel Street, Newton, MA 02160
- Educational Due Process Services, Box 57387, Washington, DC 20037

- Epilepsy Foundation of America, 1828 L Street, NW, Washington, DC 20036
- ERIC Clearinghouse on Disabilities and Gifted Education, The Council for Exceptional Children (CEC) 1920 Association Drive, Reston, VA 22091–1589
- Gifted Child Society, Inc., 59 Glen Gray Road, Oakland, NJ 07436
- Gifted Students Institute for Research and Development, 611 Ryan Plaza Drive, Suite 1149, Arlington, TX 76011
- Institute for Research on Learning Disabilities (identification, assessment, and placement) 350 Elliot Hall, 75 East River Road, University of Minnesota, Minneapolis, Minnesota 55455
- International Association of Parents of the Deaf, 814 Thayer Avenue, Silver Spring, MD 20910
- Latino Institute, Research Center, Project REACH, 1760 Reston Ave. Suite 101, Reston, VA 22090
- Learning Disabilities Research Institute (attentional deficits), The University of Virginia, Department of Special Education, 152 Ruffner Hall, Charlottesville, VA 22903
- Muscular Dystrophy Association, 810 Seventh Avenue, New York, NY 10019
- National Association for Gifted Children, 217 Gregory Drive, Hot Springs, AR 71901
- National Association for Parents of the Visually Impaired, 2011 Hardy Circle, Austin, TX 78756
- National Association for Retarded Citizens, 2709 Ave E East, Arlington, TX 76011
- National Association for the Deaf-Blind, 2703 Forest Oak Circle, Norman, OK 73071
- National Association of the Deaf, 814 Thayer Ave., Silver Spring, MD 20910
- National Center for Law and the Deaf, 7th St. and Florida Ave., NE, Washington, DC 20002
- National Council for the Gifted, 700 Prospect Avenue, West Orange, NJ 07052
- National Cystic Fibrosis Research Foundation, 3379 Peachtree Road NE, Atlanta, GA 30326
- National Easter Seal Society, 2023 West Ogden Avenue, Chicago Il 60612
- National Federation of the Blind, 1800 Johnson Street, Baltimore, MD 21230
- National Information Center for Children and Youth With Disabilities (NICHE), PO Box 1492, Washington, DC 20013–1492
- National Network of Parent Centers, 9451 Broadway Drive, Bay Harbor, FL 33154
- National Society for Autistic Children, 621 Central Avenue, Albany, NY 12206
- National/State Leadership Training Institute on the Gifted and Talented, 316 West Second Street, Suite 708, Los Angeles, CA 90012
- Office of the Gifted and Talented, US Office of Education, Washington, DC 20202
- Oration Society, Inc., 8415 Beeline Lane, Baltimore, MD 21204

- PACER Center, Parent Advocacy Coalition for Educational Rights, 4701 Chicago Avenue South, Minneapolis, MN 55407
- Parents Educational Advocacy Center, 116 W. Jones Street, Raleigh, NC 27611
- Research Institute in Learning Disabilities (LD adolescents) University of Kansas, Room 313, Lawrence, KS 66045
- Spina Bifida Association of America 343 S. Dearborn Street, Suite 319, Chicago, IL 60604
- The American Association for the Gifted, 15 Gramercy Park, New York, NY 10003
- The Association for the Gifted (TAG), The Council for Exceptional Children, 1920 Association Drive, Reston, VA 22091
- The Educational Resources Information Clearinghouse on Handicapped and Gifted, The Council for Exceptional Children, 1920 Association Drive, Reston, VA 22091
- The National Association for Creative Children and Adults, 8080 Spring Valley Drive, Cincinnati, OH 45236
- United Cerebral Palsy Association, 66 E. 34th Street, New York, NY 10016
- United Epilepsy Association, 111 W. 57th Street, New York, NY 10019
- Volta Speech Association for the Deaf, 1537 35th Street, NW, Washington, DC 20007

Selected Journal Publications on Exceptional Children

- Academic Therapy
- Accent on Living
- American Annals of the Deaf
- American Educational Research Journal
- American Journal of Art Therapy
- American Journal of Mental Deficiency
- American Journal of Occupational Therapy
- American Journal of Psychology
- American Sociological Review
- American Speech and Hearing Association Journal
- Analysis and Intervention of Developmental Disabilities
- Applied Research in Mental Retardation
- Behavior Disorders
- Behavior Therapy
- Behavioral Science
- British Journal of Mental Subnormality
- Bulletin of Prosthetics Research

- Bulletin of the Orton Society
- Career Development of Exceptional Individuals
- Career Education Quarterly
- Child Psychiatry and Human Development
- Childhood Education
- Day Care and Early Education
- Developmental Psychology
- Disabled U.S.A.
- Early Years
- Education and Training of Children
- Education and Training of the Mentally Retarded
- Education Forum
- Education of the Visually Handicapped
- Educational Horizons
- Educational Medicine
- Educational Researcher
- Exceptional Children
- Exceptional Parent
- Focus on Exceptional Children
- Gifted Child Quarterly
- Gifted/Creative/Talented Children
- Harvard Educational Review
- Health Services report
- Hearing
- Instructor
- Journal for the Education of the Gifted
- Journal of Abnormal Child Psychology
- Journal of Abnormal Psychology
- Journal of Applied Behavior Analysis
- Journal of Career Development
- Journal of Career Education
- Journal of Consulting and Clinical Psychology
- Journal of Creative Behavior
- Journal of Experimental Education
- Journal of Language, Speech, and Hearing
- Journal of Learning Disabilities
- Journal of Music Therapy

- Journal of Nervous and Mental Disease
- Journal of Personality and Social Psychology
- Journal of Personality Assessment
- Journal of Rehabilitation
- Journal of Rehabilitation of the Deaf
- Journal of Social Issues
- Journal of Social Psychology
- Journal of Special Education
- Journal of Special Education Technology
- Journal of Speech and Hearing Disorders
- Journal of Teacher Education
- Journal of the Association for Persons with Severe Handicaps
- Journal of the Division of Early Childhood
- Journal of Visual Impairment and Blindness
- Language, Speech, and Hearing Services in the Schools
- Learning Disabilities Focus
- Learning Disabilities Quarterly
- Learning Disabilities Research
- Mental Retardation
- Perceptual and Motor Skills
- Personnel and Guidance Quarterly
- Physical Therapy
- Psychology in the Schools
- Reading Research Quarterly
- Rehabilitation Digest
- Rehabilitation Literature
- Rehabilitation Research and Practice Review
- Rehabilitation Teacher
- Remedial and Special Education
- Research in Education
- Review of Educational Research
- Roeper Review: A Journal on Gifted Child Education
- School Psychology Digest
- Sign Language Studies
- Teacher Education and Special Education
- Teacher of the Deaf
- Teaching Behaviorally Disordered Youth

- Teaching Exceptional Children
- The Creative Child and Adult Quarterly
- The Deaf American
- The Gifted Child Quarterly
- The Journal for the Education of the Gifted
- The Journal of Creative Behavior
- The Sight Saving Review
- The Volta Review
- Today's Education
- Topics in Early Childhood Special Education
- Vocational Guidance Quarterly

Publishers of Materials for the Gifted

- Academic Press, 111 Fifth Avenue, New York, NY 10003
- Adapt Press, 1209 West Bailey, Sioux Falls, SD 57104
- Aldine-Atherton, 529 South Wabash Avenue, Chicago, Il 60605
- Allyn and Bacon, 470 Atlantic Avenue, Boston, MA 02210
- Arno Press, 3 Park Avenue, New York, NY 10017
- Bantam Books, 666 Fifth Avenue, New York, NY 10019
- Basic Books, 10 East Fifty-Third Street, New, York, NY 10022
- William Brown Company, 2460 Kerper Blvd., Dubuque, IA 52001
- Citation Press, 906 Sylvan Avenue, Englewood Cliffs, NJ 07632
- Collier, 866 Third Avenue, New York, NY 10022
- Council for Exceptional Children, 1920 Association Drive, Reston, VA 22091
- Creative Learning Press, PO Box 320, Mansfield Center, CT 06250
- Creative Publication, PO Box 10328, Palo Alto, CA 94303
- Doubleday and Company, 245 Park Avenue, New York, NY 10017
- Duke University Press, 6697 College Station, Durham, NC 27708
- E.P. Dutton and Company, 201 Park Avenue, New York, NY 10016
- Grune and Stratton, 111 Fifth Avenue, New York, NY 10003
- Fearon-Pitman Publishers, 6 Davis Drive, Belmont, CA 94002
- Goodyear Publishing Company, 1640 Fifth Street, Santa Monica, CA 90401
- Harper and Row Publishers, 10 East Fifty-Third Street, New York, NY 10022
- Harvard University Press, 79 Garden Street, Cambridge, MA 02138
- D.C. Heath and Company, College Department, 125 Spring Street, Lexington, MA 02173
- Holt, Rinehart and Winston, 383 Madison Avenue, New York, NY 10017

- Houghton Mifflin Company, One Beacon Street, Boston, MA 02107
- Little Brown and Company, 34 Beacon Street, Boston, MA 02106
- Macmillan Publishers, 866 Third Avenue, New York, NY 10022
- Charles Merrill Publishing, 1300 Alum Creek Drive, Columbus, OH 43216
- M.I.T. Press, 28 Carleton Street, Cambridge, MA 02142
- Monarch Press, 1230 Avenue of the Americas, New York, NY 10020
- Oxford University Press, 200 Madison Avenue, New York, NY 10016
- Prentice Hall, Englewood Cliffs, NJ 07632
- Rand McNally and Company, PO Box 7600, Chicago, IL 60680
- Random House, 400 Hahn Road, Westminster, MD 21157
- Science Research Associates, 155 North Wacker Drive, Chicago, IL 60025
- Charles Scribner's Sons, 597 Fifth Avenue, New York, NY 10017
- Teachers College Press, Columbia University, 1234 Amsterdam Avenue, New York, NY 10027
- Teaching Resources Corporation, 100 Boylston Street, Boston, MA 02116
- United States Government Printing Office, Public Documents Department, Washington, DC 20402
- Viking Press, 625 Madison Avenue, New York, NY 10022
- John Wiley and Sons, 605 Third Avenue, New York, NY 10016
- Winston Press, 420 Oak Grove, Minneapolis, MN 55403
- World Future Society, 4916 Elmo Avenue, Washington, DC 20014

Organizations and Publications for the Gifted

- The American Association for the Gifted, 15 Gramercy Park, New York, NY 10003
- American Mensa, 1701 West Third Street, Brooklyn, NY 11223
- The Association for the Gifted (TAG), The Council for Exceptional Children, 1920 Association Drive, Reston, VA 22091
- Creative Education Foundation, State University College at Buffalo, 1300 Elmwood Avenue, Buffalo, NY 14222
- Gifted Child Society, Inc., 59 Glen Gray Road, Oakland, NJ 07436
- Gifted Students Institute for Research and Development, 611 Ryan Plaza Drive, Suite 1149, Arlington, TX 76011
- The National Association for Creative Children and Adults, 8080 Spring Valley Drive, Cincinnati, OH 45236
- National Association for Gifted Children, 217 Gregory Drive, Hot Springs, AR 71901
- National/State Leadership Training Institute on the Gifted and Talented, 316 West Second Street, Suite 708, Los Angeles, CA 90012

- Office of the Gifted and Talented, U.S. Office of Education, Washington, DC 20202
- The Educational Resources Information Clearinghouse on Handicapped and Gifted, The Council for Exceptional Children, 1920 Association Drive, Reston, VA 22091

Publications for the Gifted

- The Creative Child and Adult Quarterly, The National Association for Creative Children and Adults, 8080 Spring Valley Drive, Cincinnati, OH 45236
- The Gifted Child Quarterly, The National Association for Gifted Children, 217 Gregory Drive, Hot Springs, AR 71901
- Gifted/Creative/Talented Children, G/C/T Publishing Company, Box 66654, Mobile, AL 36606
- The Journal for the Education of the Gifted, The Association for the Gifted, 1920 Association Drive, Reston, VA 22091
- The Journal of Creative Behavior, Creative Education Foundation, State University College at Buffalo, 1300 Elmwood Avenue, Buffalo, NY 14222
- Roeper Review: A Journal on Gifted Child Education, Roeper City and Country School, 2190 North Woodward, Bloomfield Hills, MI 48013

Selected Readings on Instruction and Management for the Disabled

- A Survival Kit for the Special Education Teacher—Pierangelo
- Adaptive Play for Special Needs Children-Strategies to Enhance Communication and Learning—Musselwhite
- At Risk Youth in Crisis-A Team Approach in the Schools—Morgan
- Beyond Behavior Modification-Behavior Management in the School—Kaplan and Drainville
- Bilingual Education and Bilingual Special Education—Fradd and Tikunoff
- Bilingualism and Special Education—Cummins
- Can't Your Child See? A Guide for Parents of Visually Impaired Children—Scott, Jan, and Freeman
- Career Ladders for Challenged Youths in Transition from School to Adult Life—Siegel, Robert, Greener, Meyer, Halloran, and Ross
- Children on Medication—Gadow
- Children's Arithmetic-How They Learn It and How You Teach It—Ginsburg
- Computers and Exceptional Children—Lindsey
- Conferencing Parents of Exceptional Children—Simpson
- Coping With Noncompliance in the Classroom—Walker and Walker

- Counseling Persons on Physical Disabilities—Marshak and Seligman
- Curriculum Development for the Gifted—Maker
- Effective Discipline—Smith and Rivera
- Effective Instruction for Special Education—Mastropieri and Scruggs
- Families of Handicapped Children—Fenwell and Vadasy
- How to Create a Curriculum for Autistic and Other Handicapped Children—Romanczyk and Lockshin
- How to Integrate Autistic and Other Severely Handicapped Children Into a Classroom—Koegel
- How to Reduce Autistic and Severely Maladaptive Behaviors—Luce and Christian
- How to Teach Autistic and Other Severely Handicapped Children—Koegel and Schreibman
- How to Teach Prevocational Skills to Severely Handicapped Persons—Mithaug
- How to Teach Sign Language to Developmentally Disabled Children—Carr
- How to Treat Self-Injurious Behavior—Favell and Greene
- How to Use Sensory Extinction—Rincover
- Interventions for Students With Emotional Disorders—Morgon and Reinhart
- Language Arts-Teaching Exceptional Children—Wallace, Cohen, and Polloway
- Language Interaction in Curriculum and Instruction—Gruenewald and Pollak
- Life Skills Instruction for all Students with Special Needs—Cronin and Patton
- Limiting Bias in the Assessment of Bilingual Students—Hamayan and Damico
- Management of Autistic Behavior—Simpson and Regan
- Medical Problems in the Classroom—The Teacher's Role in Diagnosis and Management—Haslam and Valletutti
- Meeting the Needs of Culturally and Linguistically Different Students—Fradd and Weismantel
- Models of Curriculum-Based Assessment—Idol, Nevin, and Whitcomb
- PEEK-Peabody Early Experiences Kit—Dunn, Chun, Crowell, Dunn, Halevi and Yacket
- PLDK-Peabody Language Development Kits—Dunn, Smith, Dunn, Horton and Smith
- Preventing School Dropouts-Tactics for At-Risk, Remedial, and Mildly Handicapped Adolescents—Lovitt
- Remedial Techniques in Basic School Subjects—Fernald and Idol
- Teaching Behavioral Self-Control to Students—Workman
- Teaching Mathematics to the Learning Disabled—Bley and Thornton
- Teaching Secondary Students With Mild Learning and Behavior Problems—Masters, Mori, and Mori

- The Challenge of Complex School Problems—Norby, Thurlow, Christenson, and Ysseldyke
- The Resource Room-Organization and Implementation—Wiederholt, Hammill, and Brown
- The Resource Teacher-A Guide to Effective Practices—Wiederholt, Hammill, and Brown
- Tools for Transition: Preparing Students With Learning Disabilities for Postsecondary Education—Aune and Ness
- Transition Goals for Adolescents With Learning Disabilities—Trapani
- Visual Handicaps and Learning—Barraga and Erin

Selected Readings on Assessment and Testing for the Disabled

- Eighty-five Tests for Special Educators—Compton
- A Consumer's Guide to Tests in Print—Hammill, Brown and Bryant
- A Guide to Vocational Assessment—Power
- A Psychoeducational Assessment of Students Who Are Visually Impaired or Blind—Johnson
- Assessing the Abilities and Instructional Needs of Students—Hammed
- Auditory Processes—Gillett
- Educational Assessment of Learning Problems—Wallace, Larsen, and Elksnin
- Handbook on the Assessment of Learning Disabilities—Swanson
- How to Write an I.E.P.—Arena
- Infant Toddler Assessment—Rossetti
- Learning Process Skills—Riley
- Limiting Bias in the Assessment of Bilingual Students—Hamayan and Damico
- Models of Curriculum-Based Assessment—Idol, Nevin and Whitcomb
- Prescriptive Teaching From the DTLA–2—Banas
- Psychoeducational Assessment of Hearing Impaired Students—Johnson and Evans
- Test Critiques-Volumes I–X—Keyser and Sweetland
- Testing Children—Weaver
- Testing Young Children—Culbertson and Willis
- Tests-A Comprehensive Reference for Assessment in Psychology, Education and Business—Sweetland and Keyser
- The I.E.P. Primer—School and Cooper
- The WISC-III Companion—Truch
- Understanding Children's Testing—Aylward
- WAIS–R Tutorial Workbook—Swiercinsky

Selected Readings for Parents on Specific Disabilities

Brain Injury

- Cognitive Rehabilitation of Closed Head Injured Patients—Adamovich, Henderson, and Auerbach
- Community Re-Entry for Head Injury Adults—Ylvisaker and Gobble
- Educational Dimensions of Acquired Brain Injury—Savage and Wolcott
- Head Injury Rehabilitation—Ylvisaker
- Psychopathology and Education of the Brain-Injured Child—Strauss, Lehtinen, and Kephart
- Traumatic Brain Injury in Children and Adolescents—Mira, Tucker, and Tyler
- Traumatic Brain Injury—Bigler

Early Intervention

- Atypical Infant Development—Hanson
- Early Intervention—Hanson and Lynch
- High-Risk Infants—Rossetti
- Infant-Toddler Assessment—Rossetti
- The Medically Fragile Child—Krajicek and Tompkins

Speech/Language Disorders

- Alaryngeal Speech Rehabilitation—Salmon and Mount
- Children's Phonetic Disorders—Hoffman, Schuckers, and Daniloff
- Cleft Palate—Karlind, Moller, and Starr
- Clinical Management of Childhood Stuttering—Wall and Meyers
- Clinical Management of Voice Disorders—Case
- Clinical Methods on Communication Disorders—Leith
- Clinical Research in Communicative Disorders—Hegde
- Communication Disorders Following Traumatic Brain Injury—Beukelman and Yorkston
- Counseling the Communicatively Disordered and Their Families—Luterman
- Developmental Apraxia of Speech—Hall, Jordan, and Robin
- Evaluation and Treatment of Swallowing Disorders—Logemann
- Genetic Syndromes in Communication Disorders—Jung
- Handbook of Clinical Phonology—Elbert and Gierut
- Introduction to Communicative Disorders—Hegde
- Keep Your Voice Healthy—Brodnitz

- Language Intervention and Academic Success—Wallach and Miller
- Laryngectomy Rehabilitation—Keith and Darley
- Later Language Development—Nippold
- Manual of Voice Therapy—Prater and Swift
- Nature of Communication Disorders in Culturally and Linguistically Diverse Populations—Taylor
- Neural Bases of Speech, Hearing, and Language—Kuehn, Lemme, and Baumgartner
- Practical Procedures for Children with Language Disorders—Nesson
- Reference Manual for Communicative Sciences and Disorders—Kent
- Research on Child Language Disorders—Miller
- Research Strategies in Human Communication Disorders—Doehring
- Targeting Intelligible Speech—Hodson and Paden
- Teaching Aphasic Children—Myers
- Treating Disordered Speech Motor Control—Vogel and Cannito
- Treatment of Communication Disorders in Culturally and Linguistically Diverse Populations—Taylor
- Treatment Procedures in Communicative Disorders—Hegde

Hearing Impaired

- Assessment and Management of Mainstreamed Hearing Impaired Children—Ross, Brackett, and Maxon
- Auditory Evoked Potentials—Hood and Berlin
- Can't Your Child Hear?—Freeman, Carbin, and Boese
- Facilitating Classroom Listening—Berg
- Hearing Disorders—Green
- Language Learning Practices With Deaf Children—McAnally, Rose, and Quigley
- Manual Communication—Christopher
- Our Forgotten Children: Hard of Hearing Pupils in the School—Davis
- Reading and Deafness—King and Quigley
- Speech Acoustics and Perception—Boothroyd
- They Grow in Silence—Mindel and Vernon

Visually Impaired

- Supporting Visually-Impaired Students in the Mainstream—Martin and Hoben
- Visual Handicaps and Learning—Barraga

Physically Disabled

- Individuals With Physical Disabilities: An Introduction for Educators—Best
- Physical and Multiple Handicaps—Bigge and Sirvis
- Teaching Individuals With Physical and Multiple Handicaps—Bigge

Learning Disabilities

- A Cognitive Approach to Learning Disabilities—Reid, Hresko, and Swanson
- Attention-Deficit Disorder Comes of Age—Shaywitz and Shaywitz
- Collective Perspectives on Issues Affecting Learning Disabilities—National Joint Committee on Learning Disabilities
- Directory of Facilities and Services for the Learning Disabled
- Handbook of Learning Disabilities–Volume I: Dimensions and Diagnosis—Kavale and Bener
- Handbook of Learning Disabilities–Volume II: Methods and Interventions—Kavale and Bender
- Handbook of Learning Disabilities–Volume III: Programs and Practices—Kavale and Bender
- Handbook on the Assessment of Learning Disabilities—Swanson
- Helping Children Overcome Learning Difficulties—Rosner
- Higher Order Thinking-Designing Curriculum for Mainstreamed Students—Carnine and Kameenui
- Learning Disabilities-Educational Principles and Practices—Johnson and Myklebust
- Learning Disabilities—Myers and Hammill
- Learning Disabilities-The Challenges of Adulthood—Patton and Palloway
- Overcoming Dyslexia in Children, Adolescents, and Adults—Jordon
- Promoting Postsecondary Education for Students with Learning Disabilities—Brinckerhoff, Shaw, and McGuire
- Reading, Writing, and Speech Problems in Children—Orton
- Resource Book for the Special Education Teacher—Lucas and Barbe
- School Survival Guide for Kids with LD—Cummings and Fisher
- Strategy Assessment and Instruction for Students With Learning Disabilities—Meltzer
- Teaching Students With Learning and Behavior Problems—Hammill and Bartel
- Teaching the Dyslexic Child—Griffiths
- The Assessment of Learning Disabilities—Silver
- The Learning Disabled Child: Ways That Parents Can Help—Stevens

- The Tuned-In, Turned-On Book About Learning Problems—Hayes
- Written Language Disorders—Bain, Bailet, and Moats

Emotional Disabilities

- Applications of Human Behavior in School and Home—Hall
- Basic Principles of Human Behavior—Hall
- Childhood Behavior Disorders—Algozzine, Schmid, and Mercer
- Depression and Suicide in Children and Adolescents—Muse
- Helping the Child Who Doesn't Fit In—Nowicki and Duke
- Life Space Intervention—Talking with Children and Youth in Crisis—Wood and Long
- Readings in Emotional Disturbance—Newcomer
- Teaching Disturbed and Disturbing Students—Zionts
- The How to Book of Teen Self-Discovery—Childre
- The Measurement of Behavior—Hall and Van Houten
- Understanding and Teaching Emotionally Disturbed Children and Adolescents—Newcomer
- Understanding and Treating Conduct Disorders—Toth
- Understanding Children and Youth with Emotional and Behavioral Problems—Zionts and Simpson

Autism

- Autism—Information and Resources for Parents, Families, and Professionals—Simpson and Zionts
- Emergence-Labeled Autistic—Grandin and Scariano
- Preschool Education Programs for Children with Autism—Harris and Handleman
- The Ultimate Stranger-The Autistic Child—Delacato

Attention-Deficit Disorder

- ADHD Adolescence: The Next Step—Robin
- ADHD in Adults—Barkley
- ADHD in the Classroom: Strategies in the Classroom—Barkley
- Attention-Deficit Disorder and Learning Disabilities: Realities, Myths, and Controversial Treatments—Ingersoll and Goldstein
- Dr. Larry Silver's Advice to Parents on Attention-Deficit Disorder—Silver
- Identification and Treatment of Attention-Deficit Disorder—Nussbaum and Bigler
- Jumping Johnny Get Back to Work—Gordon

- The ADD Hyperactivity Handbook for Schools—Parker
- Advice to Parents on ADHD—Silver
- ADD and the College Student—Quinn
- ADD Hyperactivity Workbook—Parker
- Helping Your Hyperactive Child—Parker
- Why Can't I Eat That?—Taylor
- CHADD Educators Manual—CHADD
- Driven to Distraction—Hallowell
- Attention-Deficit and the Law—Latham

Mental Disabilities

- Advances in Down's Syndrome—Dmitriev and Oelwein
- Cognitive Skills for Community Living—McClennen
- Developmental Disabilities—Baroff
- Encyclopedia of Mental and Physical Handicaps—Tver and Tver
- Individuals With Profound Disabilities—Sternberg
- Music Therapy for the Developmentally Disabled—Boxill
- Speakeasy-People With Mental Handicaps Talk About Their Lives in Institutions and in the Community—Schwier
- The Conquest of Mental Retardation—Blatt

Gifted

- Critical Issues in Gifted Education-Volume I: Defensible Programs for the Gifted—Maker
- Critical Issues in Gifted Education-Volume II: Defensible Programs for Cultural and Ethnic Minorities—Maker
- Critical Issues in Gifted Education-Volume III: Programs for the Gifted in Regular Classrooms—Maker
- Gifted and Talented Children—Pendarvis
- Gifted Children: Psychological and Educational Perspectives—Tannenbaum
- Growing Up Gifted—Clark
- Teaching the Gifted Child—Gallagher
- The Gifted and Talented: Their Education and Development—Passow

Tourette's Syndrome

- Adult Tics in Gilles de la Tourette's Syndrome; Description and risk factors. Neurology—Goetz, C., Tanner, C., Stebbins G., et al. 1992, Vol. 42; pp. 784–788.

- Advances in Neurology: Tourette's Syndrome: Genetics, Neurobiology, and Treatment. Chase, T., Friedhoff, A., Cohen, D.
- Development of Behavioral and Emotional Problems in Tourette's Syndrome. Pediatric Neurology—Singer HS, Rosenberg LA. 1989, Vol. 5; pp. 41–44.
- Developmental Perspective of the Gilles de la Tourette Syndrome. Perceptual Motor Skills—Incagnoli T, Kane R. 1983, Vol. 57; pp. 1271–1281.
- Gilles de la Tourette Syndrome—Shapiro, E., Young, J.G., Feinberg, T.
- Guide to the Diagnosis and Treatment of Tourette's Syndrome—Bruun, R.D., Cohen, D.J. Leckman, J.F.
- Neuropsychological Performance in Children With Tourette's Syndrome. Psychiatry Resources—Bornstein, R. 1990, Vol. 33; pp. 73–81.
- New England Journal of Medicine—Leckman, J.F., Schahill, L. Vol. 332, p. 1694 (letter).
- Sensory Tics in Tourette's Syndrome—Kurlan R., Lichter D., Hewitt, D. Neurology. 1989, Vol. 39; pp. 731–733.
- Tourette Syndrome and Other Tic Disorders: Diagnosis, Pathophysiology, and Treatment. Medicine—Singer H.S., Walkup J.T.. 1991, Vol. 70; 15–32.
- Tourette Syndrome Association, 42–40 Bell Blvd., Bayside, New York 11361 (718) 224-2999.
- Tourette's Syndrome and Tic Disorders: Clinical Understanding and Treatment—Cohen, D.J., Bruun, R.D., Leckman, J.F.
- Tourette's Syndrome: Current Concepts. Neurology—Kurlan, R. 1989, Vol. 39; pp. 1625–1630.

Selected Sources of Commercially Produced Instructional Software

- American Educational Corporation
- Apple Computer
- Automated Simulations
- Avant-Garde Publishing Corporation
- Computer Courseware
- Cross Educational Software
- Davidson and Associates
- Dorsett Educational Systems
- Educational Activities
- Educational Micro Systems
- Educational Teaching Aids
- Edu-Ware Services

- EMC Publishing
- Encyclopedia Britannica Educational Corporation
- Follett Software Company
- J.L. Hammett Company
- Harcourt Brace Jovanovich
- The Learning Company
- McGraw-Hill School Division
- Media Materials
- Milliken Publishing Company
- Milton Bradley Educational Division
- Pendulum Press
- Psychological Corporation
- Quicksoft
- Random House School Division
- Reader's Digest Services
- Reston Publishing
- Science Research Associates
- Scott, Foresman and Company
- Society for Visual Education
- Southeastern Educational Software

Names and Addresses of Test Publishers

Academic Therapy Publications
1539 Fourth St.
San Rafael, CA 94901

American Association for Health, Physical Education and Recreation
1201 Sixteenth St., NW
Washington, DC 20036

Bobbs Merrill Co.
4300 West 62nd St.
Indianapolis, IN 46268

American Foundation for the Blind
15 West 16th St.
New York, NY 10011

American Guidance Service
Publisher's Building
Circle Pines, Minnesota 55014

American Printing House for the Blind
1839 Frankfort Ave.
Louisville, KY 40206

C.T.B./McGraw-Hill
Del Monte Research Park
Monterey, CA 93940

Consulting Psychologists Press
557 College Ave.
Brandon, VT 05733

Educational Testing Service
Princeton, NJ 08540

Crippled Children and Adults of Rhode Island
Meeting Street School
333 Grotto Ave.
Providence, RI 02906

Denver Public Schools
414 Fourteenth St.
Denver, CO 80202

Educational Performance Associates
563 Westview Ave.
Ridgefield, NJ 07657

Educators Publication Service
75 Moulton St.
Cambridge, MA 02138

Follett Publishing Co.
1010 W. Washington Blvd.
Chicago, IL 60607

Harcourt, Brace, Jovanovich
757 Third Ave.
New York, NY 10017

Marshall Hiskey
5640 Baldwin
Lincoln, NE 68508

Houghton Mifflin Co.
110 Tremont St.
Boston, MA 02107

Ladoca Program and Publishing Foundation
East 51st Ave. and Lincoln St.
Denver, CO 80216

Charles Merrill Publishing Co.
1300 Alum Creek Drive
Columbus, OH 43216

Personnel Press
Educational Center
PO Box 2649
Columbus, OH 43216

Psychological Corporation
304 East 45th St.
New York, NY 10017

Research Concepts
1368 E. Airport Road
Muskegon, MI 49444

Science Research Associates
259 East Erie St.
Chicago, IL 60611

Stanwix House
3020 Chartiers Ave.
Pittsburgh, PA 15204

Stoelting Co.
1350 South Kostner Ave.
Chicago, IL 60623

Teachers College Press
1234 Amsterdam Ave.
New York, NY 10027

University of Illinois Press
Urbana, IL 61801

Webster Division/McGraw-Hill
1221 Avenue of the Americas
New York, NY 10020

Western Psychological Services
12031 Wilshire Blvd.
Los Angeles, CA 90025

Appendix D—Reference Lists

Gross Motor Skills

Example Activity	Approximate Age
Child able to raise chin while lying on stomach	1 month
Child raises chest while lying on stomach	2 months
Child able to reach for objects but misses	3 months
Head set forward, steady, lumbar curvature	4 months
Child able to turn over	4–6 months
Child able to sit on lap and grasp object	5 months
Child can sit in high chair and grasp dangling object	6 months
Sits with good posture	10 months
Creeps and crawls	11 months
Pulls to standing position	11 months
Climbs stair steps	13 months
Walks alone unsupported, seldom falls	18 months
Sits self in small chair	18 months
Walks carrying large objects	20 months
Raises self from sitting position with hips first	22 months
Runs well without falling	2 years
Kicks ball without overbalancing	2 years
Jumps with both feet in place	2 1/2 years
Picks up objects from floor without falling over	2 1/2 years
Stands on one foot even momentarily	3 years
Petals tricycle	3 years

Receptive Language Skills

Activity	Approximate Age
Understands few words	11 months
Points to 1 named body part on request	1 year
Stops activity to name	1 year
Stops activity to "no"	1 year
Points to familiar persons, animals, toys on request	15 months
Follows 1-step simple commands	15 months
Points to 3 named body parts on request	17 months

Follows 2-step command	20 months
Points to 5 or 6 pictures of common objects on request	21 months
Points to 5 body parts on self or doll	22 months
Follows 3-step command given in one long utterance	2 years
Understands 200–400 words	2 years
Understands 800 words	3 years
Verbalizes past experiences	3 years
Points to *big, little, soft, loud*	3 years
Follows commands with 2–3 actions	4 years
Understands approximately 1500 words	4 years

Expressive Language Skills

Activity	Approximate Age
Says first word	10 months
Shakes head and says "*no-no*"	11 months
Imitates the sounds of others	1 year
Uses 3 words in speaking vocabulary	13 months
Use of verbs appears	14 months
Uses at least 6 words	17 months
Refers to self by name	21 months
Uses "*me*" and "*you*"	23 months
Says 50–200 words	2 years
Knows full name	2 years
Uses plurals	2 years
Asks questions	2 1/2 years
Uses negatives in speech	2 1/2 years
Enunciates vowel sounds	3 years
Enunciates consonant sounds	3 years
Speech is 75–80% intelligible	3 years
Uses 3- and 4-syllable words	4 years
Says 6- to 8-word sentences	4 years
Speech is about 90–95% intelligible	4 years

Dressing Skills

Activity	Approximate Age
Can pull and tug at clothing	3–4 months

Cooperates in dressing by holding out limbs	1 year
Can remove shoes by self	14 months
Can place socks on feet by self	18 months
Can put on own hat	18 months
Can pull up pants	18 months
Can unzip	18–20 months
Attempts to put on own shoes	19 months
Can partially dress self	2 years
Pulls up pants	2 years
Undresses self	30 months
Can put on shirt and coat	30 months
Attempts to place shoes on feet	30 months
Can choose own outfit	3 years
Can unbutton clothes	3 years
Places clothing on in the correct direction	42 months
Can dress and undress with supervision, (not including shoelaces and so on)	48 months
Can button front buttons on clothing	52–56 months
Can zip up and down and can snap simple snaps	60 months
Can tie shoes with bows	66 months
Can unlace bows on shoes	66 months
Dresses self completely	66 months

Eating Skills

Activity	Approximate Age
Sucks and swallows liquids	Birth
Gagging reflex	Birth
Sucks and swallows liquids supplied from spoons	2 months
Eats strained baby foods from spoon	3 months
Brings hand against bottle when eating	3 months
Sips from a cup that is held for him/her	4 months
Becomes excited when hearing sounds of food preparation	4 months
Holds spoon but needs assistance	5 months
Can feed self soft food	6 months
Begins to bite and chew food	6 months
Holds own baby bottle	7 months
Can chew small lumpy food	8 months

Can take bottle out of mouth and replace it	9 months
Can use fingers to feed him/herself	10 months
Holds cup with two hands	1 year
Chews table food	13–15 months
Can grasp spoon and place in mouth with some spilling	15 months
Can manage spoon without assistance with little spilling	1 1/2 years
Requests food when hungry	23 months
Requests liquids when thirsty	23 months
Can hold a small glass with one hand unassisted	2 years
Can use a fork to grab food	3 years
Can spread butter on bread	3 years
Can help set table	4 years
Can use a fork to separate food	4 years
Can pour water from a pitcher into a glass	4 years
Can use a knife to cut food	5 years
Can set table without assistance	6 years

Toileting and Grooming Skills

Activity	Approximate Age
Grooming	
Holds on to side of tub and cries when removed	5 months
Splashes water with hands and feet	6 months
Grimaces when face is washed with cloth	6 months
Exhibits resistance to washing face	8 months
Can open and pull out drawers	1 1/2 years
Can wash hands and face by self but not well	2 years
Can wash front of body while in bath	2 years
Can run a brush through hair	2 1/2 years
Can brush teeth with assistance	3 1/2 years
Can wash and dry face with towel by self	4 years
Can brush teeth with no assistance	4 years
Can put away own toys by self with supervision	4 years
Can hang up coat by self on hook	4 years
Brushes hair independently	5 years
Hangs up own clothes without supervision	5 years
Washes self alone	6 years

Toileting

About 4 bowel movements a day associated with waking up	1 month
2 bowel movements a day either at waking or after being fed	2 months
Some delay shown between feeding and elimination	4 months
Stays dry for 1–2 hour intervals	7 months
May awaken at night and cry to be changed	1 1/2 years
Child may indicate wet pants	1 1/2 years
Only has occasional accidents	22 months
Uses same word for both functions of elimination	22 months
Begins to differentiate between elimination functions	2 years
Climbs onto toilet by self	2 1/2 years
Can control bladder for up to 5 hours	2 1/2 years
Begins to develop a routine for elimination	3 years
Attempts to wipe self but not successful	3 1/2 years
Stays dry at night	4 years
Can toilet self without assistance	5 years
Washes and dries own hands after toileting	5 years
One bowel movement a day	5 years

Childhood Immunization Checklist

Your child will need protection against polio, diphtheria, tetanus, pertussis (whooping cough) measles, rubella (German measles), and mumps. Make sure your child has received all shots.

Remember, your child will need all immunizations in order to be protected against these diseases.

For further information regarding immunization, please contact your physician.

2 months old	DTP (diphtheria-tetanus-pertussis)
	TOPV (trivalent oral polio vaccine)
4 months old	DTP
	TOPV
6 months old*	DTP
15 months old	measles vaccine**
	rubella vaccine**
	mumps vaccine**
18 months old	DTP (booster)
	TOPV (booster)
4 to 6 years	DTP (booster)
(school entry)	TOPV (booster)

Thereafter: Tetanus-diphtheria (Td) booster should be given every ten years or following a dirty wound if a booster has not been given in the preceding five years.

*In some regions, doctors may give an optional dose of TOPV at this age.

**Some states recommend that these be given in a combined injection (MMR). A tuberculin skin test may also be administered.

Please keep in mind that the charts give average ages. Your child may develop somewhat slower or faster. If you notice that your child has a problem in any area, and that his/her problem continues over a period of time, please call your doctor or clinic. Remember, you are the person closest to your child and in the best position to notice signs of future problems and to seek help.

Appendix E—Special-Education Tests

Intelligence Tests

Advanced Progressive Matrices (APM)—ages 11 and older

Bayley Scales of Infant Development (Mental Scale)—1 month–42 months

Cattell Infant Intelligence Scale—ages 3–30 months

Cognitive Abilities Test—grades K–12

Colored Progressive Matrices (CPM)—ages to 11 and selected populations

Columbia Mental Maturity Scale (CMMS)—ages 3.5–10

Henmon-Nelson Tests of Mental Ability—grades K–12

Kaufman Adolescent and Adult Intelligence Test (KAIT)—ages 11–85

Kaufman Brief Intelligence Test (K-BIT)—ages 4–90

Leiter International Performance Scale (LIPS)—ages 3 and older

McCarthy Scales of Children's Abilities—ages 2.6–8.6

Otis-Lennon School Ability Test—grades K–12

Peabody Picture Vocabulary Test–Revised (PPVT–R)—ages 2.5–40

Pictorial Test of Intelligence—ages 3–8

Slosson Full-Range Intelligence Test (SF–RIT)—ages 5–21

Slosson Intelligence Test–Revised (SIT–R)—ages 4–adult

Stanford Binet Intelligence Test—Ages 2–adult

Standard Progressive Matrices (SPM)—ages 6–adult

Test of Nonverbal Intelligence-2 (TONI-2)—ages 5–85

Wechsler Scales of Intelligence—ages 4 1/2–adult

Language Tests

Adolescent Language Screening Test (ALST)—ages 11–17

Assessment for Children's Language Development—ages 3–8

Assessment of Fluency in School-Age Children—ages 5–18

Bankson Language Test (BLT–2)—ages 3–7

Boehm Test of Basic Concepts—Kindergarten–grade 2

Boston Assessment of Severe Aphasia—all ages

Clark-Madison Test of Oral Language—ages 4–8

Communicative Abilities in Daily Living—adults

Comprehensive Receptive and Expressive Vocabulary Test (CREVT)—ages 4–17

Early Language Milestone Scale (ELM–Scale–2)—birth–36 months

Examining for Aphasia, Third Edition (EFA)—all ages

Expressive One-Word Picture Vocabulary Tests—ages 2–12

Figurative Language Interpretation Test (FLIT)—ages 9–16

Goldman-Fristoe Test of Articulation—ages 2–16

Goldman-Fristoe-Woodcock Auditory Skills Test Battery—ages 3–adult

Goldman-Fristoe-Woodcock Test of Auditory Discrimination (G-F-WTAD)—
ages 3.8–70

Illinois Tests of Psycholinguistic Abilities (ITPA)—ages 3–11

Kaufman Survey of Early Academic and Language Skills—ages 3–7

Khan-Lewis Phonological Analysis (KLPA)—ages 2–6

Kindergarten Language Screening Test (KLST)—Kindergarten

Language Structured Auditory Retention Span-Revised (LARS)—ages 3 1/2–adult

Minnesota Test for Differential Diagnosis of Aphasia—adult

Peabody Picture Vocabulary Test—Revised (PPVT-R)—ages 2.5–40

Photo Articulation Test (PAT)—all ages

Picture Articulation and Language Screening Test (PALST)—grade 1

Preverbal Assessment Intervention Profile (PAIP)—all ages

Receptive-Expressive Emergent Language Test (REEL–2)—infants and toddlers

Receptive-One-Word Picture Vocabulary Test—ages 2–12

Screening Test for Developmental Apraxia of Speech—ages 4–12

Speech Ease Screening—grades K–1

Stuttering Prediction Instrument for Young Children—ages 3–8

Stuttering Severity Instrument for Children and Adults (SSI–3)—ages 8–adult

Test for Auditory Comprehension of Language (TACL)-ages 3-9

Test of Adolescent and Adult Language (TOAL–3)—ages 13–25

Test of Awareness of Language Segments (TALS)—ages 4.6–7

Test of Early Language Development (TELD–2)—ages 2–8

Test of Language Development (TOLD–2)—ages 4–13

Test of Pragmatic Language (TOPL)—ages 5–13

Test of Word Knowledge (TOWK)—ages 5–17

The Assessment of Phonological Processes-Revised (APP-R)—all ages

The Speech and Language Evaluation Scale (SLES)—4.5–18

Utah Test of Language Development (UTLD–3)—ages 3–9.11

Voice Assessment Protocol for Children and Adults (VAP)—all ages

Tests for the Hearing Impaired

Auditory Perception Test for the Hearing Impaired (APT/HI)—ages 5 and up

Carolina Picture Vocabulary Test (CPVT)—ages 4–11.5

Goodenough-Draw-A-Person Test—all ages

Hiskey-Nebraska Test of Learning Aptitude—ages 3–18

Leiter International Performance Scale—ages 2–17

Rhode Island Test of Language Structure (RITLS)—ages 3–20

Screening Instrument for Targeting Educational Risk (SIFTER)—for children with identified hearing loss

Test of Early Reading Ability—Deaf or Hard of Hearing (TERA–D/HH)—primary grades

Psychological Tests

Adjustment Scales for Children and Adolescents (ASCA)—ages 5–17

Anxiety Scale for Children and Adults (ASCA)—all ages

Assessment of Interpersonal Relations (AIR)—grades 5–12

Assessment of Interpersonal Relations (AIR)—ages 10–19

Beck Anxiety Inventory (BAI)—ages 17–80

Beck Depression Scale—ages 17–80

Beck Hopelessness Scale (BHS)—ages 13–80

Beck Scale for Suicide Ideation—ages 17 and up

Behavior Assessment System for Children (BASC)—ages 4–18

Behavior Rating Profile (BRP-2)—ages 6.6–18.6

Children's Apperception Test (CAT)—ages 5–10

Children's Apperceptive Story-Telling Test (CAST)—ages 3–10

Children's Depression Inventory (CDI)—ages 7–17

Conners' Rating Scales (CRS)—ages 3–17

Culture Free Self-Esteem Inventories (CFSEI–2)—ages 5–adult

Depression and Anxiety in Youth Scale (DAYS)—children and adolescents

Differential Test of Conduct and Emotional Problems (DT/CEP)—grades K-High School

Draw-A-Person Test (DAP)—ages 6–17

Emotional and Behavioral Problem Scale (EBPS)—4.5–21

Goodenough-Harris Drawing Test—ages 5–15

Holtzman Inkblot Technique—ages 5–adult

Index of Personality Characteristics (IPC)—ages 8–17.11

Kinetic Family Drawing—ages 6–17

Million Index of Personality Styles (MIPS)—ages 18–65

Personality Assessment Inventory—ages 18 and older

Reynolds Adolescent Depression Scale (RADS)—ages 13–18

Rorschach Technique—ages 5–adult

Self Esteem Index (SEI)—ages 7–18

Sentence Completion Test—all ages

Social Emotional Dimension Scale (SEDS)—ages 5.5–18.5

Social Skills Rating System (SSRS)—ages 3–18

Student Self-Concept Scale (SSCS)—grades 3–12

Test of Early Socioemotional Development (TOESD)—ages 3–7.11

The Mooney Problem Check Lists—junior high–college

Thematic Apperception Test (TAT)—children and adults

Perceptual Tests

Beery-Buktenica Developmental Test of Visual Motor Integration—ages 4–18

Bender Gestalt Visual Motor Test (BGVMT)—children and adults

Bruininks-Oserestsky Test of Motor Proficiency—ages 4.5–14.5

Cognitive Abilities Scale (CAS)—grades K–12

Comprehensive Scales of Student Abilities (CSSA)—ages 6–16

Detroit Tests of Learning Aptitude–3 (DTLA–3)—ages 6–17

Developmental Activities Screening Inventory–II—ages birth–60 months

Developmental Test of Visual-Motor Integration (VMI)—ages 3–18

Early Screening Profiles (EPS)—ages 2–7

Frostig Developmental Test of Visual Perception—elementary-aged children

Frostig Movement Skills Test Battery—elementary-aged children

Goldman-Fristoe Woodcock Test of Auditory Discrimination—ages 3.8–70

Jordan Left-Right Reversal Test–Revised (JLRRT)—ages 5–12

K–ABC: Kaufman Assessment Battery for Children—ages 2.5–12.5

Learning Efficiency Test II–Revised (LET–II)—ages 5–adult

Lindamood Auditory Conceptualization Test—all ages

Malcomesius Specific Language Disability Test—grades 6–8

McCarthy Screening Test (MST)—ages 4–6.6

Motor-Free Visual Perception Test (MVPT)—ages 4–8

Mullen Scales of Early Learning (MSEL)-Infant Scale—birth–39 months

Mullen Scales of Early Learning (MSEL)-Preschool—ages 24–69 months

Quick Neurological Screening Test (QNST)—ages 5–18

Slingerland Screening Tests for Identifying Children With Specific Language Disabilities—grades K–5

Test of Auditory Analysis Skills (TAAS)—ages 5–8

Test of Auditory Perceptual Skills (TAPS)—ages 4–12

Test of Auditory Perceptual Skills (TAPS:Upper Level)—ages 12–18

Test of Gross Motor Development (TGMD)—ages 3–10

Test of Memory and Learning (TOMAL)—ages 5–19

Test of Pictures/Forms/Letters/Numbers Spatial Orientation and Sequencing Skills (TPFLNOSS)—ages 5–8

Test of Visual Analysis Skills (TVAS)—ages 5–8

Test of Visual Motor Skills (TVMS)—ages 2–13

Test of Visual Motor Skills (TVMS: Upper Level)—ages 12–40

Test of Visual Perceptual Skills (Nonmotor) (TVPS nm:UL)—ages 12–19

Test of Visual Perceptual Skills (Nonmotor) (TVPS)—ages 4–13

Tests of Auditory-Perceptual Skills (TAPS)—ages 4–12

Tests of Auditory-Perceptual Skills (TAPS Upper Level)—ages 12–18

Visual Skills Appraisal (VSA)—ages 5–9

Vulpe Assessment Battery-Revised (VAB–R)—ages birth–6

Wepman Auditory Discrimination Test—ages 3–8

Woodcock Johnson Psychoeducational Battery—all ages

Rating Scales and Adaptive Behavior Scales

AAMR Adaptive Behavior Scales-residential and community

AAMR Adaptive behavior Scales—school-aged children

Adaptive Behavior Inventory (ABI)—school-aged children

Barsch Learning Style Inventory—ages 14–adult

Career Inventories for the Learning Disabled (CILD)—ages 6–adult

Comprehensive Behavior Rating Scale for Children (CBRSC)—ages 6–14

Comprehensive Test of Adaptive Behavior (CTAB)—ages birth–60

Conners Rating Scales—ages 3–17

Developmental Assessment for the Severely Handicapped (DASH)—birth–60 months

Devereux Behavior Rating Scale–school form—ages 5–18

Devereux Scales of Mental Disorders—ages 5–18

Gardner Social Maturity Scale (GSDS)—ages birth to 9

Learning Disability Rating Procedure (LDRP)—ages 6–18

Light's Retention Scale (LRS)—ages 6–18

Normative Adaptive Behavior Checklist (NABC)—birth–21

Preschool Behavior Checklist (PBCL)—ages 2–5

Pupil Rating Scale Revised: Screening for Learning Disabilities—ages 5–14

Screen: Senf-Comrey Ratings of Extra Educational Need—ages 5–7

Syracuse Social Maturity Scale—all ages

The Adaptive Behavior Evaluation Scale (ABES)—grades K–12

The Attention-Deficit Disorders Evaluation Scale (ADDES)—ages 4.5–18

The Behavior Disorders Identification Scale (BDIS)—ages 4.5–21

The Learning Disability Evaluation Scale (LDES)—grades K–12

Vineland Adaptive Behavior Scale–Classroom Edition—ages 3–13

Vineland Adaptive Behavior Scale–Interview Edition—ages 0–18

Weller-Strawser Scales of Adaptive Behavior for the Learning Disabled (WSSAB)—ages 6–18

Woodcock Johnson Psychoeducational Battery—all ages

Reading Tests

Brigance Disagnostic Inventory of Basic Skills—grades K–6

Diagnostic Achievement Test for Adolescents—grades 7–12

Doren Diagnostic Reading Test of Word Recognition Skills—grades K–4

DRS–81: Diagnostic Reading Scales—grades 1–7

Durrell Analysis of Reading Difficulty—grades 1–6

Durrell Listening-Reading Series—grades 1–9

Formal Reading Inventory (FRI)—grades 1–12

Gates-MacGinitie Silent Reading Tests—grades 1–12

Gates-McKillop Reading Diagnostic Tests—grades 1–6

Gilmore Oral Reading Test—grades 1–8

Gray Oral Reading Test (GORT–3)—grades 1–college

Language Arts Assessment Portfolio (LAAP)—grades 1–6

Nelson Reading Skills Test—grades 3–9

Nelson-Denny Reading Test—grades 9–16

NewGAP—ages 7–10

Slosson Oral Reading Test (SORT–R)—ages preschool–adult

Spache Diagnostic Reading Scales—grades 1–8 and 9–12 (students with reading deficiencies)

Spadafore Diagnostic Reading Test (SDRT)—ages 6–adult

Standardized Reading Inventory (SRI)—grades preprimer–8

Stanford Diagnostic Reading Test—ages 1–adult

Test of Early Reading Ability (TERA–2)—ages 3–10

Test of Phonological Awareness (TOPA)—Kindergarten-grade 2

Test of Reading Comprehension (TORC)—ages 7–17

Wide Range Achievement Tests–Revised—ages 5–adult

Woodcock Reading Mastery Tests (WRMT–R)–Revised—grades K–12

Arithmetic Tests

Diagnostic Test of Arithmetic Strategies (DTAS)—elementary-school-aged children

Key Math Diagnostic Arithmetic Tests–Revised—preschool–grade 6

Sequential Assessment of Mathematics Inventories (SAMI)—grades K–8

SRA Achievement Series in Arithmetic—grades 1–10

Stanford Achievement Series in Arithmetic—grades 1–10

Steenburgen Diagnostic Quick Math Screening Test—ages 6–11

Test of Early Mathematics Ability—(TEMA–2)—ages 3–9

Test of Mathematical Ability (TOMA)—ages 8–19

Wide Range Achievement Test—ages 5–adult

Spelling Tests

Written: Phonic Words, Irregular Words

Wide Range Achievement Test–Revised—ages 5–adult

Diagnostic Word Patterns—grade 2–college

Mykelbust Picture Story Language Test—elementary grades

The Spellmaster Assessment and Teaching System

Diagnostic Spelling Potential Test (DSPT)—ages 7–adult

Test of Written Spelling (TWS–3)—grades 1–12

Larsen Hammill Test of Written Spelling—ages 5–15

Visual: Recognition of Sight Words

Kauffman Individual Achievement Test—ages 5–18

Peabody Individual Achievement Test—ages 5–adult

Wechsler Individual Achievement Test—ages 5–18

Writing Tests

Denver Handwriting Analysis (DHA)—ages 8–13

Diagnostic Achievement Test for Adolescents—grades 7–12

Myklebust Picture Story Language Test—7–17 years

Test of Early Written Language (TEWL)—ages 3–7

Test of Written English (TWE)—ages 6–11+

Test of Written Language–2 (TOWL–2)—grades 1–6

Writing Process Test—grades 2–12

Writing Supplement to the Iowa Tests of Basic Skills—grades 3–8

Writing Supplement to the Tests of Achievement and Proficiency—grades 9–12

Written Language Assessment (WLA)—ages 8–18+

Comprehensive Academic Skill Tests

Basic Achievement Skills Individual Screening (BASIS)—grades 1–12

Brigance Diagnostic Inventory of Basic Skills—grades K–6

California Achievement Test—grades 1–9

Criterion Test of Basic Skills (CBS)—ages 6–11

Diagnostic Achievement Battery (DAB–2)—ages 6–14

Diagnostic Achievement Test for Adolescents—grades 7–12

Differential Ability Scales (DAS)—ages 2.6–18

Hudson Educational Skills Inventory—grades K–12

Iowa Test of Basic Abilities—grades 1–9

Kaufman Survey of Early Academic and Language Skills—ages 3–7

Kaufman Test of Educational Achievement (KTEA)—ages 5–18

Metropolitan Achievement Test—grades 3–9

Multilevel Academic Survey Tests (MAST)—grades K–12

Peabody Individual Achievement Test-Revised (PIAT–R)—grades K–12

Quick Cognitive Inventory—ages (QCI) 6–8

Quick Score Achievement Test—grades 1–12

Riley Inventory of Basic Learning Skills (RIBLS)—upper-ages 8–14+

Riley Inventory of Basic Learning Skills (RIBLS)—primary-ages 6–7

Scholastic Abilities Test for Adults—ages 16–70

Test of Academic Achievement Skills (TAAS)—ages 4–12

Test of Academic Achievement Skills (TAAS–RAS)—ages 4–12

Test of Academic Performance—grades K–12

Wechsler Individual Achievement Test (WIAT)—grades K–12

Wide Range Achievement Test–3 (WRAT–3)—ages 5–adult

Bilingual Assessment Measures

Austin Spanish Articulation Test

Culture-Free Self-Esteem Inventories–2 (CFSEI–2)—ages 5–adult

Developmental Assessment of Spanish Grammar

Dos Amigos Verbal Language Scales (DAVLS)—ages 5–13

ESL/Literacy Scale (ELS)—ages 16–adult

James Language Dominance Test

Language Proficiency Test (LPT)—ages 15–adult

Matrix Analogies Test—ages 3–17

Peabody Picture Vocabulary Test-Revised (PPVT-R)—ages 2.5–40

Screening Test of Spanish Grammar

Spanish Accent Auditory Discrimination Test

System of Multicultural Pluralistic Assessment (SOMPA)—ages 5–11

Test de Vocabulario en Imagenes Peabody (TVIP)—ages 2 1/2–18

Test for Auditory Comprehension of Language (TACL)

Early Childhood and Infant Assessment Scales

AGS Early Screening Profiles—ages 2–6.11

Bayley Infant Neurodevelopmental Screen (BINS)—1 month–42 months

Bayley Scales of Infant Development—ages 1–42 months

Boehm Test of Basic Concepts–Revised—K–grade 2

Bracken Basic Concept Scale (BBCS)—ages 2.6–8

Bracken Concept Development Program (BCDP)—ages 2.6–8

Cattell Infant Intelligence Scale—ages 3 to 30 months

Child Development Inventory (CDI)—15 months–6 years

Children's Early Intervention for Speech-Language-Reading (CEI)—pre-K–early elementary

First STPE: Screening Test for Evaluating Preschoolers—ages 2.9–6.2

Gardener Social Maturity Scale (GSDS)—ages birth–9

Kindergarten Readiness Test (KRT)—kindergarten

Metropolitan Readiness Tests (MRT)—pre-K–grade 1

Miller Assessment for Preschoolers—ages 29 months–5.8 years

Mullen Scales of Early Learning—ages birth–69 months

Neurobehavioral Assessment of the Preterm Infant (NAPI)—ages 32 weeks conceptual age to term

Preschool Language Scale–3 (PLS–3)—birth–6

Screen: Senf-Comrey Ratings of Extra Educational Need—ages 5–7

Stuttering Severity Instrument for Young Children (SPI)—ages 3–8

Survey of Early Childhood Abilities (SECA)—ages 3–7

Test of Gross Motor Development (TGMD)—ages 3–10

Test of Kindergarten/First Grade Readiness Skills (TKFGRS)—ages 3.6–7

Test of Phonological Awareness (TOPA)—grades K–2

Tests of Early Reading Ability (TERA-2)—ages 3–9

The Early Childhood Behavior Scale (ECBS)—36–72 months of age

The Preschool Evaluation Scale (PES)—birth–72 months

Visual Skills Appraisal (VSA)—grades K–4

Vulpe Assessment Battery-Revised (VAB-R)—birth–6

Standardized Tests Used in an Occupational Therapy Evaluation

Certain tests are used by Occupational Therapists in their evaluations. Such measures may include:

Bruninks-Oseretsky Test of Motor Proficiency (BOT): Gross and fine motor subtests include running speed, balance, bilateral coordination, strength, upper limb coordination, response speed, visual-motor control and upper limb speed and dexterity. Age: 4 years, 6 months–14 years, 6 months.

Degangi-Berk Test of Sensory Integration: Test of sensory integration (postural control, reflex integration, bilateral; motor integration, muscle tone, ocular-motor control, vestibular function). Age: 3 years–5 years.

Denver Developmental Screening Test: Individual formalized observations of normal developmental behavior of infants and children. A screening tool for detecting infants and children with developmental delays. Areas evaluated: gross motor, fine motor, language and personal-social development. Age: birth–6 years.

Developmental Programming for Infants and Young Children: Low-volume profile designed to reduce the gap between evaluation and programs for children functioning between birth to 36 months' levels of development. Areas formally evaluated include perceptual/fine motor, cognition, language, social/emotional, self-care, and gross motor. The educator/therapist develops comprehensive and individualized developmental programs by translating comprehensive evaluation data rendered by the profile into short-term behavioral objectives that form the basis of daily activities planned to facilitate emerging skills. Age: birth – 3 years.

Developmental Test of Visual-Motor Integration (VMI or the BEERY): Test of integration of visual perception and motor behavior in young children. Subject is presented with 24 geometric forms, arranged in order of increasing difficulty, that are then copied into a test booklet. There are two forms based on age:

(a) Age: 2 years–8 years (b) Age: 2 years–15 years.

Frostig Developmental Test of Visual Perception: Test of eye-motor coordination, figure-ground discrimination, form constancy, position in space, and spatial relation. Age: 3 years–8 years.

Early-Lap: The early learning accomplishment profile for developmentally young children. Assessment of gross motor, fine motor, cognitive, language, self-help, and social-emotional development. Age: birth–36 months.

Jordan Left-Right Reversal Test (Jordan Test): An individual or group-administered instrument designed to measure letter and number reversals in the area of children's visual receptive functioning. Age: 5 years–12 years.

McCarthy Scales of Children's Abilities (MSCA): Tests of the general level of intellectual functioning, the General Cognitive Index (GCI) and profile of abilities. The profile includes six scales: verbal, perceptual performance, qualitative, general cognitive, memory, and motor. Several items also assess hand dominance. Age: 2 years, 6 months–8 years, 6 months.

Milani-Comparetti Motor Development Test: A basic neurodevelopmental screening test designed to assess a child's physical development. Administered several times over a period of months by a physician, nurse, or therapist, the test indicates trends in a child's motor development and may be employed to detect problems in this area. Age: birth – 2 years.

Miller Assessment or Preschoolers (MAP): Screenings test a child's developmental status with respect to other children his/her age. Once completed, the examiner has a comprehensive overview of the developmental status in each of 5 indices; foundations, coordination, verbal, nonverbal, and complex task. Specifically, areas tested include basic motor and sensory abilities, complex fine and oral-motor sensory abilities, cognitive language abilities, cognitive abilities not requiring spoken language, and skills requiring interaction of sensory motor and cognitive abilities. Age: 2 years, 9 months–5 years, 8 months.

Motor Free Visual Perception Test: Overall, visual-perception processing ability is tested while avoiding motor involvement. Areas tested include spatial relationships, visual discrimination, figure ground, visual closure, and visual memory. Age: 4 years–8 years.

Quick Neurological Screening Test (QNST): Individual neurological screening for maturity of motor development; skill in controlling large and small muscles, motor planning and sequencing, sense of rate on rhythm, spatial organization, visual and auditory perceptual skills, balance and cerebellar-vestibular function and disorders of attention. Age: 5 years – adult.

Riley Motor Problems Inventory (RMPI): A ten-item test to evaluate motor performance in the following areas: oral-motor tasks, fine-motor tasks, and gross-motor tasks. Age: 4 years–9 years.

Southern California Sensory Integration Test (SCIST): Series of tests for perceptual-motor development. Separate tests include figure ground, motor accuracy, perceptual motor function, and nystagmus test. Age: 4 years–10 years.

The Purdue Perceptual-Motor Survey (PPMS): Sometimes referred to as the "Kephart Scale," the PPMS is an instrument designed to provide qualitative information regarding the degree to which children demonstrate adequately developed perceptual-motor skills. Items are grouped into five basic areas: (1) balance and posture, (2) body image and differentiation, (3) perceptual-motor match, (4) ocular control, and (5) form perception. Age: 4 years–10 years.

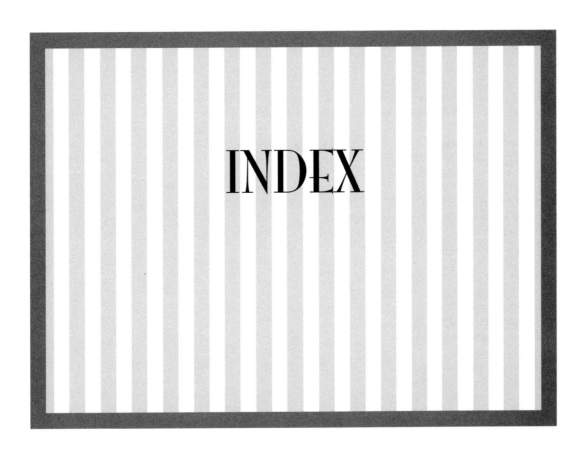

INDEX

A

Academic diploma, and implementation phase, 89
Acceleration programs, 176-77
Accrue pure tone audiometric screening, 148
Adaptive physical education, 112
Administrator, Pupil Personnel Team, 25
Alternate testing techniques, 106-7
　　and General Equivalency Diploma, 106-7
　　and implementation phase, 88
　　implementation roles and responsibilities, 107-
　　　　10
　　modifying manner:
　　　　of presentation, 103-4
　　　　of response, 104-5
　　modifying process used to derive response,
　　　　105
　　and Scholastic Aptitude Test, 106
American Foundation for the Blind, 150
Americans with Disabilities Act (ADA), 262-63
American Sign Language, 150
Analysis, 178
Annual review, 91-93
　　definition of, 91-92
　　parent's preparations checklist for, 93
　　participation in, 92
　　record-keeping during, 93

Anorexia nervosa, 187
Anticonvulsive medications, 205
Antidepressants, 197-98, 202-3
Antipsychotic medications, 194-97, 201-2
Antisocial personality disorder, 191
Anxiety disorders, 190
　　medication for, 198-200, 203-4
Anxiety disorders of childhood:
　　avoidant disorder of childhood/adolescence,
　　　　186
　　overanxious disorder, 186
　　separation anxiety disorder, 185-86
Apartment living, and the mentally disabled child,
　　　　137
Approachability factor, 216
Arthogryposis multiplex congenita, 141
Arthritis, 113
Articulation disorders, 159
　　treatments and remediation of, 161
Articulation skills, 22
Art therapy, 112
Associating, 178
Astigmatism, 144
Ataxia, 141
Athetosis, 141
Attendance problems, and the emotionally dis-
　　　　abled child, 133
Attendance records, examining, 64

Attention Deficit Disorder (ADD), 106
Attention Deficit Hyperactive Disorder, 75, 152
Attention/Deficit/Hyperactivity Disorder (ADHD),
    75, 152-57
    classroom management techniques, 154-57
      academic skill areas, 156-57
    diagnostic criteria for, 152-53
    medications for, 193-94
    treatments plans, 153-54
Attention problems, and the learning-disabled
    child, 125
Attivan, and anxiety disorders, 199-200
Audiologist, 165
Audiometric evaluation measures, 147-48
Auditory learner, 130
Auditory training, 148
Autism, 74, 163-66, 181
    criteria used to diagnose, 163-64
    description of, 181
    educational implications, 181
    interdisciplinary diagnosis of, 165-66
    least-restrictive educational setting, 181
Avoidance behavior patterns, 36-37
Avoidant disorder of childhood/adolescence, 186

B

Balance and equilibrium guidelines, physical ther-
    apy evaluations, 117
Behavioral guidelines, physical therapy evalua-
    tions, 116
Behavioral play audiometry, 148
Behavior modification, 154
Bilingual assessment, 60
Bilingual and culturally disadvantaged child, 170-
    72
    CSE referral requirements, 171-72
    IEP program for, 170-71
Blind, 144
Board and care homes, and the mentally disabled
    child, 137
Borderline personality disorder, 191
Bruninks-Oseretsky Test of Motor Proficiency
    (BOT), 317
Bulimia nervosa, 187-88

C

Caption decoder, 150
Catapres, and Tourette's Syndrome (TS), 197
Cataracts, 146
Categorizing, 178
Cerebral palsy, 113, 140-41

Certificate of attendance, and implementation
    phase, 89
Challenges to authority, and the emotionally dis-
    abled child, 133
Child development:
    normal development, 7-19
      principles of, 7-8
Child development milestones:
    eighteen to twenty-four months, 14-15
    fifteen to eighteen months, 13-14
    four to five years, 18-19
    newborn, 8-9
    nine to twelve months, 12
    one to three months, 9-10
    six to nine months, 11
    thirty to thirty-six months, 16-17
    three to four years, 17-18
    three to six months, 10
    twelve to fifteen months, 13
    twenty-four to thirty months, to, 15-16
Childhood immunization checklist, 307-8
Chronic motor/vocal tic disorders, 168
Classifying, 178
Classroom Observation Report Form, 69-71
Classroom teacher, Pupil Personnel Team, 26
Cluster grouping, 177
Cluttering, 159
Cognitive development, 22
Commercially produced instructional software,
    299
Committee on Preschool Special Education
    (CPSE), 47-48
Committee on Special Education (CSE), 73-74
    agreement to withdraw CSE referral, 277-78
    how recommendations are made by, 73-75
    medical report for, 276
    procedures of, 76-77
    referrals to, 29, 31-32
    specific responsibilities of, 77-79
    suggested materials for, 267-69
      academic data, 223-24
      CSE packet checklist, 270-71
      data processing sheet, 267-69
      early childhood screening program check-
        list, 280
      elementary screening program, 280-81
      initial referral to CSE from parent/guardian,
        271
      learning profile, 278-79
      parental consent for evaluation, 271-72
    and testing modifications, responsibilities of,
      107-10
Communication, 214-17
    connective discussion, 214-15

direct love, 215-16
labeling feelings, 214
nonverbal misinterpretation, 215
triggers, 215
as a two-way street, 214
verbal attacks, 214
written, 215
Communication disorders, 157-63
articulation disorders, 159
treatments and remediation of, 161
characteristics of, 159-60
critical questions about, 158-59
definition of, 157-58
determining presence of, 161-63
fluency disorders, 159
treatments and remediation of, 162
language disorders, 160
treatments and remediation of, 162
normal language development, summary of,
160-61
voice disorders, 159
treatments and remediation of, 161-62
Communication guidelines, physical therapy evaluations, 116
Communications modes, hearing-impaired child,
148-49
Comparing, 178
Complexity, 179
Computers/applications, and implementation
phase, 88-89
Conditioned Orienting Reflex Audiometry
(CORA), 165
Conduct/discipline, and implementation phase, 89
Conduct disorder, 184-85
categories of, 184
description of, 184
educational implications, 184
least-restrictive educational setting, 184-85
Conductive hearing loss, 146
Connective discussion, 214-15
Convergent thinking, 178
Cooperative educational services, 83
Council for Exceptional Children, 47
CPSE, See Committee on Preschool Special
Education (CPSE)
Creative thinking, 178
Criterion-referenced tests, 72
Critical thinking, 178
CSE, See Committee on Special Education (CSE)
Cued speech, 148-50
Cumulative school record, examining, 64
Curiosity, 179
Curriculum, and implementation phase, 88

Cylert, and Attention Deficit/Hyperactivity
Disorder (ADHD), 153, 194
Cystic fibrosis, 142

D

Deaf, 74
Deduction, 178
Degangi-Berk Test of Sensory Integration, 317
Denver Developmental Screening Test, 317
Depression, medication for, 197-98
Desensitization, 208
Developmental disorders, 180-81
anxiety disorders, 190
anxiety disorders of childhood, 185-86
eating disorders, 187-88
elected mutism, 189
expressive language disorder, 183
functional encopresis, 188-89
functional enuresis, 189
mathematics disorder, 182
mental disabilities, 180-81
mood disorders, 190
personality disorders, 190-92
pervasive developmental disorders, 181
phonological disorder, 183
reading disorder, 182-83
receptive language disorder, 184
writing disorders, 182
Developmental guidelines, physical therapy evaluations, 117
Developmental Programming for Infants and
Young Children, 317-18
Developmental Test of Visual-Motor Integration,
318
Development areas, 22-23
articulation skills, 22
cognitive development, 22
expressive/receptive language development, 22
motor development, 22
physical development, 23
Dexedrine, and Attention Deficit/Hyperactivity
Disorder (ADHD), 153, 194
Diabetic retinopathy, 146
Differential Aptitude Test, 273
Diplegia, 141
Direct love, 215-16
Discipline, 211-13
choosing your battlegrounds, 212
concealing problems with your child, 213
consistency of consequence, 211
delaying, 213
focusing on inappropriate behavior, 212
forced choice technique, 213

limited punishment, 211-12
projecting a united front, 212
punishment, 211
    trading for reward, 212
relinquishing power to your spouse, 213
and rewards, 211
setting limits/guidelines, 211
temper tantrums, 212-13
Disruptive behavior disorders, 185
    conduct disorder, 184-85
    oppositional defiant disorder, 185
    separation anxiety disorder, 185-86
Divergent thinking, 178
Dopamine, 201
Double hemiplegia, 141
Down's Syndrome, characteristics of, 139-40
Due process, 95-98
    impartial hearing:
        definition of, 96-98
        record-keeping during, 98
        requesting, 98
    summary of assurances, 95-96
Duration of symptoms, 35
Dyslexia, 127-28, 223
    primary characteristics, 127
    secondary characteristics, 127-28
Dysthymia, 190

E

Early-Lap, 318
Eating disorders, 187-88
    anorexia nervosa, 187
    bulimia nervosa, 187-88
Educational evaluation, 272
Educationally disabled child, 157
Educational performance, 157-58
Education of the Handicapped Amendments of
        1990 (P.L. 101-476), 227
Eighteen- to twenty-four-month-olds, 14-15
Elaborate thinking, 178
Elavil (Endep), and depression, 197
Elected mutism, 189
Elementary screening program, 280-81
Emotionally disabled child, 74
    attendance problems, 133
    challenges to authority, 133
    characteristics of, 132-33
    child's difficulty in remaining seated, 134-35
    directions, helping child follow, 135
    inappropriate verbalizations, 133-34
    incomplete classwork and homework, 133-34
    instructional considerations, 133-35
    outbursts, 133-34

potential suicide risk:
    behavioral indications, 136
    warning signs of, 135-36
social relationships, helping child develop, 135
stimulating attention of, 135
tardiness, with, 133
Endurance guidelines, physical therapy evalua-
        tions, 117
Enrichment programs, 175-76
Equipment guidelines, physical therapy evalua-
        tions, 117
Evaluation, triennial, 94-95
Evaluation process, 57-72
    Classroom Observation Report Form, 69-71
    components of, 60
    definition of, 57
    due-process guarantees during, 71-72
    intake form, example of, 65-67
    observation scales, 67-71
    parental consent for, 60-61, 62
    pupil behavior rating scale, 59
    school intakes and interviews, and parents, 61-
        63
    school records, examining, 63-65
    social and developmental intakes, 65-67
    student rating scale, 58
    tests, 72
Evoked response audiometry, 148
Exceptional children, definition of, 21
Expressive language disorder, 160, 183
Expressive/receptive language development, 22

F

Feelings, labeling, 214
Feingold, Ben, 154
Fifteen- to eighteen-month-olds, 13-14
Flexible thinking, 178
Fluency disorders, 159
    treatments and remediation of, 162
Fluent thinking, 178
Forced choice technique, 213
Four- to five-year-olds, 18-19
Freedom of Information Law, 63
Frequency of symptoms, 35
Frostig Developmental Test of Visual Perception,
        318
Functional encopresis, 188-89
    description of, 188
    educational implications, 189
    least-restrictive educational setting, 189
Functional enuresis, 189
Functional hearing loss, 147

Functional mobility, physical therapy evaluations, 117

G

Gait pattern guidelines, physical therapy evaluations, 117
Gifted and talented child, 172-80
    characteristics of, 179-80
    classroom activities, examples of, 174-75
    educational programming, approaches to, 175-76
    intelligence tests, 172-73
    organizations for, 289-90
    program management, comment characteristics of, 177-78
    publications for, 289-90
    publishers of materials on, 288-89
    terminology for, 178-79
Glaucoma, 146
Group homes, and the mentally disabled child, 137
Grouping, and implementation phase, 88
Group IQ test information, examining, 64
Guidance counselor, Pupil Personnel Team, 26

H

Haldol:
    and psychosis, 195
    and Tourette's Syndrome (TS), 197
Handwriting, and the mentally disabled child, 138
Hard of hearing, 74
Hearing-impaired child, 146-50
    audiometric evaluation measures, 147-48
    causes of hearing impairments, 146-47
        American Sign Language, 150
        finger spelling, 150
    communications modes, 148-49
    degrees of impairments, 150-51
    oral-aural approach, 148-50
        auditory training, 148
        caption decoder, 150
        cued speech, 148-50
        manual communication, 150
        teletypewriter assistance for the deaf, 150
    sound intensities, examples of, 151
    total communication, 150
    technological devices, 150
Hearing impairments, 113
Hemiplegia, 140
Hemophilia, 141

High-risk students, school symptoms exhibited by, 33-34
High school credentials, and implementation phase, 89
High-school equivalency, and implementation phase, 89
Historical disturbance, 26
Homebound instruction, 81
Homogeneous grouping, 177
Hospital setting, 81, 83-84
Hynotics, 200-201
Hyperopia, 144
Hypertonia, 141

I

IDEA, *See* Individuals with Disabilities Education Act (IDEA)
Imagination, 179
Impartial hearing, definition of, 96-98
Impedance audiometry, 148
Implementation phase, 87-91
    arranging for implementation, 90-91
    considerations in, 87-88
        diploma options/requirements, 89-90
        educational considerations, 88-89
        parental considerations, 90
    definition of, 87
    record-keeping during, 91
Inappropriate verbalizations, and the emotionally disabled child, 133-34
Inclusion, 81-83
Incomplete classwork and homework, and emotionally disabled child, 133-34
Indirect love, 216
Individual counseling, 111
Individual Education Plans (IEPs), 32, 47, 79
    alternate testing techniques:
        and General Equivalency Diploma, 106-7
        implementation roles and responsibilities, 107-10
        modifying manner of presentation, 103-4
        modifying manner of response, 104-5
        modifying process used to derive response, 105
        and Scholastic Aptitude Test, 106
    guidelines for, 99-106
        alternate testing modifications, 103
        CSE recommendations, 100-101
        current placement data, 100
        evaluative measures, 102-3
        general identifying data, 99
        goals/objectives, 101-2
        mastery levels, 102

testing modifications, student eligibility and criteria for, 105-6
Individualized Preschool Service Plan (IPSP), 46
Individualized Transitional Education Program (ITEP), 231-32
Individuals with Disabilities Education Act (IDEA), 21, 47, 75, 227
Induction, 178
In-school services:
    group counseling, 111-12
    individual counseling, 111
    questions to ask about, 120-21
    what to expect from, 121
Institutional setting, 81
Institutions, and the mentally disabled child, 137-38
Instructional software, commercial, 299
Intake form, 65-67
    academic history, 66-67
    developmental history, 66
    identifying data, 65-66
    social history, 67
Intensity of symptoms, 35
Itinerant services for hearing impaired, 112
Itinerant services for visually impaired, 112

J

Jordan Left-Right Reversal Test (Jordan Test), 318
Journals, on exceptional children, 285-88
Juvenile rheumatoid arthritis, 141

L

Labeling feelings, 214
Language-based disorders, 131
Language disorders, 160
    treatments and remediation of, 162
Language problems, and the learning-disabled child, 125
Learning disabilities:
    causes of, 223
    definition of, 223
    frequently asked questions concerning, 223-24
    recognizing, 221-23
        academic requirements, 221
        background requirements, 222
        behavioral requirements, 222-23
        exclusion requirements, 221
        intellectual requirements, 221
        processing requirements, 221-22
    referrals, 224
    symptoms of, 224

Learning-disabled child, 74, 123-92
    diagnosing, 123-26
        academic criteria, 124
        background criteria, 125
        behavior criteria, 125-26
        exclusion criteria, 124-25
        intellectual criteria, 123-24
        process criteria, 124
    identifying, 126
    instructional techniques, 128-30
    mathematical disabilities, 131
    phonetically inaccurate spellers, 130-31
    reading disabilities, 131
    readings:
        on assessments and testing for, 292-93
        on instruction/management for, 290-92
        for parents on specific disabilities, 293-98
    severe learning discrepancy, 126-28
    writing disorders, 130
        mechanical, 130
Learning profile, 278-79
Learning style, 208
Least-restrictive educational services (LRE), 79-81
Legally blind, definition of, 144
Legislation, special education, 3-4
Librium (Libretabs), and anxiety disorders, 199
Limb deficiency, 141
Limbic system, 198
Limited punishment, 211-12
Local school district, as recommended placement, 83
Low vision, 144

M

McCarthy Scales of Children's Abilities (MSCA), 318
Macular degeneration, 146
Manual communication, 150
Math, and the mentally disabled child, 138
Mathematical disabilities, 131, 182
    description of, 182
    educational implications, 182
    least-restrictive educational setting, 182
Mediation, 96
Medical history records, examining, 64
Medical report, for CSE, 276
Medical terminology, 252-57
Medication, 193-205
    for ADHD, 193-94
    for anxiety or panic disorders, 198-200
    by category, 200-205
    for depression, 197-98
    for psychosis, 194-97

for Tourette's Syndrome (TS), 196-97
Mellaril, and psychosis, 195
Memory problems, and the learning-disabled child, 125
Mental disabilities, 180-81
  description of, 180
  educational implications, 181
  least-restrictive educational setting, 181
  types of, 181
Mentally disabled child, 74-75
  Down's Syndrome, characteristics of, 139-40
  instructional considerations, 138-39
    general, 138
    handwriting/spelling, 138
    improving work habits, 139
    math, 138
    reading, 138
  residential alternatives, 137-38
Mental retardation, 113
Mentor programs, 177-78
Milani-Comparetti Motor Development Test, 318
Mills vs. *Board of Education of the District of Columbia*, 3
Mixed hearing loss, 147
Mongolism, 139
Mood disorders, 190
Motivation/attitude problems, and the learning-disabled child, 125
Motor abilities, and the learning-disabled child, 125
Motor Free Visual Perception Test, 318
Multiply handicapped classification, 75
Muscle skeletal problems, 113
Muscular dystrophy, 113, 141
Music therapy, 112
Myopia, 144

N

National Association for the Deaf, 150
Navane, and psychosis, 195
Neighboring school district, as recommended placement, 83
Neuroleptic drugs, 194-97, 201-2
Neuromuscular guidelines, physical therapy evaluations, 117
Newborn, 8-9
  reflexes of, 9
Nine- to twelve-month-olds, 12
Nonacademic activities, and implementation phase, 88
Nondisabled children, 158
Nonverbal misinterpretation, 215

Normal language development, summary of, 160-61
Norm-referenced tests, 72
Norpramin, and depression, 198
Nurse teacher, 26

O

Observation scales, 67-71
Observing behaviors:
  avoidance behaviors, 36-37
  determining the severity of the problem, 35-36
  division of energy:
    high tension level, 39-41
    model development, 38-39
  school symptoms exhibited by high-risk students, 33-34
  symptomatic behavior, 34-35
Obsessive-compulsive disorder, 190
Occupational education, and implementation phase, 89
Occupational therapy, 112, 113-21
  assessments unique to, 114
  evaluation guidelines, 113-19
  legal aspects of, 118-19
  problems requiring, 115-16
  service delivery, 117-18
Occupational therapy terminology, 259-62
One- to three—month-olds, 9-10
Open-ended referral form, 55
Oppositional defiant disorder, 185
Oral-aural approach, to hearing-impaired child, 148-50
Orap, and Tourette's Syndrome (TS), 196-97
Organization problems, and the learning-disabled child, 125
Organizations, for exceptional children, 282-85
Original thinking, 178
Orthopedically impaired classification, 75
Osteogenesis imperfecta, 141
Outbursts, by the emotionally disabled child, 133-34
Outside reports, 273
Overanxious disorder, 186

P

Pain guidelines, physical therapy evaluations, 117
Pamelor, and depression, 198
Panic disorders, *See* Anxiety disorders; Anxiety disorders of childhood
Paraplegia, 140

Parental consent, for evaluation process, 60-61, 62, 271-72
Parenting suggestions, 207-26
    communication, 214-17
        connective discussion, 214-15
        direct love, 215-16
        labeling feelings, 214
        nonverbal misinterpretation, 215
        triggers, 215
        as a two-way street, 214
        verbal attacks, 214
        written, 215
    discipline, 211-13
        choosing your battlegrounds, 212
        concealing problems with your child, 213
        consistency of consequence, 211
        delaying, 213
        focusing on inappropriate behavior, 212
        forced choice technique, 213
        limited punishment, 211-12
        projecting a united front, 212
        punishment, 211
        relinquishing power to your spouse, 213
        and rewards, 211
        setting limits/guidelines, 211
        temper tantrums, 212-13
        trading punishments for rewards, 212
    helping children with homework, 207-10
        avoiding finishing assignments for child, 210
        avoiding negative nonverbal messages, 210
        checking assignments, 210
        checking problems first, 208-9
        checking small groups of problems, 209
        darkening page lines, 210
        discussing homework questions, 209
        homework schedule, 208
        learned helplessness, creation of, 208
        placing textbook chapters on tape, 209-10
        prioritizing assignments, 208
        setting reasonable homework periods, 209
    retention, 224-26
    self-esteem, improving child's, 217-20
Parents:
    primary rights of, 2
    and testing modifications, responsibilities of, 109-10
Partially sighted, definition of, 144
Partially sighted classification, 75
Passive-aggressive personality disorder, 192
Pennsylvania Association for Retarded Children vs. *Commonwealth of,* 2
Percent-based mastery level, 102

Perceptual problems, and the learning-disabled child, 125
Personality disorders, 190-92
    antisocial personality disorder, 191
    borderline personality disorder, 191
    passive-aggressive personality disorder, 192
    schizoid personality disorder, 190-91
Pervasive developmental disorders, 181
Phonological disorder, 183
Physical examination, 60
Physically disabled child, 140-42
    causes of physical disability, 140-41
    infectious diseases, modes of transmission, 142
Physical therapy, 112, 113-21
    assessments unique to, 114
    evaluation guidelines, 113-19
    legal aspects of, 118-19
    service delivery, 117-18
Physical therapy terminology, 259-62
Postsecondary schooling, 243-46
    advice for students considering, 243-46
        Buckley Amendment, 244
        examinations, 246
        laundry, 244
        legal advice, 245
        nutrition/health, 244
        parental contact, 245
        phone usage, 244
        plagiarism, 244
        syllabus, 245
        testing modifications, 245
        time management, 245-46
        tutoring, 245
Postural deviations, 113
Posture guidelines, physical therapy evaluations, 117
Potential suicide risk:
    behavioral education, 136
    behavioral indications, 136
    warning signs of, 135-36
Preschool special education, 43-48
    determination of a disability, criteria for, 46-48
    Early Intervention Program, 45-46
    eligibility for services, 46
    parents as family specialists, 44-45
Private approved schools:
    changing a student's classification or placement, 85-86
    as recommended placement, 84
Prolixin, and psychosis, 195
Prozac, and depression, 198
Psychological evaluation, 60, 272
Psychological terminology, 257-59
Psychosis, antipsychotic medication, 194-97

Psychostimulants, 200
  and Attention Deficit/Hyperactivity Disorder
    (ADHD), 193-94
Public Law 94-142, 1
Public schools, and the mentally disabled child,
  137
Pullout programs, 177
Pupil behavior rating scale, 59
Pupil Personnel Team, 25-26
  observation scales used by, 67-69
  options of, 28-30
    language evaluation, 29
    psychoeducational evaluation, 29
    psychological evaluation, 30
    referral, 30
  questions considered by, 26-28
Purdue Perceptual-Motor Survey (PPMS), 319
Pure tone audiometric screening, 147
Pure tone threshold audiometry, 147

Q

Quadriplegia, 140
Qualitative orientation, 208
Quantity orientation, 208
Quick Neurological Screening Test (QNST), 318

R

Range of motion guidelines, physical therapy
    evaluations, 117
Ratio-based mastery level, 102
Reading, and the mentally disabled child, 138
Reading disorder, 131, 182-83
  description of, 182
  educational implications, 183
  least-restrictive educational setting, 183
  symptoms of, 183
Reading teacher, Pupil Personnel Team, 26
Reading teacher's report, 273
Receptive language disorder, 160, 184
Recommendation phase, 73-87
  Committee on Special Education (CSE), 73-74
    how recommendations are made by, 74-75
    procedures of, 76-77
    specific responsibilities of, 77-79
  continuum of services, 79-81
  definition of, 73
  inclusion, 81-83
  individual educational program development,
    79
  least-restrictive educational services (LRE), 79-
    81

parental guarantees during, 84-85
participation suggestions, 85
Public Law 504, conditions of, 75-67
recommended placements, 83-84
record-keeping during, 85
student classification or placement, changing,
    85-87
Record-keeping:
  during annual review, 93
  during due process, 98
  during implementation phase, 91
  during recommendation phase, 85
  and referrals, 52
Reference lists, 303-8
Referrals, 49-57, 224
  contents of, 49-50
  initial referral to CSE from school staff, 52-53
  learning disabilities, 224
  open-ended referral form, 55-56
  parental guarantees, 50-51
  parental participation, 51-52
  parents referral letter to the CSE, example of,
    53
  rating scale, 57
  record keeping, 52
  referral to the CSE from school staff, 54
Regional facilities, and the mentally disabled
    child, 137
Regular class placement, 80
Regular classroom, maintaining gifted student in,
    177
Regular education teacher, and testing modifica-
    tions, responsibilities of, 109
Related services, 110-21
  adaptive physical education, 112
  art therapy, 112
  in-school services:
    group counseling, 111-12
    identifying need for, 119-20
    individual counseling, 111
    questions to ask about, 120-21
    what to expect from, 121
  itinerant services:
    for hearing impaired, 112
    for visually impaired, 112
  music therapy, 112
  physical and occupational therapy, 112, 113-21
  sign language interpreter, 112
  speech/language therapy, 112
Residential school, 81
Respiratory problems, 113
Respite services, 46
Retinitis pigmentosa, 146
Retrolental fibroplasia, 146

Reversals, importance of, 224
Right to notification of action, 95
Riley Motor Problems Inventory (RMPI), 319
Risk taking, 179
Ritalin, and Attention Deficit/Hyperactivity
Disorder (ADHD), 153, 194

S

Salicylates, 154
Scheduling, and implementation phase, 88
Schizoid personality disorder, 190-91
    description of, 190
    educational implications, 191
    least-restrictive educational setting, 191
School Abilities Index (SAI), 172
    examining, 64
School district screening model, 25-31
    Pupil Personnel Team, 25-26
        options of, 28-30
        questions considered by, 26-28
School intakes and interviews, and parents, 61-63
School principal, and testing modifications,
        responsibilities of, 108
School records, examining, 63-65
Screening procedures, 21-32
    development areas, 22-23
        articulation skills, 22
        cognitive development, 22
        expressive/receptive language development,
        22
        motor development, 22
        physical development, 23
    school district screening model, 25-31
    screen, definition of, 21-22
    screening requirements, 23-24
    See also School district screening model
Second language instruction, and implementation
        phase, 88
Sedatives, 200-201
Selective forgetting, as avoidance behavior, 36
Self-esteem, child's, improving, 217-20
    allowing children right to make decisions, 219
        allowing children to make mistakes, 220
        allowing disagreement, 220
        alternate solutions, 219
        proper labeling, 219
        repeating successful experiences, 219
        reward system, 220
        setting realistic goals, 220
    solution-orientation, 219
Sensorineural hearing loss, 146-47
Separation anxiety disorder, 185-86
    description of, 185

educational implications, 185
    least-restrictive educational setting, 186
Severe learning discrepancy, 126-28
Sheltered workshops, and the mentally disabled
        child, 137
Sign language interpreter, 112
Situational disturbance, 26
Six- to nine month olds, 11
Skeletal and joint condition, physical therapy
        evaluations, 117
Skin and soft tissue guidelines, physical therapy
        evaluations, 117
Social behavior, and the learning-disabled child,
        125
Social and developmental history form, 274-76
Social and developmental intakes, 65-67
Social history, 60
Social relationships, helping emotionally disabled
        child develop, 135
Social worker:
    and autism, 165
    Pupil Personnel Team, 26
Sounded field audiometry, 148
Sound intensities, examples of, 151
Southern California Sensory Integration Test
        (SCIST), 319
Special class in a regular school, 80
Special day school outside the school district, 81
Special education:
    court cases, 3
    forms, 267-81
    least-restrictive environment, education in, 4
    legislation, 3-4
    modern history of, 1-5
    primary rights of parents, 2
    Public Law 94-142, 1
    right to due process and equal access, 5
    right to a free appropriate public education, 4
    terminology, 248-66
Special-education process, 49-98
    annual review, 91-93
    due process, 95-98
    evaluation, 57-72
    implementation, 87-91
    recommendation, 73-87
    referrals, 49-57
    triennial evaluation, 94-95
Special education teacher:
    and autism, 165
    Pupil Personnel Team, 26
    and testing modifications, responsibilities of,
        108-9
Special-education tests, 308-19
    arithmetic tests, 314

bilingual assessment measures, 316

comprehensive academic skills tests, 315-16

early childhood/infant assessments scales, 316-17

hearing impaired, test for, 310

intelligence tests, 308

language tests, 309-10

perceptual tests, 311-12

psychological tests, 310-11

rating scales/adaptive behavior scales, 312-13

reading tests, 313-14

spelling/writing tests, 314-15

standardized, used in occupational therapy evaluation, 317-19

writing tests, 315

Special schools, and the mentally disabled child, 137

Speech audiometry, 147

Speech and hearing clinic, 165-66

Speech-impaired child, 157, 158

Speech and language evaluation, 273

Speech and language teacher, Pupil Personnel Team, 26

Speech and language therapy, 112

Spelling, and the mentally disabled child, 138

Spina bifida, 141-42

Spinal cord injury, 142

Spotlight behaviors, as avoidance behavior, 37

State-operated schools, as recommended placement, 84

Stelazine, and psychosis, 196

Structured referral form, 9-109-10

Student classification or placement:

changing, 85-87

by parents, 85-86

by the school, 86-87

Student rating scale, 58

Subject matter acceleration, 176

Sweep testing, 147

Symptomatic behavior, 34-35

Synthesis, 178

T

Tangible Reinforcement Operant Conditioning Audiometry (TROCA), 165

Tardiness, and the emotionally disabled child, 133

Teacher anecdotal records, examining, 64

Telescoping, 176

Teletypewriter assistance for the deaf, 150

Temper tantrums, 212-13

Testing, and implementation phase, 88

Test publishers, 300-302

Tests, 72

Thirty- to thirty-six-month-olds, 16-17

Thorazine, and psychosis, 196

Three- to four-year-olds, 17-18

Three- to six-month-olds, 10

Tic disorders, 188

See also Tourette's Syndrome (TS)

Time-based mastery level, 102

Tofranil (Janimine), and depression, 197-98

Tourette's Syndrome (TS), 75, 166-69, 188

classroom strategies for children with, 169

complex motor tics, 167

complex phonic tics, 167

description of, 188

diagnostic criteria for, 167-68

educational implications, 188

least-restrictive educational setting, 188

medication for, 196-97

and pharmacotherapy, 168-69

antidepressants, 169

clonodine, 168

narcoleptics, 168

simple motor tics, 166

simple phonic (sound) tics, 166-67

symptoms of, 188

Transient tic disorders, 167

Transitional services, 106, 227-46

from school to work, 239-40

Individualized Transitional Education Program (ITEP), 106, 227-46

sample of, 235-38

postsecondary schooling, 240-41

advice for students considering, 243-46

considerations about, 241-42

student and family participation, 232-35

Transitional Planning Timeline, 233-35

to posthigh-school programs, 240

vocational assessments, 228-31

Transportation, and implementation phase, 89

Traumatic accidents, 113

Traumatic brain injury, 142

Triennial evaluation, 94-95

definition of, 94

parental guarantees during, 94

participation in, 95

record-keeping during, 95

Triggers, 215

Trilafon, and psychosis, 196

Trisomy, 139

Twelve-month special service, 90

Twelve- to fifteen-month-olds, 13

Twenty-four to thirty-month-olds, 15-16

U

Undifferential Attention Deficit Disorder, 152
Unfinished classwork, as avoidance behavior, 37
Usher's syndrome, 146

V

Valium, and anxiety disorders, 199
Variability in performance, and the learning-disabled child, 125
Verbal attacks, 214
Vision guidelines, physical therapy evaluations, 117
Visual impairment, 113
Visual learner, 130
Visually handicapped, definition of, 144
Visually impaired child, 75, 143-46
    causes of visual impairments, 144-46
    characteristics of visual impairments, 143
    disability terminology, 144
    legal and administrative definitions, 144
Vocal tic disorders, 168

Vocational assessments, 228-31
    field-of-study assessments, 230
    general assessments of postsecondary education skills, 230
    levels of, 229-30
Vocational evaluation, 60
Vocational evaluation-aptitude test results, 273
Voice disorders, 159
    treatments and remediation of, 161-62

W

Writing disorder, 130, 182
    description of, 182
    educational implications, 182
    least-restrictive educational setting, 182
    symptoms of, 182
Written communication, 215

X

Xanax, and anxiety disorders, 199